Personal Development

for SMART PEOPLE

Hay House Titles of Related Interest

YOU CAN HEAL YOUR LIFE, the movie, starring Louise L. Hay & Friends
(available as a 1-DVD program and an expanded 2-DVD set)
Watch the trailer at: **www.LouiseHayMovie.com**

✦ ✦

ATTITUDE IS EVERYTHING FOR SUCCESS: Say It, Believe It, Receive It,
by Keith D. Harrell

THE COMPASSIONATE SAMURAI: Being Extraordinary in an Ordinary World,
by Brian Klemmer

HOW SUCCESSFUL PEOPLE WIN, by Ben Stein

*INTERPERSONAL EDGE: Breakthrough Tools for Talking to Anyone,
Anywhere, about Anything,* by Daneen Skube, Ph.D.

THE RICHES WITHIN: Your Seven Secret Treasures, by Dr. John F. Demartini

SECRETS OF SUCCESS: The Science and Spirit of Real Prosperity,
by Sandra Anne Taylor and Sharon A. Klingler

*SUCCESS INTELLIGENCE: Essential Lessons and Practices from the World's
Leading Coaching Program on Authentic Success,* by Robert Holden, Ph.D.

21 DISTINCTIONS OF WEALTH: Attract the Abundance You Desire,
by Peggy McColl

✦ ✦

All of the above are available at your local
bookstore, or may be ordered by visiting

Hay House USA: **www.hayhouse.com**®
Hay House Australia: **www.hayhouse.com.au**
Hay House UK: **www.hayhouse.co.uk**
Hay House South Africa: **www.hayhouse.co.za**
Hay House India: **www.hayhouse.co.in**

✦ ✦

Personal
Development
for SMART PEOPLE

The Conscious Pursuit of Personal Growth

STEVE PAVLINA

HAY
HOUSE

HAY HOUSE, INC.
Carlsbad, California • New York City
London • Sydney • Johannesburg
Vancouver • Hong Kong • New Delhi

Published and distributed in the United States by: Hay House, Inc.: www.hayhouse. com • *Published and distributed in Australia by:* Hay House Australia Pty. Ltd.: www. hayhouse.com.au • *Published and distributed in the United Kingdom by:* Hay House UK, Ltd.: www.hayhouse.co.uk • *Published and distributed in the Republic of South Africa by:* Hay House SA (Pty), Ltd.: www.hayhouse.co.za • *Distributed in Canada by:* Raincoast: www.raincoast.com • *Published in India by:* Hay House Publishers India: www.hayhouse.co.in

Editorial supervision: Jill Kramer • *Design:* Tricia Breidenthal

Library of Congress Cataloging-in-Publication Data

Pavlina, Steve.
  Personal development for smart people : the conscious pursuit of personal growth / Steve Pavlina. -- 1st ed.
       p. cm.
  ISBN 978-1-4019-2275-7 (hardcover : alk. paper) -- ISBN 978-1-4019-2276-4 (tradepaper : alk. paper) 1. Self-actualization (Psychology) 2. Maturation (Psychology) I. Title.
  BF637.S4P385 2008
  158--dc22
                                                    2008021487

Hardcover ISBN: 978-1-4019-2275-7
Tradepaper ISBN: 978-1-4019-2276-4

11 10 09 08   4 3 2 1
1st edition, October 2008

Printed in the United States of America

For Erin.
Thank you for teaching me how to love.
Our souls are dancing.

Contents

———————————→

Introduction

> "When I'm working on a problem, I never think
> about beauty. I think only how to solve the problem.
> But when I have finished, if the solution
> is not beautiful, I know it is wrong."
>
> — R. BUCKMINSTER FULLER

Do you remember the exact moment you first became interested in personal development? I certainly do. It happened in January 1991 while I was sitting in a jail cell. I'd just been arrested for felony grand theft. This wasn't my first run-in with the law, so I knew was in trouble. I was 19 years old.

I began stealing shortly after moving to Berkeley, California, during my first semester at UC Berkeley. I didn't steal for money or to build a reputation—I stole for the thrill. I was addicted to the surge of adrenaline. The compulsion to steal was so strong that shoplifting was part of my routine, nothing more than my daily espresso. Usually I didn't care what I stole; it was the act of stealing that seduced me. On a typical outing, I'd lift a dozen candy bars and then drop them off in a public place, figuring that other people would eat them. I didn't eat the candy because I didn't think it was healthy.

As I sat in jail for several days that January with nothing to do but wallow in my own stupidity, the reality of my situation came crashing down upon me. In high school I'd been a straight-A honors student, president of the math club, and captain of the Academic Decathlon team. My future as a computer-science major looked unbelievably bright, but somehow I'd torn it to shreds. Now I was expecting to spend the next year or two behind bars.

Upon returning to my studio apartment after three days in jail, I received a letter from UC Berkeley informing me in no uncertain terms that I'd been expelled. Apparently schools do that sort of thing when you don't bother showing up to classes and your grade point average starts with a decimal point. In that moment, I realized I had two basic options for how to deal with my situation: grow up or give up.

During the next few months while waiting for my court date, I was in a total funk. Most days I slept until well past noon. I buried myself in video games, sometimes for 18 hours at a time. (We're talking single-player Nintendo games here, not massive multiplayer online games.) It's hard to feel motivated when you're expecting to go to jail for a while.

Eventually I secured a lawyer and met with him at his office to discuss my situation. Before I could open my mouth, he blurted out, "Steve, I've reviewed your case, and since this is your first offense, I'm pretty sure we can get it reduced to petty theft. If we plead no contest, you'll get off with a lesser conviction and end up with some community service. I'm on great terms with the district attorney, so I'm sure he'll go for it. I strongly advise against going to trial, as the evidence against you is overwhelming, seeing as you were caught red-handed."

Immediately my thoughts began to race. *First offense? Is he deluded? Why does he think this is my first offense? Doesn't he know about my priors? If he thinks this is a first offense, will the rest of the court think so, too? Should I correct him on this serious oversight?*

While trying to decide how to respond, I heard a voice in the back of my mind: *Keep your damned mouth shut!* I realized that speaking up now might backfire on me later, but there was a slim chance it could "frontfire," too. I figured that the worst case was that I'd have an angry lawyer somewhere down the road, but the best case was too good to pass up. Grand theft is a felony; petty theft is only a misdemeanor. I decided I had to risk it. Taking risks was an all-too-familiar pastime.

Several weeks later we went to court, and I was a nervous wreck. My plan was to keep my mouth shut as much as possible and only say the absolute minimum. Outside the courtroom, I reviewed the posted documents about my case. None of my priors were listed. Was it human or computer error? Either way, it was one huge mistake in my favor.

Sure enough, when my lawyer and I entered the courtroom, the court remained under the assumption that this was a first offense and diligently processed it as such. I pled no contest to the reduced charge of petty theft and received 60 hours of community service. My head was spinning as I raced out of the courtroom. The next two years of my life were mine again.

I did those 60 hours like I was at a dream job, knowing full well my sentence could have been 17,520 hours. It's hard to imagine a more joyful time in my life than those days spent picking up trash at the Emeryville Marina. You have no idea how good freedom feels until you expect to lose it. I felt immensely grateful for this second chance, a chance I felt I didn't deserve.

I wish I could say my recovery after these events was fast and easy, but it wasn't. Despite this amazing gift, turning my life around was still incredibly difficult. I said good-bye to my Berkeley friends and moved back to my hometown of Los Angeles. I landed a minimum-wage job in retail sales. Even with a criminal record, I probably could have found a more lucrative position, but I just didn't want one. I only wanted to play it safe, stay below the radar, and eke out a "vanilla" life devoid of stress and excitement. Courage had become my enemy.

During this year of quiet, uneventful living, I worked on myself. I gradually developed a new code of ethics to guide me, integrating values such as honor, honesty, integrity, humility, and fairness. This conscious reconstruction process would continue for at least a few more years. As the months went by, I began to feel good about myself again, and I decided it was time to go back to school. I figured that if I could earn my degree in computer science, it would somehow erase my past mistakes.

In the fall of 1992, I enrolled at California State University–Northridge (CSUN), starting over as a freshman. CSUN's computer-science program wasn't impacted, meaning that it had plenty of room for new students. I was guaranteed admittance just by filling out an application, so they didn't care that I'd flunked out of UC Berkeley.

Now 21 years old, I was no longer the same person I'd been at 18. Something was different. I'd developed a passion for personal growth, and I felt an intense desire to do my absolute best this time.

In my mind, I was already three years behind, and I couldn't stomach the thought of taking four more years to graduate. I knew I was responsible for this situation, and I intensely desired to speed things along. So I set the ambitious goal of earning my degree in only three semesters by taking triple the normal course load. Those who knew me thought I'd gone insane, but they couldn't see into my heart. I was 100 percent committed, and I knew that nothing could stop me from achieving this goal. It was the only way I could honor my tremendous gift of freedom.

To prepare myself for the heavy workload, I studied time-management techniques and immediately applied what I learned. I listened to motivational tapes every day to keep my attitude positive. I exercised daily to manage stress, and I found creative ways to increase my productivity. I experienced a tremendous flow of energy and drive because I knew I was finally doing my best. I worked hard and aced my classes. I even added a double major in mathematics along the way. At my graduation, I was given a special award for being the top computer-science student of the year.

In my final semester, I also worked as a contract programmer, developing several computer games for a local games studio, and I served as vice chair of the school's computer club. It took a lot of hard work and conscious effort, but I successfully achieved my goal of graduating from college in three semesters. Somehow this achievement helped me release the pain and guilt of my past while retaining the valuable lessons I'd learned.

During the months after my graduation, I launched my own computer-game development business and began dating my future wife, but personal growth remained my top priority. Little did I know at the time, my lifelong pursuit of conscious growth was only beginning. Over the next several years, I read hundreds of books and listened to dozens of audio programs on a diverse selection of personal development topics, including psychology, motivation, success, productivity, career development, problem solving, health, wealth, conscious living, spirituality, meditation, and more.

Admittedly, most of the self-help information I absorbed wasn't very helpful. The authors were enthusiastic, but their ideas were often unoriginal, inconsistent, incongruent, incomplete, impractical, or simply incorrect. I suspected that many of them exaggerated their results. If you're an avid reader of such works, I'm sure you've encountered similar problems, such as buying a diet book and discovering that it's nothing more than a disguised sales pitch for expensive supplements. Nevertheless, I did encounter some nuggets of wisdom that gave me new insights and helped me improve my life. However, my greatest breakthroughs usually came from personal experimentation, not from devouring information products.

I ran my computer-games business for many years (sometimes successfully, sometimes unsuccessfully) while maintaining a passionate interest in personal development on the side. But as time went by, I lost interest in game publishing, and running my business became less fulfilling. I decided it was time to expand my personal development hobby into my primary career.

Creating StevePavlina.com

In 2004, my wife and kids and I moved from Los Angeles to Las Vegas, and in October of that year I officially retired from computer-game publishing to launch a new online personal development business, StevePavlina.com. I started a blog, wrote articles, and recorded audio programs to share what I'd learned from more than a decade of personal-growth efforts. Within three years I'd created enough material to fill about 20 books, and I still felt as though I was just getting started. I shared all of this content for free. The Website generated income from advertising, affiliate programs, promotional offers, and donations.

Although I had virtually no credibility in the personal development field when I began, StevePavlina.com exploded with traffic, quickly becoming the most popular personal development Website in the world with readers in more than 150 countries. This happened by word of mouth, since people who benefited from the free content often referred their friends, family members, and co-workers to the site. I never spent a dime on marketing or promotion. Soon the site was bringing in tens of thousands of dollars a month, even though I had no products, no employees, and no customers. This drew even more visitors, since people wanted to know how I could be earning so much money by giving everything away for free. All of this free content is still available on the site today, with more being added every month.

Running StevePavlina.com massively advanced my personal-growth knowledge because I had the opportunity to communicate with so many people about their unique challenges. After thousands of interactions with my readers, I began to detect recurring patterns and themes. I also noticed that when I wrote an article on a specific subject, often someone would take a general concept from the piece and find a way to apply it to a totally different area. For example, if I wrote about sleep, someone would figure out how the same general advice could be applied to their business. I began to suspect that there was a hidden order beneath our seemingly chaotic growth experiences.

What Is Personal Development for Smart People?

Personal development for smart people is a phrase I use to describe my approach to personal growth. Instead of going after the low-hanging fruit and solving the easy problems, such as how to make healthier food choices or earn more money, I wanted to answer a really tough question: what does it mean for us to grow as conscious human beings, and how do we intelligently guide that process?

There were two threads in my life that led me to tackle this question. The first thread was my long-term fascination with the concept of intelligence. The second thread was my direct study of the field of personal development.

While earning my computer-science degree, I specialized in artificial intelligence (AI). I learned how difficult it is to create intelligent computer programs, largely because we don't really understand intelligence. I incorporated basic AI techniques in some of my early computer games, but those programs only mimicked intelligent be-havior and couldn't be considered truly intelligent. I soon asked my-self: *How do I actually know that I'm intelligent?* I couldn't find an an-swer that satisfied me. Eventually my pursuit of personal development led me to adopt a new definition of intelligence that satisfied both my logic and intuition. You'll learn that definition in Chapter 7.

While studying personal development for many years, I learned that this field is very broad and fragmented. Any area of your life can rea-sonably slide under the umbrella of self-improvement, including your health, career, finances, relationships, and spiritual beliefs. Each subset of this field has its own purported experts, all of them sharing different ideas, rules, and advice. Relationship experts tell you how to maintain successful relationships, wealth experts teach you how to manage your money, and health experts help you improve your body.

Unfortunately, these experts often disagree with each other. Some people recommend a high-protein diet; others recommend high carb. Some say you can achieve success through hard work and self-disci-pline; others advise letting go and allowing God or the universe to handle the details. Some experts encourage you to change; others say you should accept yourself as you are. If you try to incorporate all these different ideas into your life, you'll end up with a fragmented, incongruent mess.

I soon realized that an intelligent approach to personal develop-ment would have to resolve these incongruencies somehow. Such an approach would have to make logical and intuitive sense, satisfying both head and heart. It would have to appear logically correct in order to satisfy the left brain, and it would have to feel intuitively correct in order to engage the right brain.

Qualities of the Core Principles

The laws of physics are universal. Although their specific appli-cations can vary tremendously, these governing laws don't change based on our location, our culture, or our moods; the core principles are the same whether we're dealing with rockets or submarines. Why should the field of personal development be any different? Couldn't universal laws of consciousness exist as well?

I decided to tackle this problem head-on, doing something I've never seen done before. I set out to find the common pattern behind all successful growth efforts, to identify a complete set of core principles that would be universally applicable. To define what this set of principles would have to look like, I outlined several criteria, all of which would have to be satisfied by the final solution. These criteria include universality, completeness, irreducibility, congruency, and practicality:

First, these principles must be universal. They must be applicable by anyone, anywhere, in any situation. They must work equally well for all areas of life: health, relationships, career, spiritual growth, and so on. They must be timeless, meaning that they can still be expected to work 1,000 years from now, and they would have worked 1,000 years ago. They must be culturally independent. They need to work for all those living on Earth, as well as for people aboard a space station in orbit. They must work both individually and collectively, so they're effective for any group of any size.

Second, these principles must be collectively complete, so all the critical elements are present and none are missing. It should be possible to trace all other effective universal laws of personal growth back to these basic building blocks. Ideally, these principles should lend themselves to a structure that is both simple and elegant.

Third, the primary principles must be irreducible, similar to prime numbers in mathematics. They must serve as the fundamental atomic building blocks of conscious human growth. Therefore, it must be possible to combine two or more primary principles together to form secondary principles, and the resulting combinations must also be inherently sound and universally applicable.

Fourth, these principles must be internally congruent. They can't be in conflict with each other. They must be logically and intuitively consistent.

Finally, these principles must be practical. They must be able to generate intelligent real-world results. You should be able to use these ideas to diagnose personal development challenges and devise workable solutions. Knowledge of them should accelerate your personal growth, not obfuscate it.

Consider the statement "Love your neighbor as yourself." This concept can and does assist many people on their path of personal growth, but unfortunately it violates most of our criteria, so we can't include it as part of our framework. First, the concept isn't universal. It applies well to some areas of life such as relationships and even business, but it doesn't make as much sense if we try to apply it to improve our physical health. Second, it isn't irreducible. This statement actually derives from the more general principle of oneness, and oneness itself can be derived from the principles of truth and love (see Chapter 4). Taken in isolation, this statement is incomplete, so it only provides partial guidance. "Love your neighbor as yourself" is sound advice that may help you improve your interpersonal relationships, but it probably won't help you pay your bills. There are many similar concepts that have positive applications but that we can't include as part of our underlying framework because they don't satisfy all of our criteria.

Finding the hidden order behind all conscious human development is extremely difficult because the solution has to be fairly general and abstract, but it must also have abundant practical applications. Because we're dealing with the realm of pure conscious thought, the solution won't be as crisp as a mathematical formula, but it should bring us as close to that ideal as we can reasonably get.

I researched various philosophical, psychological, and spiritual frameworks that had previously attempted to address this challenge. Some had clearly identified one or more of the core concepts, but none provided satisfactory explanations of the big picture. I racked my brain again and again, asking repeatedly: *What is the underlying pattern?* There were clues everywhere, but the complete structure remained a mystery. The task seemed nearly impossible, and I had no guarantee there even was an answer. I ended up rejecting an almost endless progression of partial solutions. It was frustrating to find a solution that looked good at first glance, only to discover that it was full of holes.

Introducing the Seven Principles

It took me almost two and a half years, but I eventually found the solution I was looking for. It consists of just three core principles: *truth, love,* and *power.* Four secondary principles are directly derived from the first three: *oneness, authority, courage,* and *intelligence.* Oneness is truth plus love. Authority is truth plus power. Courage is love plus power. And intelligence is the total combination of truth, love, and power. Consequently, we can say that the intelligent, "smart people" approach to personal development is the direction that moves you into greater alignment with truth, love, and power. As you'll learn in Chapter 7, this also provides us with a very elegant definition of intelligence: *Intelligence is alignment with the principles of truth, love, and power.*

Don't worry if you don't understand these principles yet. We'll spend a full chapter exploring each one, and several additional chapters will address their practical applications. Once you learn these seven principles and recognize how they operate in all areas of your life, you'll never look at personal development the same way again.

Some of these principles will appear to be common sense at first glance. The principle of truth is intuitively understood by any scientist. The principle of love is common to all major religions. And the principle of power shows up repeatedly in business and government. Unfortunately, our society tends to compartmentalize these principles. We're taught to favor truth during our early education, while our power is simultaneously weakened by external authority figures. We're encouraged to align with love in our relationships and spiritual practices while truth and power are de-emphasized. And we're conditioned to seek power as we build our careers and improve our finances, while truth and love take a backseat in these areas. This is an enormous mistake. These principles are universal; they cannot be successfully compartmentalized without sacrificing something far more important—our true nature as conscious beings.

The goal of this book is to teach you how to bring all areas of your life into alignment with these universal principles. This requires injecting truth into your relationships, aligning your career with love, and bringing power to your spiritual practice. This is what it means to live as a conscious, intelligent human being. The more your life aligns with these principles, the smarter you become.

This book offers you a new way of thinking about personal growth from high-level concepts to practical actions. You won't need different rules for maintaining your health, building your career, and caring for your relationships. The core principles of growth don't change from one area of life to the next, nor do they vary from person to person. Once you understand how they work, you'll be able to use them to improve your results in any endeavor.

How to Read This Book

This book is organized in two parts. Part I explores the seven fundamental principles of personal development, starting with the three primary principles of truth, love, and power. By internalizing these basics, you'll build a solid foundation for improving your growth efforts in all areas of your life. Your goal for reading this part of the book is simply to gain an understanding of these seven principles. There are some suggested application exercises to deepen your understanding, but you don't need to do them on your first pass. Those exercises are mainly intended to illustrate how the ideas can be applied through action. Because some of these principles build on those before them, it's best to read these first seven chapters in order.

Part II is the down and dirty application section. This half of the book explains how to apply the seven principles to generate positive, practical results in your life. Every chapter tackles a different area of life, including your career, health, relationships, and more. You can read these chapters in any order, so feel free to jump straight to the section that interests you most. However, it's best if you read all the chapters in Part I before progressing to Part II.

This is a very content-rich book, packed with fresh ideas. Take as much time as you need to read it, and don't feel you have to race to the end. This book is meant to serve you in your pursuit of personal growth, and how that plays out is up to you.

If you want extra help or if you'd just like to explore personal development with like-minded folks, be sure to take advantage of the Personal Development for Smart People discussion forums at **www. StevePavlina.com/forums**. There you'll find a welcoming and supportive community of thousands of growth-oriented individuals from around the world. The forums are completely free, too, so there's no catch to participate.

Incidentally, some Web pages will be mentioned in this book to refer to you additional free content at StevePavlina.com. Rest assured that this book is complete as is. These Web pages are offered as supplemental resources, such as the discussion forums mentioned above. If for some reason you don't have Web access at home or at work, take note that most public libraries provide it for free.

My promise to you as you read this book is threefold. First, in accordance with the principle of truth, I'll be completely honest and straight with you. I have no interest in filling your head with false notions and leading you astray. Second, in accordance with the principle of love, I'll do my best to connect with you, human being to human being. I'm here to serve as your friend and guide, not your guru. And finally, in accordance with the principle of power, I intend to help you embrace *your* true power and face your fears. Sometimes that means I'll be encouraging and supportive; other times it means I must challenge you. Applying what you learn from this book won't be easy for you. It hasn't been easy for me, either. Real conscious growth is seldom undemanding, but it's always worthwhile.

Let us now begin our journey into conscious personal growth.

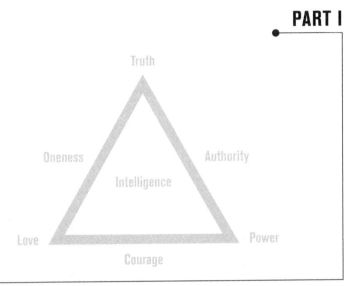

PART I

Truth

Oneness   Authority

Intelligence

Love   Power

Courage

Fundamental Principles

Chapter 1

TRUTH

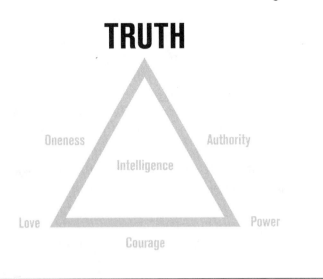

Oneness

Authority

Intelligence

Love

Power

Courage

> *"Life has no other discipline to impose, if we would but realize it, than to accept life unquestioningly. Everything we shut our eyes to, everything we run away from, everything we deny, denigrate or despise, serves to defeat us in the end. What seems nasty, painful, evil, can become a source of beauty, joy and strength, if faced with an open mind. Every moment is a golden one for him who has the vision to recognize it as such."*
>
> — HENRY MILLER

Truth is the first principle of personal development. We primarily grow as human beings by discovering new truths about ourselves and our reality. You'll certainly learn some important lessons no matter how you live, but you can accelerate your growth tremendously by consciously seeking truth and deliberately turning away from falsehood and denial.

Genuine personal growth is honest growth. You can't take shortcuts through the land of make-believe. Your first commitment must be to discover and accept new truths, no matter how difficult or unpleasant the consequences may be. You can't solve problems if you don't admit they exist. How can you achieve a fulfilling career if you won't admit that your current job is wrong for you? How can you improve your relationship situation if you refuse to accept that you've been feeling empty and alone? How can you better your health if you won't accept that your current habits don't serve you?

Reality is the ultimate arbiter of truth. If your thoughts, beliefs, and actions aren't aligned with truth, your results will suffer. Positioning yourself in this way isn't enough to guarantee success, but siding with falsehood is enough to guarantee failure. When you align yourself with truth, your troubles won't fix themselves overnight, but you'll be taking an important step in the right direction.

When you deny your problems, you turn away from truth. The lies you tell yourself spawn more lies, infecting your mind with falsehoods that weave themselves into your identity. You become disconnected from your true self, living as a mere shadow of the brilliant being you were meant to be. You aren't here to endure such an existence. You're here to learn how to create a life of your own choosing. It's not for me to say what that life should look like, but I'll do my best to help you figure it out.

For the remainder of this chapter, I'll take you on a guided tour of truth. This will help you understand how to identify and accept what's true for you. These ideas can be fairly abstract, so your goal here is simply to familiarize yourself with the high-level concepts. In Part II of this book, you'll learn to apply these concepts to all areas of your life, so you'll see exactly how they can be used to improve your results.

Let's begin with an exploration of the key components of truth: *perception, prediction, accuracy, acceptance, and self-awareness.*

Perception

Perception is the most basic aspect of truth. If you want to improve some part of your life, you have to look at it first. For example, if you want to know how your relationship is doing, a good place to start is to ask yourself: *How do I feel about this relationship? What parts are working well? What parts need improvement?* Ask your partner the same questions and compare your answers. Figuring out where you stand will help you decide what changes you'd like to make.

Perception is a key component of personal growth because we react to what we perceive to be true. Facing the truth of your situation causes you to trigger new desires. When you step on the scale and see that you weigh more than you'd like, you think, *I want to lose weight.* When you get clear about what you don't want, you gain clarity about what you do want. These new desires can help drive you in a positive new direction, but nothing will change until you first admit that you'd like it to.

The first step on your path of personal growth must be to recognize that your life as it stands right now isn't how you want it to be. It's perfectly okay to be in this position. It's okay to want something and have no idea how to get it, but it's not okay to lie to yourself and pretend everything is perfect when you know it isn't. The closest you'll get to perfection will be to enjoy the experience of lifelong growth, including all its temporary flaws.

It's easy for me to say that you should face the truth about your life, but in practice this can be very difficult to do. It's hard to admit that you've become dissatisfied with your relationship. It's hard to accept that you made the wrong career choice. It's hard to look at yourself in the mirror and realize that you don't like the person you've become. But despite how difficult this is, it's still necessary. You can't get from point A to point B if you stubbornly refuse to acknowledge that you're *at* point A. Denying A, fighting A, or otherwise resisting A only keeps you stuck at A.

What do you perceive about your life that you'd like to change? Are there any addictions or destructive habits you'd like to break? Would you find more fulfillment in a new career? Would you rather be living somewhere else? Open your eyes. Look around you and notice what you like and dislike about your life. Don't worry about setting specific goals just yet; just become aware of what you perceive and how you react to those perceptions.

Prediction

Prediction is the mechanism by which you learn from experience, thereby enabling you to discover what is true. As you observe any new situation or event, one of two things can happen: either the experience will meet your expectations, or it won't. When an experience meets your expectations, your mental model of reality remains intact. But when an experience violates your expectations, your mind must update its model of reality to fit the new information. This is how you learn from experience and discover new truths.

Your predictive powers are extremely flexible. When you learn something new, your mind tries to generalize from the experience. It favors storage of general patterns instead of specific details. Your ability to recall the finer points will be fuzzy, but you'll normally have a strong recollection of high-level patterns. For example, you can understand written language, but you don't recall when and where you learned each word. You know what certain foods taste like, but you don't remember every meal.

Your mind automatically makes predictions about the future, even when you aren't aware of it. When you see the edge of an object on a shelf, your mind can predict that it will be a book if you pick it up. You expect the book to have a certain weight, texture, and appearance. As long as your expectations are met, the mental pattern remains intact.

Based on your previous reading experience, you already have certain anticipations about what you'll find in this book. If it satisfies all your expectations, you won't learn anything new and reading this will have been a waste of your time. In order to help you grow, this book must violate your expectations and give you some unexpected "Aha!" moments.

Your mind continually generalizes from your specific experiences, stores those general patterns, and then applies them to predict the outcome of new events. This happens automatically, usually without your conscious knowledge. However, once you become aware that this is how your mind works, you can deliberately take your intelligence to a whole new level.

There are two powerful ways you can apply your mind's predictive powers to accelerate your personal growth. First, by embracing new experiences that are unlike anything you've previously encountered, you'll literally become more intelligent. New situations shift your mind into learning mode, which enables you to discover new patterns. The more patterns your mind learns, the better it gets at prediction, and the smarter you become.

Read a book on a topic that's completely alien to you. Talk to people you'd normally avoid. Visit an unfamiliar city. Stretch beyond the patterns your mind has already learned. In order to grow, you must repeatedly tackle fresh challenges and consider new ideas to give your mind fresh input. If you merely repeat the same experiences, you'll stagnate, and your mental capacity will atrophy.

What you learn in one area can often be applied to others. For example, Leonardo da Vinci, considered a genius by any reasonable standard, achieved competence across a diverse set of fields, including art, music, science, anatomy, engineering, architecture, and many others. While some would argue that such wide-ranging interests were a result of his intelligence, I think it's more likely that they were the cause of it—or at least a major contributing factor. By exposing himself to such a rich variety of input, da Vinci found patterns that others never noticed. This vastly amplified his problem-solving abilities. What's considered commonplace in one field often has creative applications in other disciplines.

Excessive routine is the enemy of intelligence. Exposing yourself to the same types of input over and over again won't help you grow. You'll merely satisfy your mind's expectations instead of pushing it to form new patterns. If you want to become smarter, you must keep stirring things up. Establish basic routines only to provide a stable foundation for branching out into unexplored territory. Push yourself to do things you've never done before. Keep exposing yourself to new experiences, ideas, and input. The more novel situations you encounter that violate your expectations, the faster you'll learn and the smarter you'll become.

The second way to apply your mind's predictive powers is to make conscious, deliberate predictions and use those predictions to make better decisions. Think about where you're headed and ask yourself: *How do I honestly expect my life to turn out?* Imagine that a very logical, impartial observer examines your situation in detail and is assigned to predict what your life will look like in 20 years, based on your current behavior patterns. What kind of future will this person predict for you?

If you're brave enough, ask several people who know you well to give you an honest assessment of where they see you in two decades. Their answers may surprise you.

When you become aware of your mind's long-term expectations, you bypass the pattern of denial and stare truth straight in the eye. This gives you the opportunity to reinforce your positive predictions and to make changes to prevent negative predictions from occurring.

Your emotions are part of your mind's predictive output. Positive feelings stem from positive predictions, and negative feelings result from negative ones. When you feel good, your mind is anticipating a positive outcome that you desire. When you feel bad, your mind expects an unfavorable outcome. Negative emotions serve as a warning that you must change your behavior now in order to prevent unwanted predictions from coming to pass.

Listen to your honest expectations. Don't fight with them or try to deny them, since that will only drive you into self-doubt. Learn to accept your expectations and work with them. When you notice that you're anticipating a negative outcome, look behind those beliefs to find the cause, and keep making changes until your expectations change. When you uncover positive expectations, notice what's working for you and keep doing more of it.

Accuracy

The closer your internal model of reality matches actual reality, the more capable you become. Greater accuracy means greater fitness for life as a human being. With an accurate map, you're more likely to make sound decisions that will take you in the direction of your desires. With an inaccurate map, you're more likely to experience setbacks and frustration.

Total clarity is a rarity. When you pursue a particular career, you'll never know if a different one might have turned out better. When you're in a relationship, you can never be certain that a more compatible partner isn't right around the corner. Whenever you make one decision, you'll never know what would have happened if you made a different choice.

The worst part is that even when you do feel certain, that's still no guarantee you're correct. You've been wrong before, haven't you? History says it's a safe bet that there's something you think you know right now that will later prove to be false.

You can try to gain as much clarity as possible about a given situation, and that's generally a good idea, but you can never eliminate all uncertainty. So you have two basic options: deny the unpredictability of life and create your own false sense of security, or accept the vagaries of life and learn to live with them. In the first case, you're drawing your map of reality the way you want it to be, regardless of what the actual terrain looks like. In the second case, you're striving to make your map as accurate as possible, even though you may dislike how it looks. The second option is better.

When you accept the inherent uncertainty of life, your decisions will increase in accuracy. You'll find it easier to avoid mistakes like gambling away all your money or falling into an abusive relationship, and you'll be in a better position to capitalize on genuine opportunities. You needn't be paralyzed by the unpredictability of life. The key is to intelligently manage risks instead of denying their existence. Learn to thrive on uncertainty, and even enjoy it.

Another problem is that your predictions could be incorrect. Some inaccuracies will self-correct as you gain additional experience and deepen your understanding of reality, but many times those errors can worsen and become self-reinforcing. Here are some examples of how your mind's predictive powers can fail you:

— **Overgeneralization.** You have a few bad dating experiences, so your mind learns the pattern that dating is disappointing. Consequently, you avoid going on any more dates because you see the activity as something to avoid. Unfortunately, this means you'll never again have a *positive* dating experience, which would have allowed your mind to correct this belief. Old patterns persist as long as they remain unchallenged.

— **Prejudice.** You overhear your co-workers complaining that someone who was just hired is apparently a real pain to work with.

This causes you to harbor negative expectations about the new hire. During your first assignment with this person, you naturally expect trouble, so you resist working together cooperatively. The other person picks up on your negative treatment and responds in kind, thereby fulfilling your expectations. Making snap judgments without the benefit of direct experience often leads to erroneous conclusions.

— **Self-fulfilling prophecy.** A number of your friends try to start their own online businesses, but they all fail and eventually give up. From their example, your mind learns that starting an online business is difficult and will most likely lead to failure. A year later you decide to launch your own Web-based enterprise. You subconsciously sabotage yourself by making avoidable mistakes, and eventually you give up, just as your friends did.

These problematic patterns all share a common element: their predictions are overly pessimistic. Such patterns can magnify fear, lower self-esteem, and induce negative emotions like worry and stress. In the worst cases, overly pessimistic predictions can cause depression, helplessness, and even suicide. On the other hand, being too optimistic is just as problematic and can lead to overconfidence, unreasonable risk taking, and manic behavior.

The best predictions are the most accurate ones, but where self-reinforcement is concerned, it's better to strengthen high self-esteem, positive emotions, and a reasonable degree of initiative, as opposed to low self-esteem, negative emotions, and undue timidity. These predictions aren't just passive observations—they're active causes unto themselves.

Acceptance

Once you've identified what's true for you with a reasonable degree of accuracy, your next task is to fully and completely accept the truth. This includes accepting the long-term consequences of your predictions.

Consider your physical body. Is it healthy, fit, and strong? Or is it unhealthy, flabby, and weak? What do you predict will happen if you continue with your current health habits? Do you accept the truth of where you'll likely end up? Are you willing to live with those consequences?

What about your finances? Are you creating such an abundance of value that you'll never know scarcity? Or are you headed for the poorhouse? What do you honestly expect to happen if your current financial patterns continue? Do you accept the complete truth of your situation?

Of course there's tremendous uncertainty in trying to predict where your life is headed, but you can still aim for the most reasonable, rational expectation based on the available evidence. If you were looking at someone else's life that shared the same qualities as yours and you had to place a wager on the outcome, how would you place your bet? Pretend you're Sherlock Holmes looking at the evidence and trying to predict the outcome. What do you honestly expect?

One of the most important skills to develop in the area of personal growth is the ability to admit the whole truth to yourself, even if you don't like what you see and even if you feel powerless to change it. When you face unpleasant truths, you'll often encounter strong internal resistance. This resistance pushes you to avoid facing the truth, running through endless cycles of distraction, escapism, denial, and procrastination. Only by staring directly into these truths can you summon the strength to deal with them consciously. A simple rule of thumb is this: whatever you fear, you must eventually face.

Whenever you're faced with a part of reality you don't like, and you feel powerless to change it, the first step is to accept the truth of your situation. Say to yourself: *This situation is wrong for me, yet I lack the strength to change it right now.*

Openly admit to yourself that even though you're stuck with complete responsibility for every area of your life, you may not have the ability to fix what isn't working at this point. Simply accept that this is how things are for now, but don't deny the truth of the situation. Never pretend to enjoy a job you hate. Never pretend to be happy in an unfulfilling relationship. Never pretend that your finances are strong when they're really weak. If you want your situation to improve, you must first come clean with yourself and admit the whole truth.

When you fully accept reality, you'll begin making better decisions because they'll be based on truth instead of fiction. If you admit that your body is terribly out of shape, you'll stop pretending that you're in good health. You'll stop subscribing to the delusion that your poor eating habits and lack of exercise are acceptable to you. You'll begin to see that you've got to start making different decisions if you want your situation to change—it isn't going to happen on its own. Once you fully surrender to what is, you can finally begin to create what you want.

Self-Awareness

As you strive to bring more truth into your life, you must cultivate a high degree of self-awareness. This includes becoming aware of your strengths, weaknesses, talents, knowledge, biases, attachments, desires, emotions, instincts, habits, and state of mind.

As human beings, we're often filled with conflicting desires. One part of us wants to be healthy, happy, and highly conscious. Another part wants nothing more than to eat, sleep, have sex, and be lazy. Without the presence of consciousness, we fall into reflexive patterns by default, living more like unconscious animals than fully sentient human beings.

Recognize that your level of awareness doesn't remain constant. Sometimes pure logic dominates your thinking; other times you're overwhelmed with emotional concerns. Sometimes you feel incredibly spiritual; other times you're worried about your finances. Sometimes you eat for good health and energy; other times you satisfy yourself with all the processed junk you can devour.

When you make decisions from a certain state of mind and act upon them, you reinforce that same state, thereby increasing the likelihood you'll respond similarly in the future. For example, if you act out of anger, you'll strengthen your mind's anger response. If you act out of kindness, you'll reinforce a kind response. Any given level of awareness has a tendency to perpetuate itself, so you'll likely find yourself cycling through the same ones repeatedly. A significant part of personal development involves working to release your attachment to the lower states as you draw yourself into higher consciousness on a more consistent basis. On a practical level, this means letting go of addictions, negative emotions, and fear-based behaviors and replacing them with consciously chosen, principle-centered actions. And in order to successfully change your behaviors, you must first develop an awareness of your thoughts.

A good way to build your awareness is to make your important decisions from the most reasonable thinking you can muster. The best point to make new choices is when you feel alert, clearheaded, and intelligent. That's the time to consider making big transformations in your life such as a career change, a relationship change, or moving to a new city. Learn to trust those higher states of consciousness. Put the decisions in writing and fully commit yourself to them. When you inevitably sink back down to lower states and lose sight of that higher perspective, continue to act on those decisions even though you may no longer feel as committed to them. Over time, your external circumstances will change in ways that reinforce those higher states. Living consciously gets easier with practice.

One time when I was in a state of very high awareness, I made the decision to switch careers from computer-game development to personal development. That was a stretch for me, especially since my games business was doing well, and I still had several large projects on my plate. However, I felt good about the decision, and I knew it was correct. But of course a few weeks later, I was still bogged down working on the games business with no end in sight. As I slipped into a lower level of awareness, I began to second-guess my determination to switch careers. I had to remind myself that I'd made the choice from a high level of awareness; and it was a sound, intelligent decision. This helped me let go of my resistance and trust the original choice I'd made.

My decisions may not be perfect, but when I use this process, I can at least trust that I made them correctly and from a place of truth.

When you consistently make key decisions from a high level of awareness, they will become more congruent. You'll avoid getting stuck in that state of ambivalence where you keep shifting back and forth between alternatives and can't make up your mind. Recognize that when you make choices from a place of anger, fear, sadness, or guilt, you cannot be aligned with truth because your predictions will be negatively biased by those lower states.

Self-awareness is really truth-awareness. When your awareness is high, you're closer to truth than when your awareness is low. If you aren't aligned with truth, your decisions will produce inferior results. Truth-aligned decisions are more accurate and will tend to yield better results than those made from low awareness. The key is to use your self-awareness to recognize when you're aligned with truth and when you aren't, and strive to make your important decisions only when this core principle is on your side.

Blocks to Truth

There are several blocks that prevent us from fully aligning with truth. They increase the chance of forming inaccurate mental patterns. Many of these false patterns are self-reinforcing and can be difficult to correct. However, once you become aware of these blocks, you'll be less likely to succumb to them.

Media Conditioning

Media companies generate profits largely from advertising, and for advertising to be effective, you must eventually buy something—whether it be a car, a drug, or a meal. People who hold an accurate model of reality only buy what they actually want or need, so advertisers frequently promote half-truths and outright falsehoods to boost profits. For example, if a brewery can convince you that drinking alcohol will make you feel popular or sexy, they can generate more revenue than if they portray a more accurate depiction of alcohol consumption.

In order to fully trust the information provided by a media source, you must be able to trust that the source will not sacrifice truth to a conflicting value. The problem with corporate-owned media is that when there's a conflict between profit and truth, truth doesn't always win.

The cumulative effect of mass-media exposure is to condition you to adopt a false view of reality—one that upholds pro-advertiser values. The more you expose yourself to mainstream media such as television, the more skewed your mental model of reality becomes. Furthermore, the more time you invest in media consumption, the less time you invest in learning from direct experience. This is a path of long-term laziness, apathy, and decay, not intelligent self-actualization.

You can reduce the effect of this block by learning to find joy in the direct experience of life instead of the pale substitute of mass media. Whenever you're exposed to media conditioning, remain aware that certain people have a vested financial interest in reshaping your beliefs about reality in a way that often conflicts with truth. I'm optimistic, however, that society will eventually outgrow the need for media ma-nipulation as more people realize that power and truth needn't be in conflict. As you'll learn in Chapter 5, power and truth work much better as allies; together they form the principle of authority.

Social Conditioning

Social conditioning is a close cousin to media conditioning. The society in which you live—including your family, friends, co-workers, and acquaintances—contributes heavily to your understanding of reality. Through your interactions with others, you're continually in-fluenced by social, cultural, educational, and religious ideas. Unfor-tunately, such conditioned beliefs often place other values ahead of truth, so you may feel compelled to do the same. In the long run, this disconnection from truth leads to self-doubt, causing you to give away your power out of weakness and confusion. Realigning yourself with truth enables you to reclaim that power.

Sometimes social conditioning serves us well. For example, a com-mon language helps us communicate and connect with each other. Other times, social conditioning installs false beliefs that weaken us, such as an unwarranted fear of public speaking.

It's important to develop an awareness of your socially conditioned beliefs and examine them consciously. When you sense a conflict between your beliefs, your behavior, and your feelings, ask yourself if you really believe what you've been taught. Are your beliefs truthful and accurate? Are they congruent with your perceptions? In order to align yourself with truth, you must eventually release erroneous, inaccurate, and inconsistent beliefs.

I was raised Catholic and attended Catholic school for 12 years. All of my family and most of my friends were Catholic, too, so I had virtually no exposure to other belief systems in my youth. Nevertheless, in my late teens, I began to doubt what I'd been taught because it often conflicted with my direct observations of reality. When I finally admitted that Catholicism no longer resonated with me, I felt free to explore my true spiritual beliefs. I was sometimes ostracized for this decision, but I learned that self-trust is more important than social conformity. My intent isn't to denigrate any particular belief system but simply to recommend that you put your greatest trust in your own judgment, even when others disagree with you. Cultivating self-trust frees you; self-doubt enslaves you.

False Beliefs

False learning occurs when you adopt a belief that's either partially or completely untrue. Such beliefs may be acquired accidentally or installed deliberately by others. The effect is that your future decisions become more error-prone, and your results are sabotaged.

When I started my computer-game development business after college, I was filled with false beliefs about how a real-world business should work, so I made dumb mistakes that wasted my time and money. For example, I mistakenly assumed that a signed contract would always be honored by the other party, failing to consider the inherent risk in any transaction. I closed important deals and soon became dependent on them for income, only to see them later collapse. It took years to rid myself of these false beliefs, but as I uprooted them one by one, my decisions improved, and the failing business finally became profitable.

A large part of conscious growth involves identifying and purging false beliefs. Do your best to remain open to fresh ideas and input, and challenge your assumptions when you suspect you may be clinging to falsehood. Later in this chapter, I'll provide some simple exercises to help you do that.

Emotional Interference

Strong emotions can corrupt your ability to perceive reality accurately. Feelings such as fear, anger, grief, guilt, shame, frustration, being overwhelmed, and loneliness block you from thinking clearly, causing you to mistake falsehood for truth. Similarly, positive emotions can make you overly optimistic, encouraging you to take unreasonable risks and to make overaggressive promises you won't keep.

By cultivating your self-awareness, you can learn to recognize when your judgment is impaired by strong emotions. Your feelings may prevent you from perceiving reality accurately, but a high degree of self-awareness can help you avoid acting on those misperceptions.

Important decisions should be made when you're clearheaded and rational, not when you're overly optimistic or pessimistic. However, your feelings have a powerful intelligence of their own that can assist you in making sound decisions. Think of your emotions as a condensed version of your mind's predictive output, so it's wise to make decisions that produce positive feelings.

Addictions

Addictions such as smoking, drinking, or excessive Web surfing make it harder to accept reality because these behaviors reinforce ignorance and denial. For example, if you smoke cigarettes every day, your pattern of behavior makes it difficult for you to accept evidence that smoking is hazardous to your health. If you fear that quitting will be too great a challenge, you're likely to avoid seeking the truth about smoking because it will compel you to face your fear and attempt to quit.

Addictions provide rich soil for cultivating further falsehood. Many people are ashamed and embarrassed by their addictions, so they do their best to hide them. Maintaining a false front becomes more important than truth; and secrets, deception, and lies take the place of honest communication.

The first step in overcoming any addiction is to admit the truth: *I am addicted.* Even though overcoming the addiction may be a struggle, if you can admit and accept the truth of your situation, it will help prevent you from succumbing to further falsehood. It's perfectly okay to say to yourself, *I am addicted and want to change, but right now I lack the strength to do so.* Being completely honest with yourself is vastly superior to living in denial. You'll often find that upon taking that first step, the internal and external resources you need to break your addiction will soon come into your life, and the response from others will be compassionate and supportive instead of disdainful and judgmental.

Immaturity

A certain degree of maturity is required to fully accept reality, and this comes from experience. The more fresh experiences you acquire, the faster your thinking will mature. The more you seek shelter and comfort through diversion, escapism, and fantasy, the longer you'll suffer from immature and inaccurate thinking.

Children have the most inaccurate models of reality because they lack experience, so their minds are less adept at making accurate predictions. It's easy to fool an inexperienced child with a trick that an adult would catch. The adult has enough experience to accurately predict the outcome; the child does not.

You can't align yourself with truth and flee from it at the same time. If you wish to live as a fully conscious human being, you must release the immaturity of escapism and embrace the deeper growth experiences that only maturity can bring.

Secondary Gain

Secondary gain is a common problem that occurs when you temporarily benefit (gain) by embracing falsehood. For example, you may tell a lie at work in order to avoid being fired, you may deny your relationship problems in order to preserve the peace, or you may eat unhealthy food for the sake of convenience.

Distancing yourself from the truth is never a wise long-term decision. It stems from a lack of acceptance of your own predictions and a refusal to deal with them openly and honestly. When you look behind secondary gain, you'll invariably find a deeper falsehood you've been fiercely denying. Your refusal to deal with that lie perpetuates an ongoing downward spiral. Apparent short-term benefits replace true advancement, drawing you ever deeper into a life of repression and denial. The more you succumb to the lure of secondary gain, the phonier you become as a human being.

For example, suppose you work in a job that you intuitively feel is wrong for you; you know it's a dead end. When you look ahead, you see nothing but a soulless void. You just can't bring yourself to accept the truth of your situation, so instead you live in denial, pretending that everything will somehow turn out okay. Instead of facing the truth, you search for other ways to fill the emptiness, and eventually you're seduced by the substitute of secondary gain. Instead of your true purpose, you pursue money, recognition, or comfort. Instead of genuine growth, you settle for climbing the corporate ladder. Instead of abiding friendship and human intimacy, you settle for a sea of casual contacts, none of whom know, accept, and love the real you. Instead of worthwhile challenges, you settle for the illusion of security.

The pursuit of secondary gain leads to persistent dissatisfaction, emptiness, and unhappiness. It's a temporary drug that can never fulfill you. If you find yourself caught up in this addictive cycle, take the time for some deep introspection. Even if you aren't ready to deal with the long-term consequences yet, at least admit the truth to yourself. Don't waste your life defending a string of false accomplishments.

How to Become More Truthful

It's perfectly normal to find plenty of falsehood and denial in your life, and you may worry that realigning yourself with truth will be an overwhelming task. Don't be discouraged. Every step you take in the direction of truth will make it easier to continue on the path of greater honesty, self-awareness, and acceptance. You don't need to fix every problem overnight.

Here are some simple, practical exercises you can use to help realign yourself with truth.

Self-Assessment

One of the best ways to bring more truth into your life is to conduct a quick self-assessment. Assign a numerical rating to each area of your life using a simple 1–10 scale. A 1 means you're definitely not getting what you want in this area of your life; a 10 means you're absolutely experiencing what you desire. Please take a minute to do this now. Here are the areas to rate:

Area of Your Life	Your Rating (1–10)
Habits & daily routine	_____
Career & work	_____
Money & finances	_____
Health & fitness	_____
Mental development & education	_____
Social life & relationships	_____
Home & family	_____
Emotions	_____
Character & integrity	_____
Life purpose & contribution	_____
Spiritual development	_____

Your answers should provide a nice snapshot of how you're doing. Usually you'll find that some areas lag behind the others, sometimes far behind. Interestingly, it's in our weakest spots that we most often succumb to falsehood and denial, since those are the most difficult areas to face. But those areas can't improve until you face and accept the truth.

Now I want you to look at those same numbers from a different perspective. Take every rating that isn't a 9 or 10, cross it off, and replace it with a 1. So now each of them must be a 1, 9, or 10.

You see, if you can't rate a given area of your life a 9 or 10, then obviously you don't have what you really want in that area. This can be especially hard to admit when you think you have a 7. A 7 looks pretty good at first glance, but the true 9s and 10s are way beyond 7s. The 10s are so far out there that you probably can't even see them from the position of a 7.

A 7 is what you get when you allow too much falsehood and denial to creep into your life. It's a phony rating to begin with, a 1 in disguise. Either you have what you want, or you don't. A 6, 7, or 8 is the answer you give when you know you don't have what you want, but you aren't ready to face up to it yet.

I know this sounds unreasonably harsh, but based on my own experience as well as what I've observed in others, people commonly rate some part of their lives a 7 (or thereabouts) when they've disconnected themselves from the truth. A 7 is a job instead of a purpose-driven career. A 7 is a comfortable living arrangement instead of a deeply fulfilling relationship. A 7 is an income that covers your basic expenses instead of providing true abundance. When you rate any part of your life as a 7, you're really saying: "This isn't what I want, but I'm not sure I can do better, so I'll pretend it's good enough. It could be worse." However, the truth is that if you aren't experiencing what you want, you're already in the worst possible situation.

An honest rating has more to do with your path than your position. For example, I absolutely love my current career. I'd definitely rate it a 10. I've enjoyed a certain level of success in this field, but that isn't why I rate it so highly. If I went back in time to when I first started, I'd still have rated my career as a 9 or 10. Even though I had virtually no external evidence of success back then, I knew I was on the right path. My position didn't matter. The high rating came from knowing I was headed in the right direction.

When you rate some part of your life a 7, it means you're on the wrong path but you don't want to accept it. You don't want to acknowledge that you're approaching a dead end, so you base your rating on your position instead. "Look how far I've come down the wrong path," you say. You assign yourself a 7 based on your location along the route, even though the path itself is really a 1. Your position doesn't matter. Your rating must come from the path. You can be starting from scratch in a new career, a new relationship, or a new spiritual journey and still rate that part of your life a 9 or 10 if you're on the right track.

Now look at each area of your life again, and ask yourself, *What do I truly want? What is my dream, my grand vision? What is the deep desire I've been longing for, the one I hesitate to admit because I don't think I can have it? What path do I most want to experience?* Accept that you want what you want, and stop living in denial of your true desires.

Journaling

Journaling is one of the easiest and most powerful ways to discover new truths. By getting your thoughts out of your head and putting them down in writing, you'll gain insights you'd otherwise miss.

While some people use journaling merely to record their thoughts and experiences in a "Dear Diary" fashion, the real power of journaling lies in its ability to help you move beyond sequential thinking and examine your thoughts from a holistic, bird's-eye view. Use this tool to solve tricky problems, brainstorm new ideas, bring clarity to fuzzy situations, and evaluate progress toward your goals. Instead of a mere record-keeping tool, your journal can vastly accelerate your personal development if you devote it to that purpose.

Many people use paper journals, others prefer a word processor, and some like special journaling software. I used paper journals for many years, but in 2002 I switched to journaling software and never went back. The advantages are numerous. Typing is faster than writing; your entries are stored in a secure, private database; you can use the built-in search feature to instantly find old entries; you can assign entries to categories for better organization; and you can easily make secure backups. The more robust programs even allow you to insert images, audio recordings, videos, spreadsheets, files, Web links, and more. Once you try journaling software, you'll never want to go back to pen and paper.

If you'd like to see an actual entry from my personal journal, you'll find it included as part of an article on journaling at **www.Steve Pavlina.com/journaling**. I wrote that particular journal entry a few months before launching StevePavlina.com, as I was trying to figure out how I'd be able to generate income from a personal development Website. It was funny to look back and see that I nearly dismissed the approach I eventually ended up using.

Media Fasting

A great way to reduce the impact of media conditioning is to go on a 30-day media fast. For 30 days straight, keep the television turned off and avoid all newspapers, magazines, and online media sources. Unplug yourself completely and see what happens.

I documented my personal results with media fasting in the article "8 Changes I Experienced After Giving Up TV" (**www.StevePavlina. com/notv**). I found that when I went 30 days without television, I felt free to focus on more important activities, I spent more time connecting with friends, and I went outside more often. It was an eye-opening experience, and I encourage you to give it a try. You'll learn more about 30-day trials in Chapter 8.

✦ ✦

I want to conclude our exploration of truth by sharing one of my all-time favorite poems with you, "The Guy in the Glass." I first heard it when I was a teenager, and it had a powerful effect on me. I hope you treasure it as much as I do. Incidentally, the word *pelf* in the first line of the poem means "wealth."

When you get what you want in your struggle for pelf,
And the world makes you King for a day,
Then go to the mirror and look at yourself,
And see what that guy has to say.

For it isn't your Father, or Mother, or Wife,
Who judgement upon you must pass.
The feller whose verdict counts most in your life
Is the guy staring back from the glass.

He's the feller to please, never mind all the rest,
For he's with you clear up to the end,
And you've passed your most dangerous, difficult test
If the guy in the glass is your friend.

You may be like Jack Horner and "chisel" a plum,
And think you're a wonderful guy,
But the man in the glass says you're only a bum
If you can't look him straight in the eye.

You can fool the whole world down the pathway of years,
And get pats on the back as you pass,
But your final reward will be heartaches and tears
If you've cheated the guy in the glass.

© 1934 by Dale Wimbrow (1895–1954) Used by permission.

I recommend that you follow the instructions in the first stanza of the poem literally. Go to a mirror and look at yourself. Is the person staring back from the glass your friend?

If you want to grow as a conscious human being, you must learn to embrace truth and relinquish falsehood. Truth enhances growth; falsehood destroys it. Whenever you feel you've fallen off track in your life, stop and ask yourself: *Am I aligned with truth?* If the answer is no, direct your efforts toward bringing more truth, awareness, and acceptance to your situation.

Now let's turn our attention to the primary mechanism through which we discover truth: the principle of . . .

✦ ✦ ✦ ✦

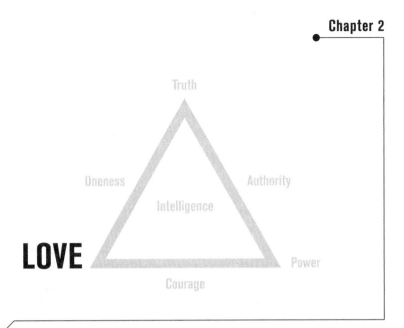

Chapter 2

Truth

Oneness · Authority
Intelligence

LOVE · Power

Courage

"Anything will give up its secrets if you love it enough."
— GEORGE WASHINGTON CARVER

Love is the second principle of personal development. Obviously love is an emotion, but it's also much more than that. One of the fundamental choices you face in every encounter is the choice to approach or avoid. You can try to connect with people, or you can pull away from them. You can immerse yourself in your day's work, or you can procrastinate. You can approach any person, place, or thing with the intention to connect, or you can remain aloof and keep your distance. The decision to connect is the essence of love.

Sometimes love arises spontaneously. You may feel a certain affinity for a person, place, or activity without knowing why. For some reason, you just perceive a strong connection. Maybe you meet someone new and have a sense you're going to become friends. Maybe you have a special fondness for playing the guitar, or perhaps you feel a soulful connection to a certain place. You might not always know why such feelings arise, but forming connections is clearly an integral part of human life. You could even go so far as to say that it's the very reason why we're here.

Every day you're compelled to make connection decisions. By your actions you decide what to link up with and what to avoid. Will you talk to your spouse or connect with the television? Will you take your next vacation at a favorite spot or go someplace new this time? Will you bond with a pet or go to a party? Whenever you choose to make one connection, you simultaneously choose not to connect with all of the other possibilities.

If you want to grow consciously, you must deliberately decide which connections you'll strengthen and which you'll allow to weaken. Such choices ultimately determine the shape of your life. In the long run, your life becomes a reflection of what you choose to connect with most often. When you feel good about your connections, you come into greater alignment with the principle of love.

In addition to *connection,* there are two other major aspects of love: *communication* and *communion.* In the upcoming sections, we'll explore all three of these elements.

Connection

In order to grow as a human being, you must master the art of forming connections. To connect means to give something your attention, to think about it, and to engage with it. In addition to connecting with people, you can connect with groups, objects, places, ideas, values, and activities. Establishing a link requires nothing but your attention. Think about your mother. Think about democracy. Think about your favorite song. Put your attention on something and you immediately connect with it.

Do you remember how you first learned about the physical universe when you were a young child? You looked around and noticed objects that grabbed your attention. Then you moved toward them, picked them up, and played with them. You learned about your environment through direct, hands-on experience. If you found something you didn't like, you tried to avoid it in the future. If you found something you liked, you gave it even more attention. Sometimes your focus put you in a state of love.

As adults we often forget that the best way to fulfill our desires is to walk right up to whatever interests us and engage with it directly. Instead, we create all kinds of silly rules that limit our ability to connect with what we want. We can't start our own business because it's too risky. We can't talk to that person because we're already in a relationship. We can't explore other belief systems because our current religion prohibits it.

Such rules are rooted in fear and disconnection, and they have no place in a life of conscious growth. When you make the commitment to live consciously, you'll often find yourself running afoul of them. If you wish to become more loving, you must be willing to connect.

Many of my best growth experiences came about when I decided to connect with something that was important to me even when others disagreed with my choice—going vegetarian is a good example. One day I decided to try eating vegetarian for a month just because it seemed interesting to me. I liked it so much that I never went back, and four years later, I progressed to a fully vegan diet. This decision to connect with something I found attractive opened up a new wave of connections with other people who shared similar values, and it allowed me to leave behind a way of eating that didn't resonate with my true self. Some people resisted my decision, but it was the right choice for me.

In order to learn and grow, you must have the freedom to connect with what you want and to disconnect from what you don't want. No one can give you that freedom. It's your birthright as a human being. You don't need anyone's permission to decide which connections are best for you. It's up to you to take the initiative to connect with what you want and to disconnect from what you don't want. By consciously making connections that feel intuitively correct to you, you bring yourself into alignment with the principle of love.

Communication

Communication is the means through which we express love. The root of the word *communicate* means "common," and it's natural to think that when we communicate with someone, we look for something we have in common. Identifying commonalities is essentially how we form new connections.

You communicate effectively by first connecting with the familiar and then branching out into the unfamiliar. When you meet someone new, the first step is to discover your shared interests, values, and attitudes. This creates a basic bond of trust and friendship. The next step is to explore and learn from your differences. People who are too different from you are difficult to bond with, and those who are too similar can't teach you very much. The best relationships provide enough common ground to form a strong bond while also stimulating growth in new directions.

The richest form of communication is basic face-to-face conversation. This allows you to pick up not only content but also vocal expressions and body language. You'll usually experience much deeper connections with people when you communicate in person instead of by phone or e-mail.

Good communication skills take time to develop. The more you practice, the better you'll get. While there are specific techniques you can learn such as smiling, maintaining an open posture, and making eye contact, don't forget that the primary purpose of communication is to create a connection with the other person. Even when you have a specific agenda in mind like persuasion, education, or entertainment, your first step is to establish a bond. Great orators, teachers, and entertainers strive to break the ice and connect with their audiences first; only after this has been achieved do they go into their main material.

Genuine communication requires mutual understanding rooted in love and trust; otherwise, you can't effectively share truth with others. It isn't enough to speak your mind and assume other people understand and accept what you're saying, nor is it enough to listen well and assume you understand what's been said. To communicate well, there must be some bond of caring between speaker and listener.

There are few greater joys in life than the experience of conscious communication with another person. No ego games, false fronts, or manipulative tactics are employed. Both individuals simply want to connect with each other for the purpose of learning and growing. Once you've experienced such open, loving communication with another human being, it's hard to settle for anything less.

Communion

Communion is the deep sense of bonding that gives rise to the emotional side of love. It's the delicious feeling of completeness that comes from sharing our true selves.

Consider your relationship with another person. Where does it actually exist? It doesn't exist anywhere in the external world. You can't simply point to it and say, "That's our relationship right there." It lives purely within your thoughts. Consequently, your connection with another person is whatever you think it is. Your belief makes the relationship real. If you cease to believe in it, then for all practical purposes, it no longer exists. The physical residue may remain, such as a particular living arrangement, but the true human connection will have been lost.

When you understand that there's no such thing as an external relationship and that all such connections exist solely in your mind, you'll become aware that the true purpose of relationships is self-exploration. Whenever you communicate in any fashion, you are in truth exploring different aspects of yourself. When you feel a deep sense of communion with another person, you're actually connecting deeply with an important part of yourself. By communing with others, you learn to love yourself more fully.

Every day I receive a large volume of e-mail feedback through my Website. Most of it comes from people who've never met me in person, nor have they ever had a single conversation with me. However, due to the large volume of personal information I've shared online, many consider me a close friend because they know so much about me, so they write to me from the perspective that we already share a bond of love. In their very first message to me, many people will tell me things about themselves they won't even share with their spouses. In their minds, they've already experienced such a strong communion with me over a period of months or years that they feel comfortable discussing their most private matters. Of course I do my best to honor such connections in the loving spirit in which they're offered.

From my own internal perspective, however, an even more powerful shift has occurred. I observe that as I've deepened my own communion with myself by exploring my thoughts in writing, my external world has shifted to reflect that internal growth. Instead of opening with shallow small talk, people begin conversations with me by immediately diving into issues of great importance to them. Even teenagers talk to me like this. The more I commune with myself on the inside, the deeper my relationships with others become. Today, my life overflows with opportunities for profound human connection. Over the years, I've seen abundant evidence that our relationships with other people always reflect our internal relationships with various parts of ourselves. If you have trouble connecting with people on the outside, it may be because you aren't communing with yourself on the inside. When you learn how to feel lovingly connected on the inside, you'll find it much easier to forge a bond with others.

The good news is that when you understand that all relationships are internal, you can consciously change how you represent them to yourself and thereby change their outward manifestation as well. If you feel disconnected with your true self, you can expect your interpersonal relationships to suffer from disconnection as well. If you want your human relationships to be more loving and accepting, you must learn to love and accept more aspects of yourself.

Loving yourself unconditionally is the result of a conscious choice. You're free to make this choice in every moment of every day. You don't need to fulfill any conditions or satisfy any rules. But in order to make this choice consciously, you must get to know yourself. No matter what hidden qualities you discover, you're still worthy of love.

Blocks to Love

Certain problems can prevent you from easily forming new connections and deepening your existing ones, holding you in a perpetual state of disconnect. Here are some of the most common blocks that keep you out of alignment with love.

Disconnected Mind-set

Consciously connecting becomes very difficult when your mind is cluttered with thoughts that keep you disconnected. The assumption that we're all inherently separate beings is among the worst of those thoughts. A belief in separation becomes a self-fulfilling prophecy. Such a disconnected mind spawns behaviors that reinforce a disconnected lifestyle. Instead of lovingly reaching out to people, you timidly hold back. Instead of offering someone a hug, you settle for a handshake. Instead of actively initiating a conversation, you passively wait for the other person to make the first move.

It's important to recognize that the notion that everyone is a completely separate being from you is an unprovable assumption. When you're asleep and having a dream, do you assume that the other dream characters are separate and distinct from you? You probably do make that assumption while asleep, but when you awaken, you know it isn't true. Those dream characters are merely projections of your mind. They exist completely inside you, not separately from you. Now what if you carried that same mind-set into your waking world?

There's no rule cast in stone that requires you to assume everyone is separate from you. Something rather magical happens when you presuppose that everyone else is a part of you, just like one of your own dream characters. The first thing you realize is that there are no strangers. There are no insignificant people in your reality. Since everyone is a part of you, everyone has something to teach you. Loving another person becomes the same thing as loving a part of yourself. Since all parts of you are worthy of love, no human being is unworthy of love either. Loving other people and loving yourself are ultimately the exact same thing.

In my early 20s, I had a chance encounter with a peculiar woman. During one of our first conversations, I found myself opening up to her very easily. I had no idea why, but I just felt completely safe with her, and I trusted her implicitly. We became very close friends over-night, and I mean that literally. I'd never experienced such a deep and rapid bonding with another person before.

Over the next several weeks, I noticed that this woman was able to establish a similar level of rapport with almost everyone she met. Total strangers would begin telling her their life stories within the first ten min-utes of conversation. I asked her how this was possible, and she explained that it was the result of a particular mind-set she had about people. She said she knew deep down that we're all parts of the same whole. She didn't have to create new connections with people. She would simply tap into the connection she believed was already there. Her mind-set brought her into strong alignment with the principle of love because she regarded everyone as being lovingly connected to her.

This was a completely alien concept to me. I firmly believed we were all separate individuals. Creating a genuine connection with someone required time, common interests, personal compatibility, and a little luck. Sometimes people connected; sometimes they didn't. Nevertheless, I couldn't deny this woman's results.

Eventually I was able to relax my skepticism, and I tried to imagine that I was already connected to everyone else. I can't say it was easy to do this consistently, but the more I imagined it, the more real it became. Emotionally I became a more loving person. I began making new friends much more easily, and my social life reached a new level of abundance. Sometimes when I'd meet people for the first time, I knew right away we'd become good friends. Almost unconsciously I began interacting with people I'd just met as if we'd been friends for years, and I noticed they'd often respond in kind.

Of course the peculiar woman who taught me how to connect at this level was Erin, who's been my wife since 1998. She still talks to everyone as if they're a part of her own soul, regardless of their job title, personality, or physical appearance. It's rare that a week goes by without someone crying with her on the phone or in person as they share a deep personal connection. By aligning herself with the principle of love, she's able to help other people grow tremendously in a fairly short period of time.

You can connect with people very easily by tuning in to the connection that already exists. Instead of having to break the ice with someone, assume that there is no ice. On some level you're already connected. As you become more aligned with this perspective, you may even find that total strangers will approach you to strike up a conversation. When you feel lovingly connected to others, you'll often see others treating you the same way.

This is a skill you can develop with patience and practice. You don't have to blindly accept the philosophy behind this idea in order to benefit from it. You can apply it just by using your imagination. The next time you're with a group of people, imagine that each person you meet is already inherently connected to you. Assume the bond of love is already there, and notice what happens.

Fear of Rejection

Fear of rejection makes minor social interactions seem like gigantic threats. Such fear creates feelings of emptiness, loneliness, and isolation, sapping you of the positive desire to connect with others and pushing you out of alignment with love.

Is there anything inherently dangerous about walking up to another person and saying, "Hi, my name is Steve. You look like someone I haven't met yet. What's your name?" Initially the other person may indeed react like you're trying to sell them something, but they'll often give you the benefit of the doubt and allow the conversation to proceed. The worst case is that you part ways and nothing happens. The best case is that you make a fascinating new lifetime friend. How many times can you afford to make a bet like that? If you open your heart and communicate with love, you're sure to meet others who respond in kind.

The irony is that when you're feeling disconnected, connecting with people is the cure. If you spend more time with positive, upbeat, interesting people, it's unlikely you'll be feeling down in the first place.

In truth, your disconnection from other people is a sign that you've disconnected from the best parts of yourself.

You're a worthy human being. When you hold back from connecting due to fear of rejection, you rob other people of the chance to get to know you. Many people would love the chance to connect with you. They want someone to understand them, someone who can remind them that they aren't alone. When you connect with people, you're giving them exactly what they want. Reaching out socially does entail some minor risk, but the long-term benefits are so enormous that the only way to fail is to refuse to try. In Chapters 3 and 6, you'll learn to build your power and courage in order to overcome this common block.

Incompatibility

While it's possible to connect with virtually anyone on a soulful level, it's easier to communicate with those who have something in common with you. A shared culture, shared values, and a similar temperament grease the wheels of communication, making it easier to form new connections and deepen existing ones. When you want to enrich your life with new connections, it's wise to seek out people with whom you're compatible, notably in terms of character qualities, values, and attitude.

Have you ever found yourself nodding along while someone else is talking, even though you disagree with everything they're saying? You know that if you choose to speak up and express your true opinion, it will only spark a pointless argument. This is a common experience when we communicate with people whose values are incompatible with ours. When basic compatibility is absent, communication becomes strained, misunderstandings increase, and it's difficult to stay aligned with truth and love.

As you continue to grow, your compatibility preferences will surely shift. This is no one's fault. Allow yourself to let go of any group, person, career, or activity that no longer resonates with you, and you'll soon attract more compatible opportunities into your life. When you feel it's time to move on, let go with love. Take your connection from the level of direct interaction and make it a timeless, treasured memory. Then file that memory away and prepare yourself for something new.

The process of letting go can be very difficult, but it's an essential part of personal growth. When you fail to release incompatibilities from your life, you settle for mere tolerance and prevent compatible new connections from forming. Moreover, you create an even bigger disconnect within yourself. Tolerance is not an act of love—it is resistance to love.

Something very powerful occurs when you fill your life with compatible connections. First, you'll feel lovingly supported and encouraged to express yourself authentically. Second, you'll find it easier to connect with people who'd otherwise be totally incompatible with you, since you know you have that stable base to return to. For example, Jesus may have communicated with people who held very different values from his, but he spent lots of time with the 12 apostles who supported and believed in him. Perhaps Judas wasn't such a great ally, but 11 out of 12 isn't bad! How would you feel if you had a dozen loyal friends who called you *Lord* and *Master* and treated you as their teacher and savior? Do you think it would empower you to branch out and connect with less fear and hesitation? Do you think it would help you stay aligned with love? Don't wait for loving connections to fall into your lap. Go out and consciously create them.

Lack of Social Skills

If you feel socially awkward and have a hard time connecting with others, the problem may simply be a lack of experience. Like any other learned ability, good communication skills take practice to develop.

While there are many books about how to improve your social skills, I can't recommend any because they're almost invariably focused on low-level tactics such as how to initiate a conversation, what kinds of questions to ask, and how to mirror the other person's body language. People who use such techniques merely mimic the surface aspects of communication, and they often come across as shallow and insincere. If you try to use silly low-level techniques to connect with others, you'll merely get better at initiating pointless conversations that leave everyone feeling empty afterward.

If you're in the right frame of mind to begin with, you won't need to worry about mimicking behaviors such as smiling and mirroring. With practice, you'll develop more comfort in a variety of social situations; and when you become comfortable, you'll express yourself naturally. Feeling at ease is the basis of effective interpersonal communication.

When you feel totally comfortable with who you are, your ego recedes into the background. You aren't obsessed with thinking about how you look, what you sound like, or what others may think of you. You're focused on the topics you're discussing and the people you're communicating with. This is true whether you're having a conversation with an old friend or giving a speech in front of hundreds of people. It's as if you're witnessing communication occurring, but you aren't even there.

In order to develop your social skills, you need to foster the conditions that allow your natural communication style to emerge. One of the best ways to do so is to begin with the most compatible, comfortable, loving group you can find. Build your skills within that group, and then leverage your connections there to expand into other areas where you aren't as comfortable.

For example, a young man who's shy about talking to women may observe that he communicates very naturally with other players in an online computer game. In the game world, he finds it easier to stay aligned with love because he brings his love of the game with him. To build experience in connecting with women, he can focus on getting to know some of the female players in the game, even if they live thousands of miles away. From there he can try to deepen some of those friendships and take them outside of the game world, such as moving to e-mail and phone calls. Once he gains comfort with those connections, he may consider joining a local gaming or computer club and connect with women face-to-face. He can continue to expand his social network as he progressively stretches his comfort level.

By starting with a compatible base (a place where you find it easy to stay aligned with love) and working to expand your connections outward, you can improve your social skills tremendously. As you gain experience in new situations, the unknown soon becomes the known, and your comfort level rises. This process can continue for the rest of your life and never really ends. Your lifelong pursuit of growth can even be regarded as the progressive expansion of loving connections.

How to Connect More Deeply

Here are some specific, nonmanipulative techniques you can use to strengthen your ability to connect with love. Some of these exercises will help you form new connections, while others will help you deepen existing ones.

The Connection Exercise

Here's a very simple exercise that will enhance your ability to connect. Think of a person you already know and love. If you can't come up with anyone suitable, then think of someone you admire or respect. Picture that person in your mind's eye, and then choose to send love to that person. Imagine your love as positive energy flowing out of you. Tune in to the connection that already exists between you. Recognize that you're both part of the same whole. Hold that thought for a moment, and notice that it feels good.

Now try this: imagine an everyday object for which you have no special feelings, such as a pen or pencil. Choose something within arm's reach, and pick it up if you can. Look at it, and tune in to the nonphysical connection that already exists between you and this object. Imagine that this object is a part of you. On some level you're both the same. Send your love energy toward that object and say to it: "I love you," and "You're beautiful." This may seem a little strange, but notice that it still feels good. If you can love an ordinary object, what else might you be able to love?

Keep looking at your everyday object. As you continue to send it loving thoughts, imagine that you can also receive its affection in return. Just pretend that this object loves you back. You can even imagine it saying: "Awww . . . I love you, too." Allow yourself to perceive a mutually loving connection between you and this object, and notice that it feels good.

In truth, you can love absolutely anything. Love is not an accident. Love is a choice to recognize the deep nonphysical connection we all share. To love is to say, "We are the same."

Am I telling you this to make you fall in love with your furniture? No, the point is to encourage you to adopt a perspective that makes it easier to give and receive love. It's easier to recognize love as something that already exists instead of assuming you must create it from scratch.

The Time-Travel Meditation

This is one of my favorite meditation exercises, and I think you'll really enjoy it, too. First, go to a place where you can physically relax. Lie down or sit comfortably, close your eyes, and breathe deeply for a few minutes. Imagine a special room in your mind's eye, one with two comfortable chairs facing each other. You're sitting in one chair, and in the other chair is your future self—the person you'll become five years from now. Your future self knows everything you know, as well as everything that will happen to you during the next five years. Now imagine having a conversation with this person. Ask anything you want, and listen for the answers.

When you're ready, ask your future self to get up and leave the room, and imagine that your past self from five years ago walks in and sits down. You are *this* person's future self. Take a moment to recall what your past self has been going through. What was your life like exactly five years ago? Imagine your past self asking you questions about how your life turned out; and see yourself answering with empathy, understanding, and reassurance. Tell your past self about some of the challenges that will be coming up in the years ahead, challenges that you've already faced.

When you're finished connecting with your past self, imagine that your future self reenters the room and all three of you stand up. Your bodies begin to glow and become translucent. You float toward each other and merge into a single being of light. When this happens, you may experience an intense release of emotion. The three of you are now an integrated whole, a single being who exists outside of time. This being is the real you.

I encourage you to try this meditation at least once, even if you've never meditated before. It will help you recognize that there's a time-less nature to your existence, that you're more than just a physical being moving forward through time. In the presence of this aware-ness, your momentary worries will shrink, replaced by feelings of ex-pansiveness and connectedness.

Sharing

One of the easiest ways to lovingly connect with other people is to share something with them. Share a conversation. Share experi-ences. Share stories. Share laughs. Share a meal. Share a game. Share yourself. Life is filled with opportunities to share interesting moments with people.

Don't be afraid to take the initiative. Sometimes when you extend an offer such as a lunch invitation, the other person won't accept. Don't let that stop you. Simply turn around and make the same offer to someone else, and soon you'll find a person who welcomes your friendly overtures.

A popular form of sharing is to immerse yourself in an activity with another person, such as by going on a date, to a party, or on a vaca-tion together. This can create lasting memories that help solidify the connection. Sharing builds trust, and trust creates stronger bonds.

Fast-Forwarding

When you want to develop a deeper bond with someone you've just met, mentally fast-forward your relationship with that person in your mind's eye. Spend a few minutes privately imagining that the two of you have been good friends for several years. Take what you already know about that person and project it forward in time. For example, if you know that he or she is a golfer, imagine that you've played numerous rounds of golf together and shared many positive experiences on your favorite course. Feel the emotional bond between you becoming stronger. The next time you see the other person, you'll likely feel that your friendship has already become stronger, and the other person may pick up on that, too.

Fast-forwarding is a natural technique you probably use without even thinking about it. It's common to daydream about a possible future with someone you like, especially a romantic interest. But you can also consciously apply fast-forwarding to build a more loving connection with a new friend, acquaintance, or business contact.

The Direct Approach

This method takes a little courage, but when it works, it tends to work extremely well. The direct approach means to verbally acknowledge your feelings of fondness for another person. During a conversation, simply make a direct statement such as, "You know . . . you're a really good friend." Unless there's some kind of underlying hostility between the two of you, the other person will almost always respond in kind. After airing such feelings out in the open, you'll probably sense that your connection has reached a new level.

Very early in our relationship, I used this approach with Erin. We hadn't even gone on a formal date yet, but one evening while we were talking on the phone, I said, "Erin, I want you to know that I really like you, and even though we've never been on an official date, I already think of us as boyfriend-girlfriend. How do you feel about that?" Fortunately, she told me that she felt the same way; and with that simple statement we took our relationship to a new level of caring, trust, and intimacy.

If you don't feel comfortable with an overly squishy application of the direct approach, you can always fall back on a more subtle version. Even a handshake and a genuine smile is a way to acknowledge your connection.

Appreciation

Another way to lovingly connect with others is to express genuine appreciation for them. Praise the other person for a recent accomplishment. Point out a unique talent or skill you admire, or simply share a small detail that impresses you. Do this only when you truly *are* impressed. Never offer insincere praise in an attempt to manipulate someone.

One of the organizations I belong to is Toastmasters International, which has thousands of individual clubs around the world. The main focus of Toastmasters is to help people develop their communication and leadership skills. At a typical Toastmasters club meeting, every speaker receives a formal evaluation from another club member. A common method for this process is called the sandwich method. First you tell the speaker what you liked, and next you offer some suggestions for improvement. Then you close with some final praise and positive encouragement. This is an effective way to deliver feedback, but it also facilitates stronger bonds between club members. Praise is built right into the meeting structure, so everyone who speaks is guaranteed to receive some appreciation for their efforts.

I've noticed that on the rare occasions a member is overly critical at these meetings, it negatively affects the spirit of camaraderie in the club, even when the criticism seems fair and accurate. I always feel more connected when we focus on the positive, including praising each other for a job well done and sharing many laughs. I leave such meetings feeling uplifted, encouraged, and supported.

Gratitude

The last connection technique is to feel grateful for the other person. Sometimes it's easiest to tap into those feelings by imagining what your life would be like without him or her. What would you miss if this person was gone from your life forever? Pay attention to whatever thoughts arise as you consider this question.

You can also apply gratitude on a communal scale. What about your family, community, country, or planet makes you feel grateful? What would you miss most if they were gone?

While many people refer to Las Vegas as "Sin City" and associate it with gambling and other vices, I chose to connect with it on different terms. This was the city that enabled Erin and me to buy our first home, to build successful careers, and to make many wonderful friends. By feeling grateful for the city of Las Vegas, I find it easy to connect with other people who live here, since we share a common bond as residents of this amazing, high energy place. If you feel grateful for your community, you'll find it much easier to connect with other residents, since this is a way of effectively honoring the connection that already exists.

✦ ✦

Love is the principle that enables you to progressively discover your true self. You accomplish this by initiating connections with others and then communicating to explore the depths of those bonds. The more connected you become with the world around you, the greater your alignment with the principle of love.

The notion that you're completely separate from everyone else is merely an illusion. Think of your relationships as external projections of the real you, and you'll realize that the purpose of every relationship is to teach you how to love yourself from the inside out. Whenever you communicate with another person, in truth you're exploring the depths of your own consciousness because that's where all your relationships exist. When you learn to love everyone and everything, you come into alignment with your true self. There is no real difference between loving others and loving yourself; the two are inseparable.

If you find it too difficult to reach out and connect with others, don't worry. Other principles will help you develop your ability to take action in this area, especially the principle of . . .

✦ ✦ ✦ ✦

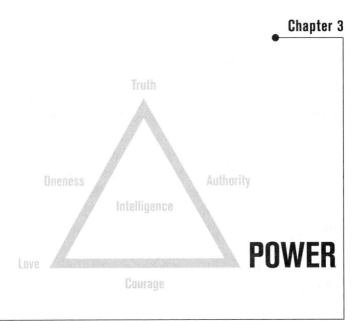

Chapter 3

"*Most powerful is he who has himself in his own power.*"

— SENECA

Power is the third principle of personal development. It is your ability to consciously and deliberately create the world around you. When your power is weak, you can't effectively satisfy your needs and desires, and you become a victim of your environment. When your power is strong, you successfully cultivate a life of your own choosing, and your environment reflects it.

To some people, the word *power* is almost a dirty word, negatively associated with abuse of force, corruption, and unbridled greed. But in truth there's nothing inherently evil or corrupt about the exercise of power. This principle can be aligned with truth and love, or it can be aligned with falsehood and disconnection. Whether power is used for good or evil is determined by the consciousness behind it.

The triad of truth, love, and power can serve as an incredible force for good. When honest, compassionate people remain powerless and only dishonest, uncaring people acquire power, we all suffer for it. The world is well served when those who are aligned with truth and love gain this third element. If you can be such a person, then I encourage you to consciously develop your power, since that decision benefits us all.

As you succeed in growing your power, you'll be able to fulfill your needs and desires with greater ease. You'll find it easier to set and achieve meaningful goals. The alternative is to wallow in powerlessness, thereby neglecting your needs and desires. If you neglect your needs, you may physically die; if you neglect your desires, you lower your consciousness and feel dead on the inside.

Some belief systems teach that powerlessness is a desirable trait, but nothing could be further from the truth. Powerlessness is neither noble nor intelligent. It's a misguided path rooted in fear, denial, and low self-worth. If you desire to live more consciously, you must learn to wield and apply power wisely, not to flee from the responsibility it entails.

Mastery of power is not remotely easy. In fact, you may find its development and correct application to be your single greatest personal development challenge. Nevertheless, power remains an essential component of conscious growth. Without it, you can be no more than a passive victim of your reality. With power, you become a conscious creator.

To deepen your understanding of power, let's explore its six key components: *responsibility, desire, self-determination, focus, effort,* and *self-discipline.*

Responsibility

It's impossible to build your power until you accept total responsibility for your life. It's certainly possible to give up control, but final accountability always rests with you. You can't duck or dodge that, no matter how hard you try. If your body is out of shape, you're the one who's out of breath after climbing the stairs. If your credit cards are maxed out, you're the one who must deal with the debt. If you don't like your job, you're the one who must suffer through your work each day.

Your experience is unquestionably your own. I can discuss your life with you, I can empathize with your situation, and I can do my best to help you. But afterward I can go home to my own life and leave yours behind. You never have that luxury.

If you try to deny or escape the burden of responsibility, it will only come back to haunt you later. You can let yourself go and slack off in your career, eat lots of junk food, and yell at your family, but the mess you create will be yours to experience. The sooner you recognize that total responsibility is inescapable, the better off you'll be.

When you were a child, others may have assumed some responsibility for your well-being, yet you and you alone must still deal with the results. Whether you were raised by loving and attentive parents or angry alcoholics, the burden of responsibility for your life now rests squarely on your shoulders. That may seem completely unfair, especially if you didn't have much control over your childhood experiences, but such are the vicissitudes of life.

It's entirely pointless to blame God, your parents, the government, or anyone else for your lot in life. Blame can only make you powerless. It doesn't matter who contributed to your current situation—all that matters is that you must live with it. No amount of blame can make that burden any easier.

I learned one of the most powerful lessons of my life after being arrested for felony grand theft at age 19. For several days as I sat in jail, all I could do was think about how I got there. At some point I realized that I'd put myself in that cell: I was in jail because I failed to wield conscious control over my life. In that moment, I finally accepted complete responsibility for my life. It still took me years to fully recover from the bad decisions I'd made, but knowing that I was responsible made it possible for me to build a new life for myself—a life of my own choosing.

No one is coming to rescue you. No one will hand you the career of your dreams, and no one will solve your relationship problems. No one will lose the extra fat on your body. If you don't proactively solve your own problems, they'll never be solved.

If you want different results, you must go out and create them yourself. Accepting full responsibility for your life means being willing to do what's necessary to create the outcome you want. You must be willing to pay the price to meet your needs and fulfill your desires. You must actively make your life happen instead of passively letting it play out. You'll surely make mistakes along the way, but you must never give up on yourself.

The bright side is that while accepting total responsibility can be very challenging, it isn't untenable. You may not have had much control over your results thus far, but the commitment to develop your power gives you the opportunity to finally create a life of your choosing. Your human will is far stronger than any obstacle in your path. You'll surely encounter challenges and setbacks while pursuing worthwhile goals, but if you simply persist in your willingness to pay the price, you'll eventually succeed.

Desire

Desire is the fuel of power. One of the sweetest benefits of life as a human being is to enjoy the progressive fulfillment of your desires through the exercise of your power. This doesn't just mean celebrating your big accomplishments. It means savoring every delicious step of the journey.

What do you want? What do you fantasize about? What do you long for so badly that you can't stop thinking about it, even if you consider it impossible? Allow yourself to dream. Spend time cultivating your deepest desires, no matter how impractical or impossible they seem. It's perfectly okay to want the impossible. It's not okay to pretend that your desires don't matter.

Never deny that you want what you want. When you deny your desires, you fall out of alignment with truth, love, and power. You distance yourself from truth by lying to yourself. You distance yourself from love by disconnecting from your core. And you distance yourself from power by cutting off the fuel of desire. If you want to develop your power, you must accept your desires as they come, no matter how strange they may seem.

Most people are out of touch with their true desires. They allow others to decide what they should want, or they settle for what they think they can get. They buy into the socially conditioned nonsense that the purpose of life is to work at a meaningless job for decades, spend themselves into debt, distract themselves with mindless entertainment, get married, have children, retire broke, and then quietly die. Consequently, they live desperate shadow lives, forever powerless and unhappy. Don't succumb to the illusion of false desire. Only *true* desire summons true power.

Self-Determination

Self-determination means that you're completely free to decide what you want. You don't need anyone's permission or approval. Your choices are yours to make and can never be dictated by others. You need never justify what you want. You want what you want, and that is enough.

In order to wield power effectively, you must accept full responsibility for your life and be willing to make decisions under all circumstances. This includes ambiguous, challenging, and risky situations. There's no rule that says you have to be right. The only rule is that no matter what happens, you're responsible. Since you can't escape full responsibility, you might as well consciously participate in the decision-making process, so you can have at least some say in determining the outcome.

When you face important crossroads in life, exercise your power to decide consciously. Offer up a definitive yes or no. Don't succumb to the blind default of silent approval. To align yourself with power, you must make real choices.

Life is constantly asking: *What do you want?* You have the freedom to answer that question however you wish. Aligning yourself with truth and love will help you evaluate the possibilities, but there are no compulsory right or wrong answers. There's only your freedom to choose. Will you answer with silence, or will you exercise your power of conscious choice?

You must break through the haze of social conditioning that says your life must obey a set of rules dictated by others. You're under no such obligation. Your only real constraints are your decisions and their consequences. You're a free and independent being. How you decide to use that freedom is up to you.

Focus

True power exists only in the present. There is no power in the past; the past is over and done with. There is no power in the future; the future exists only in your imagination. You have no power to act yesterday or tomorrow. Whenever you project beyond the present, you make yourself powerless because you're succumbing to an illusion. Consequently, it makes sense to focus your attention on the current moment since it's the only place you have any real power.

We tend to think of time as a resource that we spend, similar to how we spend money. To complete a one-hour task is to spend an hour on it. How are you spending your day? Where do you want to spend your next vacation? How will you spend your lunch break? Although this is a common way to talk about time-bound events, and I often use such language myself, the framework is technically inaccurate. Time isn't a disposable resource. You can't spend time. No matter what you do or don't do, time passes on its own. You have no choice regarding whether to spend time or not; your only choice is how you direct your focus in the present moment.

In reality, you're never in the past or future. You exist only in the here-and-now. Even when you remember the past or envision the future, you're still thinking those thoughts in the present. All you have is right now, and that's all you'll ever have. You can't control the passage of time, but you *can* control your present focus. That's it—no past, no future, just right now.

If the only thing that exists is the present moment, then what sense does it make to talk about long-term goals? How can you actually achieve anything?

Understand that you can only take action in the present moment, and you can only enjoy your results in the present as well. You can't accomplish or experience anything in the past or future because you're never there. When people learn about goal setting, they often set goals in violation of this fact. It's difficult to achieve something that's based on an inaccurate model of reality—such a goal will surely be an uphill struggle.

The purpose of goal setting isn't to control the future. That would be senseless because the future only exists in your imagination. The point of goal setting is to improve the quality of your present-moment reality. Setting goals can give you greater clarity and focus right now. Whenever you set your sights on achieving something, always ask yourself, "How does setting this goal improve my present reality?" If it doesn't improve your present reality, then the goal is pointless, and you may as well dump it. But if it brings greater clarity, focus, and motivation to your life when you think about it, it's a keeper.

Many people set goals and then assume the path to reach them will require suffering and sacrifice. This is a recipe for failure. Whenever you consider a new goal, pay attention to the effect it has on your present reality. Set goals that make you feel powerful, motivated, and driven when you focus on them, long before the final outcome is actually achieved. Avoid setting goals that make you feel powerless, stressed, or weak. Treat this process as a way to enhance your present focus, not as a way to control the future.

Suppose you set a goal to start your own business. You imagine some future point where you're enjoying being your own boss, doing what you love, and making a great income. So far, there's nothing wrong with that. Then you think about how much work it will be, the risks you'll face, and other discouraging thoughts. You've left the present and are dwelling in your future illusion. Bring your focus back to the present and realize that none of those things have happened. You're just making them up. How silly it is to dwell on results you don't even want!

Instead, try this: think about starting your own business and imagine how great it will be when everything is running smoothly. Now return your focus to the present and consider how this goal can improve the quality of your life in this very moment, not a year from now, not five years from now, not even tomorrow. What does the goal of starting your own business do for you here and now? Does it give you hope? Does it inspire you? Does it fill you with desire? Allow those thoughts to churn through your mind for a while. Consider how the goal of starting your own business improves your life right now. If you see no immediate improvement, then drop the goal and consider a different one.

Do you want to lose a certain amount of weight, begin a new relationship, or enjoy a more fulfilling career? Stop foreseeing doom and gloom on the path to get there, and imagine how each goal can improve your present reality before the goal is even achieved. What does the thought of physical fitness do for you right now? What does the thought of finding your soul mate or the prospect of a fulfilling career do for you? When you focus your attention on these goals, how does your present reality change? Do you feel more motivated? Do you feel driven to take action?

When you set a goal that improves your present reality, what does it matter how long it takes to achieve the final outcome? Whether it takes one week or five years is irrelevant. The whole path is fun and enjoyable. More important, you feel happy and fulfilled this very moment. This drives you to take action from a state of joy, so you're productive too. Instead of going after goals you think will make you happy in the distant future, focus on goals that make you happy right now.

Whenever you set goals, you can envision a path of sacrifice and suffering by focusing on the illusion of the future, or you can allow the goal to inject your present reality with excitement, enthusiasm, and motivation. Even though it seems like you're setting goals for the future, you're really doing so for the present. The better you understand this, the more easily you'll achieve what you set out to do.

If you adopt this mind-set, you'll soon learn to set different kinds of goals. As you set a variety of goals and observe how they affect you when you focus on them, a pattern will gradually emerge. You'll notice that certain types of goals consistently inspire you while others don't. The underlying pattern behind the former is your life purpose. When you become consciously aware of your life purpose, you can feel inspired and motivated whenever you want just by focusing your attention on your purpose. You'll explore life purpose in depth in Chapter 9, which includes a powerful exercise to help you discover your purpose.

By developing a clear sense of my own life purpose, I've learned that goals that lie too far outside it simply don't inspire me and are therefore a waste of my time. One time I set a goal to become a millionaire—to have a net worth of at least $1 million. Becoming a millionaire seemed like a worthy milestone on my path of personal growth, but in truth it was a pointless goal that I didn't really care about. Focusing on it caused me to disconnect from people and from my true self. I started seeing others as potential dollar signs instead of human beings. When I finally dumped that goal, I immediately felt better, and I shifted my focus to other goals that really mattered to me.

Sometimes your purpose will inspire you to set goals you'd otherwise be inclined to reject. When I first launched StevePavlina.com in October 2004, I set out to build the best personal development Website on the Internet. Many people would consider this an ill-formed goal. For starters, it's vague and difficult to measure. What does *best* mean anyway? The goal had no deadline, there were already thousands of competing sites online, and I had no budget and no specific plan for getting there. Furthermore, I had virtually no credentials to speak of—no Ph.D., no books, no coaching practice, and no workshops or seminars. I was a game developer with degrees in computer science and mathematics.

But despite these problems, whenever I focused on this goal, I felt extremely driven and motivated. I thought about all the people who'd visit the site and how they'd leave with useful ideas that would really help them. This made me feel strong and powerful, and somehow I knew that success was inevitable.

Focusing on this goal gave me tremendous motivation to write, so every week I wrote and posted new articles on the Website for free.

For the first four months, the site didn't attract much traffic and didn't generate any income at all. In its fifth month, it earned a whopping $53. But over the next three years, the site grew to include hundreds of free articles, enough to fill about 20 books. I didn't spend a dime on marketing or promotion, but purely through word of mouth, traffic grew to two million visitors per month. As a result of the traffic growth, the site began earning tens of thousands of dollars per month, mostly from advertising, affiliate programs, and donations. StevePavlina.com was soon acknowledged by many people as the most popular, practical, and down-to-earth personal development Website. The goal was achieved because it gave me the focus and motivation to take action in the present moment.

Your goals don't actually need to be specific, clear, and measurable. You don't need crisp deadlines, and you don't need detailed step-by-step plans. You simply need a burning desire to take action. Only goals that align with your truest, deepest desires can summon that kind of power.

You'll learn a lot about yourself when you discover the kinds of goals that really drive you. It took me years to learn that material goals always de-motivate me. I simply don't care enough about money, possessions, or financial independence to lift a finger toward such goals. If necessary, I'll retire on a park bench with a "Will blog for food" sign.

What really gets my juices flowing is helping people grow. I gush with joy when I see people experience breakthrough "Aha!" moments that help them move forward in life. That seems to be my best fuel for action. When I set goals centered on making a positive difference in people's lives, I feel empowered and driven to get moving.

If your goals look great on paper but don't fill you with desire and motivation when you focus on them, they're worthless. Don't settle for wimpy goals you aren't passionate about. Even if something seems solid and achievable and other people encourage you to go for it, you probably won't achieve it if it doesn't excite you. Focus your attention on goals that inspire and motivate you right now, since the present moment is the only place you have any real power.

Effort

If you want to turn your desires into reality, at some point you must take action. When you set goals that truly inspire you, you'll feel naturally motivated to take action. You'll work hard, but it won't seem like hard work because you'll be so inspired. For the most part, you'll just be doing what you love to do.

What about the Law of Attraction? Can't you just sit on your butt all day and manifest what you want through the power of intention? That would be a gross misunderstanding of how the Law of Attraction works. When you focus single-mindedly on what you want, you'll begin to notice new resources appearing in your life. If you don't take action, however, those resources will dry up, and you'll be no closer to your goals.

Your physical body is part of the process through which your intentions will manifest. True desires will compel you to get up and move. If you aren't driven to act, it means your intentions are weak. You're trying to create something you don't want badly enough, and it's dying on the vine.

If you find yourself totally unmotivated to lift a finger toward your goals, you've set the wrong goals. You need to set goals that are so inspiring to you that you can't wait to take action, and your body moves almost effortlessly. Desire is the fuel of action. If you try to fuel yourself with false desire, you simply won't move. If there's no motion, there's no motivation.

How do you move when you're about to go on an eagerly anticipated vacation? Do you lie in bed feeling lazy, whining that it's too much work to go to the airport and catch the plane? Or do you feel motivated and excited to get under way? If your goals don't inspire you at least as much as going on vacation, they're lousy goals.

Achieving meaningful goals usually requires hard work, but if yours are right for you, then such labor won't cause you to suffer. You'll still face obstacles and challenges, but you'll have the drive, motivation, and power to deal with them head-on. Pick goals that are so exciting to you that making a serious effort feels almost effortless.

Self-Discipline

Self-discipline is another one of those dirty words. We're told to take it easy. Go with the flow. Don't sweat it. The myth of *fast and easy* pervades modern society. This may convince you to buy a lot of junk you don't need, but it isn't an effective way to run your life if fulfillment and success matter to you.

Even when you're highly motivated to work on goals that truly inspire you, there will be times where your motivation wanes, and you have to tap into your willpower to keep going. Self-discipline is the willingness to do what it takes to achieve the results you want regardless of your mood. When you're feeling unmotivated, apathetic, bored, or lazy, self-discipline provides your second wind and keeps you moving. It's your fail-safe, your motivational backup system.

Being highly motivated is wonderful, but the energetic boost that motivation provides is unstable; it has its peaks and valleys. Even if you absolutely love what you do, there will still be plenty of tedious and difficult tasks that you don't enjoy much. For example, you may love your children and enjoy spending time with them, but you'll still have days when caring for them is a thankless grind. Of course, you can take a break. You can ask for help when you need it. But even when you take time for personal renewal, you'll still encounter situations where you just aren't motivated to do what it takes to get the results you want. And that's where self-discipline can save the day.

Motivation and self-discipline are the twin tools of power. Motivation is often highest at the beginning of a project. You're fresh out of the envisioning stage, your goals and dreams still dancing in your head. Maybe you've decided to start a new diet or exercise program. You take up the challenge willingly and breeze through the first few days. But after a couple of weeks, the initial motivation has faded. Now the work is just plain hard, and you wonder whether it's worth the effort to continue. This is where self-discipline can prevent you from quitting, granting you the ability to press on in spite of yourself. Motivation starts the race, but self-discipline ultimately crosses the finish line.

You see, motivation is highest when you're already in motion. When you stop moving, your motivation naturally declines. If you can summon just enough discipline to get going again, you'll often find that your momentum reboots your natural motivation to continue. It requires a lot of power to go from a state of rest to a state of action, but once you're moving, it's easier to keep going.

Self-discipline must be balanced with reason and intelligence. It isn't productive to push yourself to the breaking point, but it *is* productive to reclaim time that would otherwise be wasted. Self-discipline means taking appropriate action when it should be taken. This includes having the discipline to get things done on time without resorting to extreme measures. Pulling an all-nighter to cram for an exam isn't self-discipline—it's merely the consequence of procrastination.

There are days when I wake up feeling inspired, and my work flows easily. But there are also times when I feel lazy and unmotivated. Motivation alone would not be sufficient to drive me to complete most projects. If I relied solely on motivation, you wouldn't be reading this book because it never would have seen the light of day. Self-discipline carries me through those times when my motivation isn't high enough to compel me to act, but the powerful being inside me says, *No delays. Today we must press on.* Once I get that first half hour out of the way, I almost always want to continue.

Problems, obstacles, and setbacks are no barriers for people with high self-discipline. A disciplined person looks at a problem like a bodybuilder looks at a barbell: *I will lift you and grow stronger in the process.* Picture a 40-pound dumbbell. Is it light or heavy? That depends on how strong you are. Some people would consider that a heavy weight, while others would say it's light. Similarly, no problems are big or small except relative to your self-discipline. The more disciplined you become, the lighter your problems are.

Disciplining yourself to do what needs to be done, even when you don't feel like it, isn't easy. Building your self-discipline is one of the hardest things you'll ever do. It's so difficult that some people will do almost anything to avoid it—procrastinate endlessly, do drugs, even commit suicide. But despite the difficulty, self-discipline remains one of the most significant aspects of personal development. Without it, your life is doomed to remain a pale shadow of your potential. Imagine all the wonderful accomplishments that will be within your grasp once you become disciplined enough to consistently follow through on your best intentions. It's a wonderful feeling to set goals, knowing that you can trust yourself to do what it takes to achieve them.

Blocks to Power

Several blocks condition you to weaken yourself, either by denying your power or by attempting to give it away. As you become aware of these blocks, you'll learn to embrace your power and use it wisely. No matter how powerless you may have been in the past, your true power is still waiting for you to come and claim it.

Timidity

Timidity is the mind-set that says you're too weak, too small, and too unimportant to be deserving of real power. Who are you to live a meaningful life? You're just one insignificant person among billions.

This belief becomes a self-fulfilling prophecy. In reality, you're so powerful that you're actually turning your own strength against yourself, temporarily rendering yourself weak. You're like a god who declares, "Let me be powerless." And that's exactly what happens.

Timidity causes you to settle for puny, empty goals that don't inspire you—assuming you even set goals at all. You perform meaningless work that doesn't matter to you, live in a place you don't care for, and settle for disempowering relationships with other weak-minded people who regard you as another warm body for their pity parties. Meanwhile, your true self is practically screaming at you, but you drown its voice with idle entertainment, junk food, and other distractions.

You weren't meant to live hiding under a rock. That isn't you. You're selling yourself short, grossly underestimating your true capabilities. This is your reality, and you're responsible for it. Stop trying to live in denial of that fact, and face up to it.

You didn't come here to spend your life obsessing over trivialities. Wake up and take a good look at yourself and admit, "This is garbage.

I can do better than this!" Start listening to that powerful being inside you for once. It won't steer you wrong.

Cowardice

Cowardice is the practice of using your power to feed your fears instead of your desires. Instead of creating what you want, you create what you don't want.

When you worry that exercising your power will cause you to make too many mistakes, you feed the fear of failure. The truth is that you *will* sometimes fail. Some of your failures may even be spectacular blunders, but that's nothing to worry about. It's better to fail as the powerful being you are instead of trying to hide from the truth and live as a mouse. When you shrink from failure, you only weaken yourself. When you make mistakes and learn from them, you grow stronger.

When you worry that exercising your power will bring you too much responsibility, you feed the fear of success. The truth is that you're always completely responsible for everything in your reality. You have no choice but to carry the world on your shoulders, since you can't decline the results you witness. You can never reduce your responsibility by trying to make yourself powerless. Total responsibility is inescapable.

The only sensible choice is to consciously claim your power and do the best you can with it. Focus your attention on what you want, not on what you don't want, and accept the weighty responsibilities of power.

Negative Conditioning

You may have been misled to believe that power is somehow bad or evil. Most likely you were taught to place other values ahead of power, such as loyalty, meekness, and obedience. It's no coincidence that such qualities are often lauded by those seeking strength through coercion and control. Don't give your power away to those who prey on the weak-minded, telling you it's wrong to be strong.

If you truly believe that weakness is better than strength, then it follows logically that you should intentionally weaken yourself as much as possible. Damage your health, sabotage your career, and terminate your relationships. Make yourself as powerless as you can, and see how that feels. Of course this runs contrary to common sense, so I wouldn't expect you to behave in such a foolish way.

I encourage you to reconcile any false beliefs you may have about power with your own common sense. Do you prefer to be weak, or would you rather be strong? Would you prefer to have fewer capabilities or more? Release any negative beliefs about power that no longer serve you.

How to Build Your Power

Just like your muscle tissue, power weakens from lack of use and grows stronger when exercised. The more you train your power, the more powerful you become. Everyone has some power, but not everyone develops it to the same degree. Here are several methods to train yourself to become more powerful.

Progressive Training

A good way to build power and especially self-discipline is to progressively train yourself to tackle bigger challenges. When you train your muscles, you lift weights that are within your ability. You push your muscles until they fail, and then you rest. Similarly, you can develop your power by taking on challenges that you can successfully accomplish but that push you close to your limits. This doesn't mean trying something that's beyond your strength and failing at it repeatedly, nor does it mean playing it safe and staying within your comfort zone. You must tackle challenges that are within your current ability to handle but which are close to your limit.

Progressive training requires that once you succeed, you must increase the challenge. If you keep working at the same level, you won't get much stronger.

It's a mistake to push yourself too hard when trying to build your power. If you attempt to transform your entire life overnight by setting dozens of new goals for yourself, you're almost certain to fail. This is like a person who goes to the gym for the first time ever and packs 300 pounds on the bench press. You'll only look silly. Accept your current starting point without judging yourself harshly.

If you're starting from a very low point in your life, you may find it extremely challenging just to get yourself out of bed before noon and pay your bills on time. Later, you may progress to making dietary improvements, starting an exercise program, and breaking harmful addictions. As you gain more power over your life, you can take on bigger goals, such as building the career of your dreams and attracting a fulfilling relationship.

Don't compare yourself to other people. If you think you're weak, everyone else will seem strong. If you think you're strong, everyone else will seem weak. There's no point in doing this. Simply look at where you are now, and aim to get stronger as you go forward.

Suppose you want to develop the ability to complete eight solid hours of work each weekday. Perhaps you try to work a solid eight-hour day without succumbing to distractions, and you only manage to do it once. The next day you fail utterly. That's perfectly fine. You did one rep of eight hours. Two is too much for you, so cut back a little. Could you work with high concentration for one hour a day, five days in a row? If you can't do that, cut back to 30 minutes or whatever you can do. If you succeed, increase the challenge. Once you've mastered a week at one level, take it up a notch the next week. Continue with this progressive training until you've reached your goal.

By raising the bar just a little each week, you stay within your capabilities and grow stronger over time. When doing actual weight training, the work you do doesn't mean anything. There's no intrinsic value in lifting a piece of metal up and down. The value comes from the resulting muscle growth. However, when building your power and self-discipline, you also gain the benefit of the work you've done along the way, so that's even better. It's great when your training produces something of value and makes you stronger at the same time. That's a double win.

Master the First Hour

It's been said that the first hour is the rudder of the day, meaning that the way you start your day will tend to set the tone for the rest of it. If you adopt a disciplined routine for your first waking hour, you'll probably enjoy a highly productive day. But if you squander that first hour, it's likely the rest of the day will be equally unspectacular. Conquer that first hour by exercising, reading, cleaning, writing, or doing other productive tasks.

Many people have told me that whenever they complete an important task first thing in the morning, they gain a tremendous feeling of well-being and energy that lasts for hours. I've experienced this as well. Finishing an important task early in the day is motivating and energizing. When you conquer that first hour, you feel that no matter what else happens, your day is already a success.

Personal Quotas

Just as a salesperson might have a monthly sales quota to meet, you can use the concept of quotas to improve your performance in any endeavor. Establish a daily minimum output goal for yourself in some area of your life. This ensures constant forward progress and is a fantastic way to develop your self-discipline.

You can use any metric you want as long as it works for you. A writer could set a daily quota of words, paragraphs, or pages to write each day. If you're organizing your finances, you could set a quota of processing a certain number of transactions or receipts per day.

I've experimented with both action-based and outcome-based quotas. At first I preferred the former because the targets were more controllable. It's easier for me to commit to writing for two hours per day versus writing 2,000 words per day. Unfortunately, I found that when I used action-based quotas, my results were weaker. I'd put in the time, but I wouldn't maintain the same compulsion to closure. Today I prefer outcome-based quotas, such as completing a new article, because I find them more effective and motivating.

I encourage you to experiment with daily quotas to see what works best for you. Start with small ones that you can easily achieve, and gradually increase them to keep yourself in the sweet spot of challenge.

Worst First

If you have something difficult on your plate, get it done first thing in the morning. Arrange your daily tasks from hardest to easiest. Many people begin their days with routine tasks like checking e-mail. When you do that, however, you'll often expand your easy tasks as a way to procrastinate because you know that something more difficult is coming up next. There's no motivation to work quickly because you'll only be punished for your efforts with a harder task ahead, so you'll naturally slow down. This habit will frequently lead to the most difficult tasks being put off until the next day. This kills your power because the challenging tasks you delay are often those that will have the biggest positive impact.

On the other hand, if you complete your tasks in order of decreasing difficulty and do the worst first, then whenever you finish a task, you're always rewarded with an easier job next. This will motivate you to maintain a fast tempo throughout the day. There's no reason to slow down when you have something easier coming up. Put the routine tasks at the end of the day, and watch how much faster you get your work done.

I've been absolutely amazed by how big a difference this habit has made for me. I used to check my e-mail first thing in the morning, and it would take me about an hour to handle each day's correspondence. Now I prefer to process my e-mail later in the day, and it takes me an average of 15 to 30 minutes. I type simpler, more concise messages because when I'm finished, my workday is over.

Take your personal rewards at the end of the day, not the beginning. Saving the best for last will give you something to look forward to, and you'll find that your evenings are much more rewarding. Get your work done early each day; then relax and enjoy yourself.

Competition

If you're a competitive person, then use your inherent nature to your advantage. Competition can be very motivating, and the drive to win can help you build your power. People will often work harder to win something than they will for personal results alone. Competition causes the cream to rise to the top.

I've competed in several speech contests because the competition drives me to work harder on my skills. I must be more disciplined in how I write my speech, rehearse it, and deliver it if I want to win a contest against other skilled speakers versus if I'm only giving it for the benefit of the audience. The experience of competition increases my power to write better speeches when I'm not competing.

Contests are common in sales and sports, but where else can you apply this idea? Can you start an office pool to see who can lose the most weight in a month? Can you challenge a friend to see who can earn the most money in 90 days? Can you compete with your spouse to see who can read the most new books in a month?

The nice thing about competition is that even when you lose, you win. You may lose the contest, but you'll still see positive results, probably more than you would have if you'd never competed. A contest is a great way to break out of a rut and raise your power to a whole new level.

Rest

Rest is a key component of any weight-training program, and it's also crucial to building your power. Use cycles of exertion and relaxation to lift yourself up to higher levels of performance. Once you've successfully completed a challenge, rest for a while before tackling the next one. Stretch. Go for a walk. Take a short nap. Give yourself a chance to relax and recuperate.

Just as overtraining is a risk when working with weights, it's also a risk when building power. If you've been feeling burned out and un-motivated for several days in a row, you're pushing yourself too hard. Get away from your work for at least a couple days. Take a vacation. Psychologically restore yourself for the next challenge so you can re-turn to work even stronger.

You aren't here to be weak and passive. You're here to shine. Devel-oping your power will require hard work, but it's well worth the effort. The greater your power, the more success you'll enjoy at creating the life you desire. The deeper you can dig, the more treasure you'll find.

Building a successful career is challenging. Maintaining a success-ful relationship is challenging. Achieving financial abundance is chal-lenging. These rewards won't simply fall into your lap. You must earn them. Accept responsibility for your life, and rise to the challenges in front of you. Your problems exist to help you to grow, not to beat you down. The weights are supposed to be heavy.

Building your power isn't just about you. When you align your power with truth and love, you can become a tremendous force for good. But in order to reach that level, you must first grasp the prin-ciple of . . .

✦ ✦ ✦ ✦

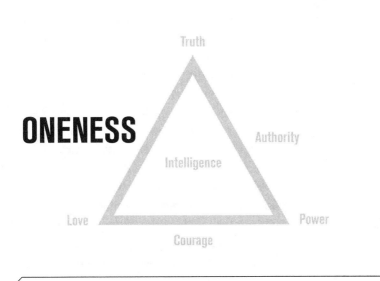

ONENESS

"All differences in this world are of degree, and not of kind, because oneness is the secret of everything."

— SWAMI VIVEKANANDA

Now that we've explored the three primary principles of truth, love, and power, it's time to address the secondary principles of oneness, authority, and courage. These secondary principles are derived from the pairings of the first three. Oneness is truth plus love. Authority is truth plus power. And courage is love plus power. These secondary principles will help deepen your understanding of conscious living. The three-part combination of truth, love, and power is intelligence, which I'll address in Chapter 7.

Oneness is the principle that results from combining truth and love. Whereas love is the ability to connect by choice, oneness is the recognition that being connected is your natural state. Love is *choosing* to connect. Oneness is *knowing* you're already connected. Oneness has no specific target; it's an omnidirectional feeling of connection to everyone and everything at the same time. Oneness is pure unconditional love.

One day several years ago, I was having lunch in my backyard while watching some birds. I tried to imagine what it would be like to experience a sense of total oneness. Soon I felt my consciousness expanding beyond my body. I instantly grasped that the birds in front of me were just as much me as my physical body was. My field of awareness continued to expand, and I sensed that the wall at the edge of the yard was also me. And finally this feeling stretched to encompass everything in my field of vision and beyond. My consciousness was no longer localized; it was everywhere. I still saw everything through my body's eyes, but my inner senses told me I was much more than this singular point of reference. I felt an intense surge of positive emotion, but it was so overwhelming that it knocked me out of that state.

Although this experience lasted only seconds, it had a deep and enduring impact on me. For several weeks, my mind struggled to catch up. I had to discard my old model of reality that assumed the world was made up of completely separate individuals and objects. I stopped seeing a world of independent individuals, and I began seeing reality as one giant body composed of individual cells. Some cells were totally unaware of the body and were inadvertently competing against their fellows. But other cells noticed the body and were working for its good. The most intelligent cells understood that the health of the body and the health of the cells were inextricably connected. The body cannot survive without the cells, nor can the cells survive without the body. Oneness is the deep realization of this simple truth.

With some practice, I learned to re-create this joyful expansion of awareness at will. It was like listening to a familiar radio station. The station was always broadcasting, but I had to tune myself to the right frequency to hear it. I found that the easiest way to tune in was to ask myself, *Where is the joy?* That question would help me listen for the right frequency, and once I got the frequency, the volume would gradually increase until I was feeling extremely joyful and connected.

The mind-set of oneness cannot be compartmentalized. It isn't some side project you add to your personal development to-do list, only to fade back into separateness when you head to work the next day. If you resonate with oneness, it changes you from top to bottom. You can no longer continue treating everyone as completely separate from you.

Let's go deeper into the principle of oneness by exploring its various aspects: *empathy, compassion, honesty, fairness, contribution,* and *unity.*

Empathy

Oneness creates an empathic connection between you and everyone else. You realize you're not an island unto yourself, and you begin to see that invisible threads connect you to others. In some ways the realization of oneness is a blessing, while in other ways it's a curse. It's a blessing to realize we're all inherently connected. It's a curse to notice that many people still live without this awareness.

Because oneness empathically connects you to others, it invites feelings of deep joy as well as deep sorrow. When you accept its pleasure, you also accept its pain. As Kahlil Gibran wrote in *The Prophet:*

> *The deeper that sorrow carves into your being, the more joy you can contain.*
>
> *Is not the cup that holds your wine the very cup that was burned in the potter's oven?*
>
> *And is not the lute that soothes your spirit, the very wood that was hollowed with knives?*
>
> *When you are joyous, look deep into your heart and you shall find it is only that which has given you sorrow that is giving you joy.*
>
> *When you are sorrowful look again in your heart, and you shall see that in truth you are weeping for that which has been your delight.*

While in a state of oneness, you tune in to the joy as well as the sorrow of the larger body, transcending the lower single-cell level of awareness. Sometimes this state induces the most exalted feelings you can imagine, while other times it feels like being hollowed out with knives.

The truth aspect of oneness determines the emotional impact. When you predict a positive outcome for the larger body and you feel that humankind is headed in a positive direction, you feel wonderful. When you predict a negative outcome, you feel intensely sad that the larger body is off course. You can never completely insulate yourself from the fate of the larger whole. Humanity's triumphs are yours to celebrate; the mistakes are yours to commiserate. It isn't enough to do no wrong. To honor the principle of oneness, you must commit yourself to doing good.

Compassion

The experience of oneness is the key to expressing compassion and kindness. In this state of being, you feel a natural affinity for everyone else. Loving actions don't require willpower or effort when you recognize that everyone is you. You don't have to remind yourself to treat your neighbor as yourself. You know that your neighbor and you are one, so behaving in accordance with this principle is effortless.

One morning while I was out for a walk, I saw a homeless man sifting through trash cans in an outdoor shopping center. None of the stores were open yet, so he and I were the only people in the area. Prior to my experience of oneness, I would have passed him by without making eye contact. But this time I knew in my heart that he wasn't separate from me. He *was* me. I didn't have to convince myself of this—I felt it with a deep sense of inner knowing. Without hesitation I walked up to the man, smiled at him, gave him some money, and told him I wished him well. He looked at me with gratitude and thanked me. I didn't connect with him because I thought it would make me feel good. I did it because when I'm in the state of oneness, compassion is my natural way of connecting with the world.

My old self would have seen this man as totally separate from me. I might have felt sorry for him. I might have assumed that if I gave him money, he'd spend it on alcohol. I might have felt what I thought was compassion, but it would have only been a shadow of the real thing. On that day, however, none of those negative thoughts were present. I simply looked at that man and saw myself. I saw a fellow cell in the larger body of humanity. I saw a cell that seemed to be struggling a bit, and I wanted to offer some help and encouragement. I wasn't really giving anything. I was just helping out a part of myself.

Oneness makes compassion unconditional. It doesn't matter what race, religion, sexual preference, or lifestyle people have. It doesn't matter if they behave hurtfully toward you. You are connected to everyone. No one is undeserving of love.

Honesty

When we resonate with oneness, lying becomes anathema to us because dishonesty creates distance and disconnection. Honest communication comes naturally to us when we recognize that we're inherently connected. Lying to others is no different from lying to ourselves.

Imagine what would happen if the cells of your body started lying to each other—or merely withholding the truth. Suppose some of your white blood cells signal that everything is okay, but in reality they're losing ground to a spreading infection. Perhaps they justify it by claiming they didn't want to worry anyone. Do such actions serve the greater good of the body?

In your communication with others, strive to be direct and forthright. Don't allow yourself to succumb to lies and deceit. Hold yourself and others to the standard of truth.

Is brutal honesty always the best policy? Genuine honesty is truth tempered with love. Using truth as a weapon is not a loving act, but shedding light on an otherwise dark situation is certainly in our best interests.

Even when it seems painful and embarrassing to tell the truth, you do more damage by holding back. There's no need to wear a public mask over your private self. In order to truly experience unconditional love, you must make yourself naked to the world.

On my Website, I've publicly shared the most difficult and shameful parts of my past, such as the time I was a kleptomaniac and was compelled to steal almost every day. It was certainly cathartic for me to share such stories, but I didn't know if they would matter much to others. To my surprise, many people told me that those stories had a deep and lasting impact on them. They saw their own painful past in my stories, and this helped them heal from similar self-inflicted wounds. By sharing my own sorrow honestly, I actually helped create joy for others, which ultimately enabled me to find the joy behind my own sorrow. When we communicate from oneness, we invite a previously unknown perfection into our lives.

Fairness

The value of fairness also arises naturally from oneness. Fairness means that we learn to treat each other in ways that honor our individual well-being as well as the greater good. In practice, this means helping others align themselves with truth, love, and power.

Fairness isn't the same as equality. The cells in any given body can be considered equal only in the sense that they're all equally part of the same whole. However, in form and function, those cells are decidedly *not* equal. The cells in your body specialize for the good of the whole, becoming blood cells, brain cells, skin cells, and so on. Similarly, as human beings it isn't in our best interests to enforce equality except at the basic level of equal human rights. Our strengths lie in our differences, so it's important for each of us to explore those differences and develop them into talents. This development can still be considered fair, even though it isn't equal.

When you interact with others, do you treat everyone equally, including friends, family members, and complete strangers? Of course you don't. Embracing oneness won't change that; it won't compel you to treat everyone with blind equality. Oneness will simply provide you with a broader perspective for making decisions. Instead of being more generous with your friends and family members as opposed to strangers, oneness will encourage you to be more generous in those areas where you can have a greater impact, regardless of your current social loyalties. Sometimes that will require helping a close friend, while other times it will mean coming to the aid of a complete stranger.

When you're aligned with oneness, everyone is part of your family. You don't have the capacity to serve your billions of family members equally, but you can make reasonable decisions about where you *can* make a positive difference. That is fairness.

In a broader social context, fairness takes the form of justice. For justice to prevail, we must make decisions that fairly balance the needs of the individual with the needs of the larger whole. Ideally, this means striving to minimize conflict between these two levels. Justice isn't merely the domain of our courts of law. It must be embraced by all of us as individuals. Whenever we turn a blind eye to injustice, we embrace separation instead of oneness, and we all suffer for it.

Contribution

A sense of oneness encourages you to optimize and expand your contribution as an individual. It isn't enough to just get by in life. If you perform well below your capacity, you're denying responsibility for your role in the larger body. You're withholding value both from yourself and others.

When I decided to retire from the field of computer-game development, I'd been devoting much of my spare time to helping independent game developers, especially those who were trying to finish and release their first game. I provided free how-to articles, hosted a popular online discussion forum, and shared lots of free advice. However, once I committed to a career change, I stopped providing that level of help to game developers and transitioned to my new career as gracefully as possible. While some people were upset by this move, I considered it a fair decision because I believed I could make a more positive contribution to the greater good through the field of personal development. I didn't regret the choice at all.

Oneness can make contribution even more rewarding. Without a sense of oneness, rewards are considered only at the individual level: *What's in it for me? What do I get out of this? Why should I make the effort?* When oneness is present, this conflict dissolves because rewards are considered at a much higher level. You partake in the success of others, and another person's achievement is valued just as much as your own.

Have you ever felt genuinely happy for someone else's success? I often feel this way when reading feedback from my Website visitors about their personal development breakthroughs. I celebrate their successes as if they're my own. When one of us gains, we all gain.

Oneness doesn't conflict with individuality. The cells in a body are unique individuals, each with different characteristics. If every cell were identical, the larger body wouldn't exist. The individual health of each unit is valued, but at the cellular level there's recognition of contributing to a greater whole rather than working merely for one's own survival and happiness. If the cells don't attend to the health of the body, the body will die, taking every cell with it. Similarly, for the body to survive, the cells must be healthy as well. The body cares for the cells, and the cells care for the body.

As an individual cell, your impact is limited. If you live entirely for yourself, your life will amount to very little against the backdrop of all humanity. With few exceptions, the accomplishments of any one cell are virtually meaningless. However, by aligning yourself with the highest good of the body, your role takes on much greater significance. Now you're an agent of a giant, a contributor to magnificence, a holographic piece of consciousness itself.

Humanity's health is your health, and humanity's accomplishments are your accomplishments. Whatever anyone living or dead has ever achieved is yours to cherish as your own. Your greatness is limited only by the expansion of consciousness itself. What would you like to contribute to this expansion?

Unity

A natural extension of oneness is the development of global con-sciousness. You acknowledge that just as each individual cell is re-sponsible for maintaining the health of the whole body, you're simi-larly responsible for the health of the entire planet. You can't continue making decisions solely at the personal, family, or communal level. Now you must consider how your thoughts and actions impact the planet as a whole.

The mind-set of unity is an awesome responsibility, and many people feel overwhelmed by it initially. This is perfectly normal. To assume responsibility for the entire planet can feel like putting a huge weight on your shoulders. How can one person be responsible for so much? But to deny such responsibility is to succumb to an illusion. You can't avoid the responsibility for what happens on Earth because you're a part of it.

If you think the planet needs saving, you're responsible for saving it. If you think our leaders have gotten off track, you're responsible for getting us back on track. If you see problems in the world that aren't adequately being addressed, you're responsible for addressing those problems.

Without the experience of oneness, you'll probably disagree with me. You can't possibly be responsible for all of that. You're just one tiny individual on a planet of billions. You're just a single cell, not the whole body.

But when you embrace the truth that we're all one connected whole, you willingly accept responsibility for everything in your re-ality. It's no longer possible to shrink and hide from this awareness. Unity becomes your answer to the question: *Why should I care?*

The positive side is that unity also gives you the strength to shoul-der that responsibility willingly and without feeling overwhelmed. Unity reveals that you're never alone. You have plenty of help available.

You don't need to build a vast global operation to cure every problem on Earth. You just need to remain aware of how your actions affect the whole and start making decisions today to align yourself with the greater good. Think at the level of the body; act at the level of the cell.

The most you can expect of yourself is to do your best. And the best you can genuinely do at this time is to fully embrace oneness, to serve as an example, and to teach others to do the same. The more people who embrace oneness, the more united we become, and the better off the entire planet will be.

If you want to align yourself with oneness, you'll eventually have to leave thoughts of separation behind. Whatever divides us is incongruent with oneness. The more you immerse yourself in patterns of separation, the more you distance yourself from the experience of oneness. This includes nationalism, racism, sexism, and similar mindsets that emphasize our separateness. It also includes working at a job where you're rewarded or punished based on your ability to outperform others, a spiritual belief system where some people are saved and some aren't, and a family-relationship model based on loving certain people more than others. Regardless of how deeply ingrained these patterns may be, if you want to shift to a higher level of social consciousness, you must eventually relinquish them.

How to Experience Oneness

No one can force you into a state of oneness. It can only be experienced by conscious choice. This choice includes both a mental side and an emotional side. The mental choice involves deciding to view the world through the lens of interconnectedness, to see yourself as part of a larger body, and to accept the new level of responsibility that arises from that perspective. The emotional choice is to deliberately tune in to this ever-present connection and to experience it as joy.

In order to truly master oneness, both the mental and the emotional sides must be integrated. You must recognize the truth of oneness, as well as feel your loving connectedness to others. If you only have the mental side, you'll understand and agree with the logic of oneness, but you won't really grasp it intuitively. You'll lack the drive to turn your realizations into direct action. If you only have the emotional side, you'll intuitively sense that we're all connected on some level, but you'll lack a sensible model of reality in which your intuitive understanding can be explained. You'll feel connected and joyful at times, but you'll have a hard time integrating that into all parts of your life.

When developing a sense of oneness, it's helpful to begin by focusing on either the mental or the emotional side, depending on whether you favor your logic or intuition. Start with whichever one you prefer, and then use your progress as leverage to explore the other side. You can even switch back and forth in order to gradually elevate both aspects.

I began with the mental side of oneness. Initially, I had no real emotional sense of our interconnectedness, but I could see clearly enough that the world would be vastly improved if more people choose to cooperate instead of compete. I could logically see that nonviolence was more intelligent than violence. I could see that fairness was a better approach than prejudice. However, I didn't really feel the truth of this in my gut. When I made decisions very consciously, I could get myself to act in accordance with oneness, but it took a lot of effort to think that way, and it didn't feel natural to me.

Only when I started experiencing the emotional side did I finally grasp it on an intuitive level. At first, the responsibility that accompanied this feeling seemed overwhelming, but as I continued to tune in and feel the connectedness directly, it helped me experience oneness in a much more natural and nonthreatening manner.

Here are some specific practices you can use to develop and expand your experience of oneness. Some of these address the mental side, while others focus on the emotional side.

Oneness World

Set aside ten minutes to sit quietly, relax, and just imagine what it would be like to live in a world where everyone lives in alignment with oneness. Picture a world where all people feel joyful and connected with everyone else. Imagine a place where cooperation replaces competition. What would it be like to walk down the street past throngs of strangers and feel as if they're all close family members? How would people behave in a world where "we" thinking replaces "me" thinking, where profiting at someone else's expense never happens, and where everyone assumes personal responsibility for the well-being of everyone else?

In this world of oneness, you can always expect fair treatment, regardless of race, gender, or sexual preference. If you need help with anything, you can approach anyone at any time, and you'll be treated like family. The very notion of individual advancement at the expense of others is completely alien. This world's mantra is: "We're all in this together."

This new world has no weapons, no prisons, and no national borders. There's no violence or war. People still have differences of opinion, but they settle them by cooperating to discover the truth while treating every individual with compassion and fairness.

Allow your mind and emotions to roam freely through Oneness World. Think about what it would be like to actually live there. Pay attention to how it makes you feel.

Although this is a fantasy exercise, it will deepen your understanding of oneness. Even in the real world, you'll experience some of these benefits as you begin to align yourself with oneness. When you interact with others from a place of cooperation, fairness, and compassion, you'll tend to receive similar treatment in return. When you treat everyone as a friend or family member, you'll often find them responding in kind. Over time, you'll attract others who resonate with oneness, which will enable you to create a microcosm of the larger ideal within your own life.

Spend Time in Nature

Spending time in nature is one of the simplest things you can do to experience oneness. Even if you can only spare an hour or less, take advantage of the opportunity to check out from urban living and reconnect with your natural roots. Observe the animals. Touch the trees. Feel the wind on your face.

Recognize that you're a part of nature, and it's a part of you. You aren't a foreign visitor to this environment—you belong here. Notice how good it feels to stop doing, stop thinking, and just be among the plants and animals. Reconnect with the truth that you're part of the animal kingdom.

One of my favorite natural environments is Sedona, Arizona, which is about a four-hour drive from my home in Las Vegas. During my last trip there, I followed a trail up the side of a mountain with an amazing view of Boynton Canyon. I sat alone for an hour watching the sunset while enjoying a quiet, meditative state. I felt so peaceful that I stayed until the last possible minute, allowing barely enough daylight to make it back down the trail before it was too dark to see. Such experiences are a great way to recharge the emotional side of our oneness batteries.

Physical Contact

A very pleasurable way to experience oneness is to put yourself in loving physical contact with another willing person. Snuggle your mate in a spooning position. Hold a child in your lap. Cradle a baby in your arms. Say nothing at all—just enjoy the silent recognition of the connection between you.

As you both maintain physical contact, imagine your consciousness expanding to encompass the other person's body. In your mind, hear the words *I am you.* There is no separation, no boundary between you. You both dissolve into each other and share a singular consciousness. Enjoy this feeling of pure connectedness, free of all thoughts of separation. Don't merely think you're one; *know* you're one.

In addition to inducing a feeling of oneness, physical contact can also deepen your intimate connection with another person, a connection that may persist even after you physically let go. As this bond with another individual becomes stronger, it will subtly transform the way you interact with others. People who are in love naturally behave more consciously and compassionately.

Sometimes when I'm feeling disconnected, I'll walk up to one or both of my kids, currently ages four and eight, and give them hugs. They usually squeeze me as tightly as they can. It feels great to share a loving physical connection with them.

Connecting with animals can induce a state of oneness as well. Erin and I used to have a kitten that would purr contentedly in our laps while we petted her. Unfortunately, I was allergic to her, so we had to find her a new home, but it was very hard to give her up because it felt so good to connect with her.

The Mirror Exercise

Select a random person, such as a friend, co-worker, or celebrity. How would you describe this person? Make a short list of this individual's key character qualities. Then put a plus (+) next to the qualities you like and a minus (-) next to the ones you dislike.

Now look at the list you've created, and read it back to yourself. But this time consider it from the perspective that you're looking at a list someone else wrote to describe *you.* You'll likely gain some new insights about yourself as you recognize that this is a fair representation of what you like and dislike most about yourself.

I've offered this mirror exercise to many people around the world, and those who apply it are often stunned by what it reveals. I encourage you to try it for yourself. It only takes a few minutes, and it will help you realize that other people are not so different from you after all.

We commonly praise in others what we like most about ourselves, while condemning those qualities we resist facing in ourselves. Incidentally, did I mention what a beautiful, brilliant, and loving person you are?

Oneness is among the most challenging principles to apply consistently, largely because the world is still very aligned with separation. A major part of oneness is the ability to relinquish thoughts of separation and allow your consciousness to expand beyond the limitations of your ego. The more your individual ego dominates your awareness, the more you'll automatically disconnect from the people around you.

I wish I could say I always act from a state of oneness, but that wouldn't be the truth. I've been there intellectually, emotionally, and spiritually; and I know it's a beautiful place to be. When I'm at my best, I have the clarity to consciously embrace oneness. Unfortunately, I'm not always at my best.

Don't beat yourself up if you find it difficult to achieve and hold the state of oneness. It's enough for now that you're aware of the concept. When you feel the time is right, you can consciously begin working to improve your alignment with this principle. But for now, let's continue onward to explore the principle of . . .

Chapter 5

"*Far better it is to dare mighty things, to win glorious triumphs, even though checkered by failure, than to take rank with those poor spirits who neither enjoy much nor suffer much, because they live in the gray twilight that knows not victory nor defeat.*"

— THEODORE ROOSEVELT

Authority is the principle derived from truth and power. Truth without power accomplishes nothing. Power without truth generates wasted action. The principle of authority teaches you to purposefully blend knowledge and action to produce intelligent results.

When you live without authority, your default behavior is to squander your time. You may acquire some knowledge, but you won't apply it well. You may take some action, but your movements will be chaotic and unfocused. You have the potential to live a powerful, self-directed life of your choosing, but until you step into your true authority, this potential remains a fantasy.

With authority, you not only assume responsibility for your life, you take complete command of it. Your control won't be perfect and total, but you'll be strong enough to achieve the important goals you set for yourself. You'll have the clarity to identify the kind of life you want to live, as well as the power to actually create it.

Let's explore the principle of authority by considering its five key aspects: *command, effectiveness, persistence, confidence,* and *significance.*

Command

There's only one true authority in your life, and it's you. You make the decisions. You take the actions. If you're looking to some external authority figure, leader, or guru to tell you how to live your life, you're looking in the wrong place. That leader is you. Whether you feel ready or not, you're in command.

Despite what you may have been conditioned to believe, there's no higher authority in this life than you—not your parents, your boss, or your favorite supreme being. If you think anyone else has authority over you, it's only because you yield your authority by choice. Sometimes the consequences of not doing so are so severe that you may feel as if you have no choice, but in truth you always do. Even when threatened with suffering or death, you remain the commander of your own life. Some of your choices may be extremely limited, but they're always yours to make.

True command doesn't imply the unbridled exercise of power. An intelligent commander does not bark random orders and expect them to be blindly obeyed. Command must be rooted in truth and based on an accurate assessment of the situation. You're the one who perceives your reality, and you must decide how to act (or not act) based on your perceptions. How you deal with that information is up to you, and life awaits your orders. You may feel well prepared, or you may feel unready, but the burden of command is yours no matter what.

I was raised to believe that God—specifically, the Catholic version of God—was the ultimate authority in my life. My entire existence was a blessing bestowed by God, and my assigned role was to satisfy His expectations for how I should live. I was told I had free will; however, I'd eventually be rewarded by God if I exercised my will one way and punished if I exercised it a different way. It wasn't lost on me that the favored path was to yield my authority to those who taught this, even though their specific teachings were incongruent and often ran afoul of my common sense. I was also encouraged to give them my time and money so they could continue expanding their own power base.

At age 17, I finally recognized I was being coerced to participate instead of being offered a truly free choice, so I left. I concluded that it was best for me to make my own decisions instead of having them dictated by those who claimed to have a direct connection to the source of ultimate authority. I was willing to live with the consequences if I was incorrect.

Let me clarify that there's absolutely nothing wrong with living in a way that you feel honors your Divine Creator, but this choice must be made freely and consciously. No honor is found in blind obedience. For better or worse, you've been granted free will, so you must always bear the burden of decision. If you fall prey to the belief that some authoritarian God might punish you for exercising your free will, recognize that such a belief cannot possibly serve you, and resolve to let it go. It makes no sense for someone to give you a gift and then punish you for opening it. Learn to make your own conscious choices, independent of what you think God or anyone else expects from you. If you weren't ready for your own command, you would never have been granted free will.

If you fail to claim authority over your own life, someone else will surely claim it for you. Many people allow their spouse, parents, or boss to practically run their lives. This practice pulls you out of alignment with truth and power and drops you into a lower state of consciousness. You become increasingly helpless as you distance yourself from your true nature. You are meant to be free.

Look around you and notice the results you're currently getting. Life is simply obeying your commands. If you want different results, you must issue different orders. You're the only one qualified to make these decisions. No one else can fill the role of commander of your life but you.

Effectiveness

Since authority is grounded in truth, this principle is immensely practical. Effectiveness is the true measure of authority. Sound decisions must be backed by intelligent action to generate real results. In order to increase your authority, you must consider two questions: *Am I making the correct decisions? Am I taking the correct actions?*

As you implement your command decisions, you must return again to the principle of truth. Observe the results you're getting. Are they consistent with your predictions? Learn from your successes as well as your mistakes. Your mind will gradually improve its predictive accuracy when you face similar situations in the future. Experience is the best teacher of effectiveness.

Notice how elegantly the principles of truth and power work together to improve your personal effectiveness over time. First, you identify one of your desires and make a decision to move toward it. Then you use your predictive abilities to select a reasonable course of action. As you progress toward your goal, you need only identify the next action you predict will move you in the correct direction. You use your power to move yourself forward, one step at a time. Even as you take these microsteps, your predictive mind is always looking ahead, continually refining its selections and evaluating the results of the decisions you've already implemented.

Maybe you reach your goal; maybe you don't. Either way, you experience a powerful gain. When you succeed, your successful predictions, decisions, and behaviors are reinforced. When you fail, your mind learns that its predictions were inaccurate, and it updates your model of reality to help prevent you from repeating the same mistakes. When you suffer from blocks to truth and power, this process won't work perfectly, but you'll still gain something from it.

Try to realize that failure is your friend. While it's often disappointing to miss the goal you aimed for, there's always a consolation prize. When you fail, you become smarter. You teach your mind to become better at prediction. This is an immensely powerful result.

I started learning computer programming when I was ten years old. Most of the programs I wrote didn't work the first time I ran them. Usually they'd produce the wrong output; sometimes they'd freeze up the computer. It was nearly impossible for me to get a program to run correctly the first try. But I took note of the actual output I got, and I tried to predict what might have caused the error. Then I adjusted the program and ran it again. Usually the output was still wrong, so I took another stab at identifying the cause of failure and made more adjustments. I kept doing this until I either succeeded or got too frustrated and gave up.

What did I gain from this process? It certainly wasn't a collection of quality programs. Most of the software I wrote during my childhood didn't have much value, and I rarely finished anything substantial. My real gain was that after thousands of cycles of identifying and fixing mistakes, I became a very good programmer. Before graduating from college, I was already working as a contract programmer developing retail computer games.

You can't expect to be competent when you tackle something new, but you *can* expect that you'll improve over time. All you have to do is set a goal, make decisions that you think will lead you in the right direction, and keep taking action. Either you'll succeed, or you'll learn from your failures. If you fail a great deal, it just means you have more to learn before you're ready to succeed.

Be willing to make decisions that may fail. Even though failure may have negative consequences, it also yields important positive results. It ultimately teaches you to succeed. You can't be a true authority unless you commit to being a lifelong student.

Persistence

To become competent in any new endeavor, you may need to invest a significant amount of time, often many years. It's imperative that you give yourself sufficient time to build your effectiveness. Your mind needs to gain enough experience to make accurate predictions. If you quit too early, you'll never complete the shift from novice to expert, and the expert level is where most of the rewards are found.

During my first five years running my computer-games business, I failed miserably. I set clear goals, made detailed plans, and worked very hard, but with each passing year, I only sank deeper into debt. I made the most horrendous mistakes, but back then they seemed like pretty good decisions.

I failed because I had no business experience whatsoever. I was a computer geek who bit off more than he could chew. My predictions were downright awful, so my actions seldom produced the intended results. What I expected would yield a profit only produced a loss. What I thought was a done deal would fall apart at the last minute. People I perceived to be my allies turned around and dealt me hurtful blows. Others told me I would fail, and they were right. Those were frustrating times, but I stubbornly refused to give up. I ran out of cash and credit and had to declare bankruptcy, but I just kept on going. Somehow, I knew I'd eventually figure it out.

I was right. It took years to train myself to think like an entrepreneur instead of a programmer, but I finally learned how to stop losing money and make my business profitable. My predictions got better, and my actions started producing the results I expected. I released a product I thought would sell well, and lo and behold, it did. I closed a licensing deal I expected would bring in extra income for years, and it actually worked. Once I finally learned how to run a successful business, I didn't have any trouble keeping it profitable every year after that.

When I launched StevePavlina.com in 2004, my mind was already trained for entrepreneurial success. I felt confident I could make the new business an even bigger success, and sure enough I did. It's been consistently profitable every year since I started. People who didn't know me were shocked by how quickly I succeeded. What they didn't realize was that this was only possible because of the massive failures I worked through in my previous company. I shudder to think what a mess I'd be dealing with right now if this had been my first business.

When you hear someone say that success is easy, run the other way as fast as you can because you're about to hear a sales pitch for another get-rich-quick scam. The honest truth is that it's very difficult —nearly impossible—to succeed at something you've never done before. But that's perfectly okay. Understand that failure and success are not opposites. Failure is an unavoidable part of success. When you fail, it means you're taking action, so you're making mistakes and educating yourself. Success happens naturally once you finally learn how to take the correct actions.

Be patient with yourself as you work through this failure period. If you're pursuing a goal you really want, the kind that practically brings you to tears when you think about it because you connect with it so deeply, then you have to stick with it. No matter how hard it gets, don't give up. I mean it!

Don't pressure yourself to achieve massive success the first time out. Just do the best you can. At first, your best may be barely one notch above complete idiot—if you're lucky. Eventually you'll gain some basic competency. And farther down the road, people will call you an expert—an expert being a person who's failed enough to succeed.

When I take a moment to tune in and connect with my past self, the one who repeatedly saw his best efforts lead to disaster, I'm overwhelmed by feelings of intense gratitude. Sometimes I wish I could go back in time, give my past self a big hug, and tell him how much I appreciate what he did for me. If he hadn't persisted through those difficult times, I'd never have been able to succeed in business, nor would I be able to share what I learned.

I find it incredibly inspiring to watch people struggle through one failure after another without giving up. From the outside looking in, it may seem as though they can't possibly succeed. But they still persist. Eventually they learn what they need to learn. They successfully adapt their predictions to fit reality, and finally their actions begin producing the intended results. I don't get inspired by people who have all the external trappings of success like money and fame. I'm moved by those who I can see are destined for greatness, but no one else knows it yet. The telltale sign is always the same—persistence.

One of my favorite quotes on persistence comes from Calvin Coolidge:

> *Nothing in the world can take the place of persistence. Talent will not; nothing is more common than unsuccessful men with talent. Genius will not; unrewarded genius is almost a proverb. Education will not; the world is full of educated derelicts.*

Persistence and determination are omnipotent. The slogan "Press on" has solved and always will solve the problems of the human race.

If you're clear about what you want, settle for nothing less. Accept that success will take time, perhaps much longer than you'd like. Rid yourself of the fast and easy, something-for-nothing mind-set. Keep your head down, work hard, and know that your efforts will eventually pay off, as long as you keep learning and growing.

Confidence

As you grow into your authority, you'll gradually develop confidence. I'm not referring to the temporary "Fake it till you make it" boldness that requires you to pump yourself up, such as you might do before asking someone on a date or getting up to speak in front of an audience. I'm referring to a stronger, more deeply held belief in your capabilities, a belief molded by experience and solidly rooted in truth. This kind of confidence cannot be faked.

Real confidence isn't flashy, cocky, aggressive, or arrogant. It isn't a feeling of dominance or superiority over others. Nor is it false modesty, self-effacement, or submissiveness. In the words of Kahlil Gibran, "To be modest in speaking truth is hypocrisy." Real confidence is the deep, soulful recognition of a certain truth, the truth that you're a powerful being. When you gaze upon your power through the lens of truth, you become naturally confident.

It isn't easy to acknowledge the truth of our power. Too often we fear our own greatness. We pretend to be powerless, mistakenly thinking that this somehow frees us from the responsibility of power. It's true that we can deny ourselves access to our own might, but we can never escape complete responsibility for our lives. When we live in denial of this truth, we block ourselves from genuine confidence and settle for temporary boldness at best.

Confidence begins with a resolute commitment to truth. You can't become genuinely confident by pretending your way into it. To build your confidence, strive to become as honest as possible, both with yourself and others. The more honest you become, the more accurate your model of reality will be. As you perceive reality with increasing accuracy, your decisions will improve, and in turn so will your actions and thereby your results. Accurate beliefs lead to effective results, and confidence is the emotional residue of effectiveness. You feel confident when you can expect positive results from your actions with a high degree of certainty.

Confidence has both short-term and long-term forms. Short-term confidence is the expectation of short-term success. For example, you may feel confident about driving your car today because you've driven it so many times before, so it's reasonable to expect continued success in this area. Long-term confidence is the expectation of long-term success, even though short-term failures may occur. This type of confidence comes from recognizing that failure is an essential part of reaching goals. Although you may not expect to succeed in a new endeavor right away, you feel confident you'll eventually succeed if you persist.

I never learned to play the piano, but I expect I could eventually do so if I really committed to it. It's not my piano experience that makes me confident I could acquire this skill; it's my understanding of the success process. If I can learn to walk, talk, program computers, and run a business through trial and error, then surely I can learn to play the piano as well. I may not experience short-term confidence while attempting to play my first song, but I can still maintain long-term confidence that I'll eventually figure it out. I can see the truth that I have the power to achieve such a goal if I really want it.

Don't bother trying to fake confidence. It's disingenuous and completely unnecessary. There's no need to manipulate yourself into a false feeling of certainty when in reality you're filled with self-doubt. It's perfectly okay to feel doubtful and still take action. If you simply persist, your uncertainty will eventually fade as you build experience, and you'll earn the feeling of true confidence instead of having to constantly fake it. If you try something new and really stink at it, simply accept how bad you are without trying to pretend otherwise, and know that you'll eventually grow beyond this stage. There's absolutely no dishonor in being a beginner. Beginning is simply the first step toward winning.

Significance

People of authority focus on what really matters to them. They don't waste time and energy on trivialities. They recognize the truth that power can be applied to meaningless pursuits, or it can be channeled toward significant achievements. Such people consciously choose the latter, sometimes for the simple reason that it's the path that yields the most growth.

What's important to you in life? What's a relative waste of your time? While these are decisions you're empowered to make freely, the truth aspect of authority reminds you that you can't escape the consequences of your actions. In order to stay aligned with both truth and power, you must carefully consider those results. When you choose a course of action, you also choose the consequences.

Your ability to predict the impact of your actions certainly won't be perfect, but you can still make reasonable determinations as to whether you're wasting your time or putting it to good use. Which activities are largely pointless? Which ones will have a real impact? You can surely come up with halfway-decent answers without needing a fortune-teller.

Authority teaches you to make present-moment decisions that you predict will have positive long-term effects. There are no neutral actions. If you can't honestly predict a positive long-term impact from your actions, admit that you're wasting your time, and set some goals that really matter to you. There's no substitute for investing your life in something that has the potential to make a real difference.

Who determines what's significant and what isn't? You're the authority here, so that decision is yours to make. Tune in to your feelings. Do you sense that you're contributing to an important purpose? Or do you feel empty inside, worrying that your potential is being wasted? What's the truth of your situation? Can you feel the difference between the relevant and the irrelevant?

How to Increase Your Authority

Since authority is truth plus power, your alignment with authority will naturally improve as you align yourself with those principles, so the exercises from the truth and power chapters will be useful here as well. But since authority is more than the sum of its parts, here are some additional methods to further develop it.

Orchestrate Small Rebellions

To become the authority of your life, you must become comfortable making independent decisions, whether or not other people agree with you. You can't be an authority unless you break free of the conditioning effects of peer pressure. One of the best ways to do so is to intentionally violate others' expectations by orchestrating small rebellions.

A small rebellion is an act of free will with minimal negative consequences. You're simply asserting your independence, allowing others to react however they wish. Examples include declining an invitation you'd normally accept, styling your hair differently, or putting some unusual posters in your work space. You've done nothing seriously wrong, but you can expect that others will react.

Don't try to justify or explain these rebellions. If anyone asks why you're behaving strangely, simply tell them you felt like it. If they press you for a detailed explanation, just reply, "I appreciate your concern, but I'd prefer not to explain my actions right now."

When I was a senior in high school, one of my small rebellions was to do my math homework with unusual media. I'd turn in my assignments in crayon, on a tiny 2" x 2" piece of paper, or on the back of a cereal box. The other students thought I'd gone off the deep end, but fortunately I had an amazing teacher who was willing to tolerate my creativity. You haven't really lived until you've done calculus in crayon.

The idea here isn't to behave like a complete jerk or to violate laws that will land you in serious trouble. Your assignment is simply to break the unwritten rules of social conformity, rules you aren't required to obey but which you've been blindly following. Small rebellions remind you that you always have a choice and that you can remain independent of other people's reactions.

Triage

In battlefield medicine, the principle of triage involves dividing patients into three groups:

1. Those who will die anyway, whether they receive medical attention or not

2. Those who will survive anyway, whether they receive medical attention or not

3. Those who will survive only if they receive timely medical attention

When resources are limited, medics must attend to members of the third group before the first and second groups in order to save as many lives as possible.

Triage can also help you build your authority by focusing your attention on the most significant actions. In this case you divide your tasks, projects, and activities into three groups:

1. Projects that will fail to have a significant impact, whether you do them or not

2. Projects that will succeed anyway, whether you do them or not

3. Projects that will have a significant impact only if you complete them in a timely manner

If you focus your attention on the first group, you're just spinning your wheels while more important tasks remain undone. If you focus your attention on the second group, you're wasting your energy for no meaningful return. But if you attend to the third group, you'll put your time and energy to the best possible use. In order to focus on the most significant actions, you must withdraw your attention from the first two groups.

Practicing triage is extremely challenging because it requires repeatedly saying no to what you may instinctively feel are good choices. It's the time-management equivalent of saying no to wounded people calling for help. But if you fail to master the art of triage, many worthwhile projects will die needlessly.

This process is a challenge of consciousness. It's easy to lose sight of the big picture when you're staring at a project screaming for your attention. But you still need to muster the awareness to ask yourself: *Is this the most important thing for me to be doing right now?*

Make a list of your group-three projects and activities, and keep it handy at all times. Maybe it's a list of your key goals, but it could also be a list of the life areas you want to attend to, such as your health, relationships, and spiritual practice. Review that list every day to keep refreshing its presence in your mind. This will help you make the tough triage decisions when the need arises. It's easier to say no to groups one and two when you can see the whole battlefield.

What are the group-three projects that are dying in the trenches but that can still be saved if you reach them in time? Your health? Your relationship? Your career? Your spiritual connection? In order to make time to save them, what ones and twos are you willing to pass up?

Experiment

One of the best ways to increase your mind's predictive accuracy is through direct testing. Instead of merely learning from others, go out and create your own knowledge. Don't blindly follow the advice of experts. Find out what works best for you by conducting personal experiments. Everyone is different, so what works for you may not be the same as what works for everyone else.

Whenever you come up with a new idea for increasing your effectiveness, test it to see what effect it has. Don't dismiss any ideas until you've actually tried them. The ongoing practice of conducting experiments will condition you to be more productive because you'll always be on the lookout for ways to improve.

I've conducted some incredibly strange experiments at times, several of them documented on my Website. For example, in late 2005 I decided to see if I could successfully adapt to polyphasic sleep. Polyphasic sleep has several variations, but the form I tested was to sleep only 20 minutes at a time, once every four hours, around the clock. That's six naps every 24 hours, for a total of 2 hours of sleep per day. Most people who attempt polyphasic sleep can't adapt and give up within the first few days, but after nearly a week of brutal sleep deprivation, I was finally able to adapt. It was a fascinating experience that changed my understanding of time, but the downside was that I fell out of sync with the rest of the world. I managed to keep it up for five and a half months before eventually returning to monophasic sleep, mainly for social reasons. It was one of the most memorable and productive times of my life, but it only happened because I decided to dive in and test it instead of merely reading about it.

You don't have to conduct experiments as severe as polyphasic sleep, but you'll surely benefit by conducting your own growth trials. Are you more productive while listening to music, or do you prefer total silence? What style of clothing makes you look and feel your best? Does your significant other respond best to verbal, written, or kinesthetic expressions of affection? What effects do you notice in your body after eating different types of foods? You can spend countless hours absorbing advice from so-called experts, or you can run a quick test and discover the answers for yourself.

For every expert who tells you one thing, you'll find someone else who says the opposite. What's the best diet, spiritual practice, or form of investing? You have to make these determinations for yourself. It's fine to consult with experts, but in all cases you're the final authority.

✦ ✦

You're the commander in chief of your life. There are no ifs, ands, or buts about it. You can try to give your power away and pretend to be powerless, but the undeniable truth is that you're still in command.

Get in touch with what's most important to you in life. If you felt responsible for the entire world, what would you want to change first? If you decided to become an expert at something, what would that be? What can you say about the great spirit that dwells inside you, waiting for the opportunity to express itself through purposeful action? What really matters to you?

Even as you learn to embrace your authority, you'll still encounter situations where aligning yourself with truth and power isn't enough. In order to successfully navigate such situations, you'll need to call upon your . . .

Chapter 6

COURAGE

"Security is mostly a superstition. It does not exist in nature, nor do the children of men as a whole experience it. Avoiding danger is no safer in the long run than outright exposure. Life is either a daring adventure, or nothing. To keep our faces toward change and behave like free spirits in the presence of fate is strength undefeatable."

— HELEN KELLER

Courage is the principle that combines love and power. The power element is perhaps the more obvious of the two. When we think of courage, we imagine someone taking bold actions, and action is an expression of power. However, the love component of courage is equally important. Love is the motivational force behind courage. It's our deepest connections that inspire us to be courageous in the first place. When we feel disconnected, there's no desire to be courageous, no reason for risk taking, and no call to action.

When your mind predicts a positive long-term outcome but a negative short-term outcome from a course of action, courage is required to bridge the gap. If you want to leave an unfulfilling relationship, quit an uninspiring job, or restore an unfit body to a state of health, the long-term outlook may be wonderful, but you can also expect short-term challenges as you transition. Courage is the application of power to break through short-term challenges in order to achieve long-term goals.

Courage is an essential element of conscious living because it enables us to choose long-term gain in the face of short-term obstacles. Without sufficient courage, your default behavior will be to play it safe by favoring false security over purposeful action. Keep working at the stable job even though it doesn't fulfill you. Remain in the unsatisfying relationship even though you feel dead inside. Accept your lot in life and make the best of it. Go with the flow and don't rock the boat. Hopefully, the currents of life will pull you in a favorable direction. This is the mind-set of cowardice.

When you disconnect from your core self, you experience fear. When you then refuse to face your fear, you disconnect even more. Fear isn't something to be avoided. It's the arrow pointing back to your true self. A good rule of thumb to follow is this: whatever you fear, you must eventually face.

Let's now explore the four fundamental aspects of courage: *heart, initiative, directness,* and *honor.*

Heart

The word *courage* derives from the Latin *cor,* which means "heart," and this is precisely what courage is. It's your connection to your core self. When you succumb to fear, you live unconsciously and disconnect from your natural power. It's only through courage that you embrace the powerful being you truly are.

Consider these powerful words from Carlos Castaneda:

Before you embark on [any path] ask the question: Does this path have a heart? If the answer is no, you will know it, and then you must choose another path.

Does your path have a heart? Do you know deep down that your path is the right one for you? Castaneda also wrote: "When a man finally realizes that he has taken a path without a heart, the path is ready to kill him." I've seen this happen repeatedly to people who set their dreams aside in order to pursue a path with no heart. Some make fame and fortune their top priorities, assuming that external success will eventually make them happy. It doesn't. Some settle for unfulfilling relationships, thinking that security will substitute for love. It won't. Others drown themselves in idle entertainment, hoping it can restore passion to their lives. It can't.

If your path has no heart, you're on the wrong path. The heart-centered path is that of courage, not false security. The illusion of security is the primary aim of the false path. It tries to find heart substitutes, such as money and status, in the external world. But if you're disconnected from your heart on the inside, you'll never find it on the outside. Courage recognizes that true power lies within and that the pursuit of security only makes you powerless.

The heart-centered path is often a winding road. As soon as you think you have it figured out, it takes a surprising turn. Even after you've found the path, it's easy to wander off and get sidetracked. When you realize you've disconnected from your heart, stop and ask yourself: *Where is the path with a heart?* This will help bring you back to your core.

What if you know you're on the wrong path but you don't know how to find the right one? In that situation your first step is to get off the road you're on. Just stop. If you can't see the right path from your current location, you must go out and explore. You can't search for it while you remain committed to the wrong one.

Over the past several years, I've watched many people undergo major career, relationship, and lifestyle transitions when they finally realized they'd been pursuing a heartless path that was slowly killing them. Some of them changed abruptly, immediately quitting their jobs and boldly setting off in new directions. Others transitioned more gradually, continuing their previous work to pay the bills while pursuing a new path in their spare time. The key is that those who succeeded burned the ships behind them. They knew they had to abandon the heartless options in order to find the path with a heart. Burning the ships, however, doesn't mean burning the food and supplies, too. You must do what's necessary to meet your transitional needs, but go far enough that you aren't tempted to return to the heartless path.

It's beautiful to see people reconnecting with their hearts again. These individuals feel courageous, happy, and free long before the external transition has occurred. Exercising their courage reminds them what it's like to feel truly alive.

Initiative

Courage is an active, present-moment virtue that waits for nothing. It's always ready to take the initiative, to make the first move, and to set things in motion. Don't wait for a new career, a new relationship, or other opportunities to come to you. Go out and actively create what you want. Life is waiting for you to make the first move. Use your power.

It's a great idea to consciously intend what you want, and I highly recommend you do that, but if you don't want something badly enough to take direct action, then what does that say about your intention? Doesn't that suggest you aren't really committed to it? When you're really hungry, will you wait patiently for food to arrive, or will you get up and make something to eat? When your intentions are important to you, direct action becomes part of the manifestation process. The best instruments of the Law of Attraction are your own hands and feet.

Fear is the shroud of opportunity. Your greatest regrets in life won't be the mistakes you made; they'll be the opportunities you let slip through your fingers by failing to act. When you take the initiative, you pull back the shroud of fear and catch a glimpse of the opportunity behind it. You reveal the long-term gain behind the short-term pain.

In the long run, taking action is less painful than wallowing in fear. Fear may be imaginary, but it can produce needless suffering in the form of discomfort, worry, and stress. Such problems can last for months, years, or even a lifetime if they aren't remedied with action.

The discomfort of courage, on the other hand, is temporary, and in some cases recovery takes only minutes. The path of courage ultimately reduces pain.

Directness

People often take circuitous paths to their goals to minimize the risk of rejection. For example, they'll send out feelers through their social network to try to determine in advance whether their future requests will be accepted or rejected. What will happen if they ask for the sale, the promotion, or the date? The idea is that if they can sniff out a negative response in advance, outright rejection can be avoided. On the other hand, if a positive result seems guaranteed, then action can be taken with minimal risk.

At first glance, this approach seems reasonable. There's really just one problem with it: it's stupid. It's a completely ridiculous plan for getting what you want in life. It's weak, dishonest, and manipulative.

People who go out of their way to avoid rejection only weaken themselves in the long run. They expend enormous amounts of thought and energy trying to manipulate circumstances, meanwhile allowing golden opportunities to slip through their fingers. All of this can be avoided with a few seconds of courageous action.

If you want something, ask for it. Accept the risk of rejection, and summon the courage to take action anyway. If you get turned down, you'll survive. You'll learn from the experience and grow stronger. If you don't get rejected, you'll achieve your outcome in the fastest and simplest way possible. When you risk rejection, either you get what you want or you build some courage. Either way the outcome is positive.

Being too direct can have negative connotations, but there's no need to be annoyingly pushy or aggressive when asking for what you want. Just be honest, open, and forthright. If the other person doesn't respond positively, then at least you know where you stand. You've shed light on the situation and aligned yourself with truth. Everything is out in the open. An honest rejection is always superior to a clever deception.

Share your thoughts and feelings openly when you ask for what you want. Make it easy for the other person to give you an honest answer. For example, when asking for a date with someone you know, you might start with something like this: "Cathy, we've been friends for a while, and I have to confess I'm starting to develop feelings for you. In fact, I like you a lot. I don't know if you feel the same about me, but I'd really like to get to know you better and see if there's an opportunity for us to build a closer relationship. How do you feel about this?" Then just listen. If the response is negative, you're free to move on. If the response is positive, you can discuss the next steps. Making such a statement only takes 15 seconds of courage. Isn't this a better approach than perpetually wondering what might have been and beating yourself up for missed opportunities? Short bursts of courage can overcome many obstacles.

What if you get rejected? How will you deal with the ensuing embarrassment? There needn't be any embarrassment if you simply accept the outcome instead of resisting it. Sure, you might be disappointed, but take solace in the fact that you successfully exercised your courage. Even when you fail, facing your fear is a positive outcome in its own right. Don't worry about rejection; just accept that it's going to happen every now and then. When someone declines your offer of connection, it doesn't mean you aren't loved.

How would you react if someone asked you for something in a very conscious, straightforward manner? It's a safe bet that you'd either accept the request or at least let the other person down easy. Even if you must decline, wouldn't you have a bit more respect for someone who comes to you with honesty and openness instead of hiding their true feelings?

As a consequence of my work, I receive new requests every day. Many people want me to review their books and products on my Website. Some ask me to assist with various projects. Others want me to coach or mentor them. I have great respect for those who ask directly for what they want, human being to human being, and I give those queries fair consideration. If the requests are aligned with truth, love, and power, I'm inclined to grant them when it's reasonable to do so. But when I see phony, insincere, or manipulative communication,

I take it as an indication I'd have to deal with a person of similar qualities, which leads to an automatic rejection.

When people get to know you as a straight shooter, even if they must reject your initial requests, they'll often bring you fresh opportunities down the road because you've demonstrated your willingness to be open and honest. The rejected date becomes a new ally who plays matchmaker for you. The missed sale creates an unexpected referral. The denied promotion yields a better job offer. When you play straight with people, they'll often remember because directness stands out from the crowd.

Are you trying to live a safe life? The word *safe* is both an adjective and a noun. As an adjective it means "being free from danger." As a noun it's "an enclosed storage container with a lock." If you're living the adjective, you're living the noun. Don't trap yourself in a cage of false security by trying to avoid rejection. In the long run, building your courage is a smarter choice than running from imaginary dangers.

Honor

In addition to connecting you with your power, courage also brings power to your connections. When you exercise your courage, you feel more connected to your true self. Your bonds with others grow deeper as well because your interactions are centered in truth, love, and power, not in falsehood, apathy, or timidity. Over time, these connections become so strong that they elevate you to a new level of awareness. At this level, you consciously commit yourself to a principle-centered life. This commitment is called honor.

Honor is not loyalty to an individual or group. Such allegiance comes from superficial bonds and familiarity, but honor connects with genuine unconditional love in a way that transcends individual identity. Honor is the place where power and love reconnect with truth.

The guiding force of honor is your conscience, which is your intuitive ability to discern right from wrong. Right actions are aligned with truth, love, and power. Wrong actions are out of alignment with these principles. A sense of honor enables you to perceive the difference.

Honor recognizes that service to self and service to others are the same thing. They cannot be otherwise. The health of the body and the health of its cells are one. For the body to be aligned with truth, love, and power, the cells must also be so aligned. When you connect with the deepest parts of yourself, you're connecting with your truth, your love, and your power. When you connect deeply with others, you're connecting with their truth, their love, and their power. Honor acknowledges that these inner and outer connections are the same.

To act with honor is to act in accordance with truth, love, and power. When driven by honor, you take action because you care— you care so much that you can't settle for inaction. You commit to a principle-centered life, recognizing that upholding these principles is your sacred duty. This duty feels right, does right, and is right. This is the place where heart and mind harmoniously agree, where logic and intuition can find no discord.

When you're deeply connected with truth, love, and power, you're driven to action. The more deeply you connect, the more motivated you become. The most powerful motivator of all is love, but it takes tremendous courage to honor that simple truth.

When you feel lazy and unmotivated, the simple reason is that you're feeling disconnected. You've fallen out of alignment with truth, love, and power. When you recognize that you're in this state, stop and reconnect with the real you. Remember who you are. Reconnect with what excites you. Revisit those times in your life when you were on fire—not because of external events, but because you were aligned with your truth, your love, and your power. Turn your gaze within and ask yourself: *Where is the path with a heart, and what can I do to honor that path right now?* Whatever answer you come up with, summon the courage to take immediate action. Growl ferociously if you think it will help, but get yourself into motion no matter what.

How to Build Courage

Much like the other principles, courage grows with regular exercise and atrophies from lack of use. Here are several exercises to help you build your courage and generate practical results at the same time.

The Heart Question

Whenever you take a moment to plan your day, write out your to-do list, or think about what action to take next, stop and ask yourself, *Where is the path with a heart?* This is powerful because it will help you immediately discard the options that don't have a heart.

Even when you're sitting at home, trying to decide how to spend your evening, ask yourself the heart question. Notice how certain options feel heartless and empty, while other paths produce a tingle of excitement when you think about them. Allow your heart to help you find the right course. Note that the word *courage* is found within the word *encouragement.* When we identify the path with a heart, we feel encouraged to take action.

Perhaps instead of watching television, you're encouraged to read something that inspires you. Maybe instead of playing computer games, you're encouraged to have a deep conversation with your mate about the future of your relationship. And maybe instead of merely going through the motions at work, you're encouraged to push yourself to make the best contribution you can. The heart-centered question leads you to the path of conscious growth.

I often ask myself this question when deciding which article to write next. Due to the constant influx of reader suggestions, as well as my own growth experiments, I never suffer from a shortage of ideas, but it can be hard to choose a topic because there are so many good ones to consider. When I stop and ask myself: *Where is the path with a heart?* the right topic usually becomes clear. It's the subject that scares me a little, the one I'm not sure I can write about well, the one that stirs my soul with excitement. On those occasions when the topic doesn't become clear, it's because the heart-centered path requires doing something other than writing.

Post the heart question in a place where you'll see it every day, or set it as your computer's screen saver, so you'll be reminded of it often. Whenever you ask the question, you bring your logic and intuition into alignment.

Progressive Training

You can use the same progressive-training principle from Chapter 3 to gradually build your courage. Instead of tackling your biggest fear right away, confront your smallest fears first, and progressively work up to more significant acts of courage.

First, select a fear you'd like to overcome. It's okay if it's too big for you to tackle right away. Now see if you can identify one small step you could take to confront that fear, something that would be a fairly mild challenge for you but that would still trigger some trepidation. For example, if you're afraid to initiate a conversation with a stranger, your first goal might be to walk past a stranger and smile. If that still seems too difficult, start with an easier goal, such as making eye contact with a stranger for one second.

Train yourself with your first baby step until you feel ready to increase the challenge. There's no specific number of repetitions you need to complete for each step, but five to ten is a good ballpark estimate. Suppose you master making eye contact with strangers, being able to hold it for one full second without looking away. You may feel a little anxious about it at first, but after ten reps, you're able to do it consistently. Then increase the challenge to two or three seconds. Once you've mastered that, you may want to progress to smiling. Next, try smiling and saying hi. Within a matter of weeks, you can slowly work up to starting a conversation with a total stranger. Each baby step builds your experience, allowing you to gradually progress from novice to expert without feeling overwhelmed.

Make each training step as small as you want. Face mild challenges that you're fairly confident you can complete. Feel free to repeat as many reps as you need until you feel ready for the next step. You control the pacing.

By following this progressive-training process, you'll accomplish two things. First, you'll stop reinforcing the fearful avoidance patterns you exhibited in the past. Second, you'll condition yourself to act more courageously in future situations. Your fear will diminish while your courage grows.

Education

One of the greatest fears is that of the unknown. This can be remedied by gathering additional knowledge. Confronting fears head-on can be helpful, but if your anxiety is largely due to ignorance or lack of experience, you may be able to reduce or eliminate it simply by educating yourself.

Suppose you're afraid to leave your hometown and move to a new city, even though you'd love to have the experience. Maybe the main reason for your hesitation is ignorance. The whole notion seems overwhelming because you don't know what to expect. But you can learn what you need to know by reading Websites, connecting with residents of other cities, and taking short trips. The knowledge you acquire will help you act more courageously, and also intelligently.

It's amazing how many opportunities we deny ourselves due to lack of knowledge or experience. In this golden information age, "I don't know" is simply not a valid excuse. All the information you need is readily accessible on the Internet, in inexpensive books, or in other people's minds. If ignorance is holding you back in any area of your life, then take the initiative and educate yourself.

Commit in Advance

A simple way to build courage is to make commitments that don't require much courage to accept but that require significant courage to implement. When you put yourself on record, you'll tend to follow through. Small commitments can help you overcome complacency and build significant courage.

During my first few months as a member of Toastmasters International, I decided to enter their humorous-speech contest. I'd never competed in an adult speech contest before, but when I was asked if I wanted to participate, it didn't take much courage for me to say, "Sure, I'll do it." As the contest date drew closer, however, I began to second-guess my decision: *What have I gotten myself into here?* But since I was already committed to the contest, I followed through and did my best.

Preparing for each round of competition was hard work, but I had a lot of fun and probably advanced my speaking skills by the equivalent of 6 to 12 months of regular club attendance. After that first contest season, I felt much more confident and courageous as a speaker, and I went on to compete in other speech contests. I'm sure I wouldn't be as comfortable with public speaking today if I hadn't committed to that first competition many years ago. All it took to get moving was to open my mouth and say, "I'll do it."

Instead of avoiding your fears, make a commitment to face them. If you're afraid of public speaking, commit to giving a speech. If you're afraid of heights, enroll in a rock-climbing class. If you're afraid of the water, sign up for swimming lessons. Remember that whatever you fear, you must eventually face, including death itself.

✦ ✦

Courage is a choice. To be courageous is to confront your fear with the power that emanates from your deepest connections. As you bring your life into alignment with truth, love, and power, fear's hold on you will gradually weaken. Truth helps you see through the illusion of fear, so you can maintain authority over your life. Love motivates you to deepen your connections and achieve the fearless state of one-ness. And power provides the strength to act in spite of fear, building courage in the process.

No matter how difficult it may seem, choose to face your fears consciously. Don't die without embracing the daring adventure your life is meant to be. You may go broke. You may experience failure and rejection repeatedly. You may endure multiple dysfunctional re-lationships. But these are all milestones on the path of a life lived courageously. These are your private victories, carving a deeper space within you to be filled with an abundance of joy, happiness, and fulfill-ment. Be afraid if you must; then summon the courage to follow your dreams anyway. That is strength undefeatable.

Now that we've explored the first six principles, it's time to ad-dress the final principle that brings them all together . . .

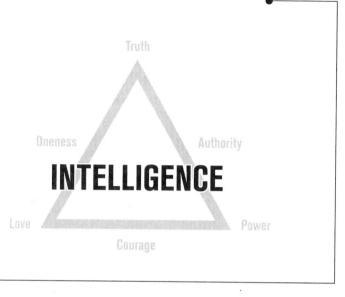

Chapter 7

Truth

Oneness   Authority

INTELLIGENCE

Love   Power

Courage

"Many difficulties which nature throws our way, may be smoothed away by the exercise of intelligence."

— Titus Livius

When truth, love, and power are harmoniously aligned, they produce the paramount principle of personal growth: intelligence. This encapsulates every idea discussed thus far into a single unified whole. When we perceive the beautiful union of truth, love, and power, we intuitively recognize intelligence.

Truth is intelligent. By embracing truth and shedding ignorance, falsehood, and denial, we create the ideal conditions for lifelong growth. We learn about ourselves by exploring physical reality, continually predicting consequences and gradually refining them for greater accuracy. As we accept each new level of truth, we progress to ever-higher levels of awareness. There can be no intelligent growth without truth.

Love is intelligent. We can't learn and grow alone in a vacuum. We must form new connections within ourselves and with others to extend our capabilities. By coming together as a community, we achieve ever-deeper levels of intimacy, thereby increasing our understanding, motivation, and creativity. There can be no intelligent growth without love.

Power is intelligent. We are immensely creative beings, free to express ourselves in physical form. By shedding idleness, timidity, and cowardice, we become capable of wielding power responsibly instead of living in fear of our own greatness. With disciplined, focused action, we create our own reality and honor the truth of who we really are. There can be no intelligent growth without power.

Intelligence is the highest form of human expression. Our intelligence is what defines us as human beings. It is our greatest strength, our staunchest ally, and our most noble pursuit. Without it, we are nothingness; we are form without substance and existence without purpose. It is only through the deliberate exercise of intelligence that we give our lives meaning, a meaning that is consciously chosen.

Our universal principles give rise to the following definition of intelligence: *Intelligence is alignment with truth, love, and power.* There is an elegant simplicity to this definition. In order to behave as a "smart person" in any area of your life, you must bring yourself into alignment with truth, love, and power. If you use these principles to guide your life, you will live intelligently. When you violate these principles, you turn your back on intelligence.

Take a moment to ponder the above definition of intelligence. Does it satisfy your logical mind as well as your intuition? When you reflect on your most intelligent choices in life, do you find that you have aligned yourself with truth, love, and power? When you consider your biggest regrets, can you identify a lack of alignment with any of these principles?

Far more than the sum of its parts, intelligence offers several emergent qualities of its own: *authenticity, creative self-expression, growth, flow,* and *beauty.*

Authenticity

Being authentic means expressing yourself congruently. The person you project on the outside is the person you truly are on the inside, whether you're communicating with an intimate friend or someone you just met. When people say, "Just be yourself," they're emphasizing the importance of authenticity. When you communicate authentically, you speak your truth without holding back. This helps others perceive you accurately and connect with you honestly and lovingly. Authentic communication empowers us.

As you interact with others, neither exaggerate nor downplay what's true for you. Be completely real. Your honesty won't always get a positive response, but allow others to have their reactions without feeling you must pretend to be something you're not. If you try to slant the truth in order to tell people what you think they want to hear, you disconnect from your true self, and you encourage others to live in denial of their own power. Denying your power is a disservice to everyone. The best course of action is to be completely honest and accept that others are free to react as they choose. You needn't agree with their reaction; just allow it to be.

For many years, I believed that the best way to relate to other people was to try to meet them at their own level of power. If someone was very timid, I'd downplay my accomplishments or hide them altogether because I didn't want to make the other person feel uncomfortable. If someone was haughty and arrogant, I'd respond in kind by trying to win their approval. I didn't have trouble making friends this way, but these were friendships rooted in falsehood, and in order to maintain them, I became increasingly disconnected with myself.

Eventually, I realized I'd rather experience a few honest friendships than settle for a plethora of connections that were corrupted by elements of phoniness. In my subsequent interactions, I did my best to stay connected to my true self. I decided to stop worrying about how other people would react to me.

At first, this approach seemed to backfire. When I expressed myself freely around some of my more timid friends, I must have scared them off, since they basically dropped out of my life. Similarly, my prideful friends fell out of my life as well, perhaps because they felt I was no longer at their level. I wish I could say I retained some middle group, but there wasn't much of a middle to speak of. People tended to fall on either one side or the other. My social life declined for a while . . . but then something very interesting began to happen.

As new people came into my life and they got to know me, they began relating to me very differently from my old friends. The most obvious change was that these relationships were rooted in genuine mutual respect. Because I stayed connected with myself, I was also more selective about the people I decided to connect with, so I sought out friends who were consciously growth oriented and not complacent or apathetic. I began to develop strong bonds much more quickly than I used to, and I felt grateful for these stimulating and genuinely caring friendships. I was soon completely convinced that total authenticity is the right choice. There's simply no point in maintaining relationships that cause us to subvert our true selves.

Being authentic doesn't mean being perfect. It means doing our best to communicate like real human beings. Sometimes that requires exposing our warts and scars, but therein lies the power of complete self-acceptance. Instead of reacting out of fear and falsehood, we can consciously choose to respond with truth, love, and power.

Creative Self-Expression

The path for intelligent human beings is to master the art of conscious, creative self-expression. This is far more important than acquiring money and possessions, which can never compensate for a lack of conscious growth. Your creativity is the very mechanism by which you'll achieve everything you could possibly want, including financial abundance, well-developed talents, fulfilling relationships, and meaningful contributions. When you commit to creatively sharing yourself with the world, it's much easier to meet your needs and satisfy your desires.

Self-expression requires both a medium and a message. Your medium is the collection of creative outlets you use. For example, I express myself creatively through writing, blogging, and speaking, so those are my media. Your message is the most powerful truth you wish to share. My message is to share conscious growth with others, and that includes the content you're reading in this book as well as what you'll find on my Website.

By embracing the principles of truth, love, and power, you accomplish two things. First, you tune in to your primary message. You discover what's most important to you, and your connectedness motivates you to share it for the benefit of all. Second, you develop the power necessary to cultivate a medium that suits your message. You invest the effort required to learn how to write, speak, act, dance, build, and so on. You do whatever it takes to create the outlets you need to share your message with the world.

When we creatively express ourselves, we're honestly sharing what's most important to us. This act of sharing connects us with others and offers them a glimpse of truth. When we enjoy the authentic result of someone else's creativity, such as a poem or painting, we can perceive the principles of truth, love, and power radiating from it.

Who are you? What do you want to share with the world? What elements of truth, love, and power can you contribute through your own acts of creative self-expression? Are you here to teach us to be more nurturing, compassionate, organized, generous, productive, honest, joyful, creative, or loving? What's the most intelligent way for you to express those qualities? Will you feed us, clothe us, teach us, motivate us, entertain us, support us, advance us, or lead us? You're the authority here. What's your decision?

Growth

A fascinating quality of intelligence is that it seeks its own improvement. Perhaps the smartest choice we can make is to attempt to become smarter, and growth is the mechanism through which this is achieved. It is intelligent to grow.

By improving your alignment with truth, you gain access to new truths. By improving your alignment with love, you increase your connectedness. And by improving your alignment with power, you become more powerful. Since intelligence is the combination of truth, love, and power, you can also see that as you increase your alignment with these three principles, you effectively become more intelligent. This is precisely how you grow as a human being.

Growth is rarely linear, so you can expect plenty of diversions and setbacks along the way. But as long as you strive to increase your alignment with these principles, you will certainly grow as a result. You won't be the same person tomorrow that you are today.

When I was 19 years old, I decided to make personal growth the guiding force of my life. At the time, I had no idea where it would lead. Initially, it was just a way to escape the hopeless situation I was in. I realized that no pain was permanent and that given enough time, I could eventually grow out of any problematic situation. I didn't fathom the principles of truth, love, and power until many years later, but focusing on growth alone was enough to turn my life around.

Three years after being arrested for grand theft, I graduated college with two degrees in only three semesters by taking triple the normal course load. A few months later, I was launching my own business with my girlfriend, who later became my wife. I still had many difficult lessons ahead, but I finally became the driving authority of my own life instead of being a slave to unconscious compulsion and addiction. A commitment to growth was the solution to all of my worst problems.

Working on your personal growth may seem like a completely selfish undertaking, but in fact it's the most selfless thing you can possibly do. As you improve your alignment with truth, love, and power, you increase your capacity to serve others. The more intelligent you become, the more good you can do. If you haven't already discovered this, you'll eventually realize that when you improve yourself, you inspire others to do the same. Those people then inspire even more people, and your positive ripples of growth ultimately impact everyone. As you improve yourself, you improve all of us. As the cells improve, the whole body improves.

If you forget everything else from this book and remember only one piece of advice, it is simply this: *The most intelligent thing you can possibly do with your life is to grow.*

Flow

With truth, love, and power on your side, you work with the natural flow of life instead of struggling against it. This doesn't mean that life becomes effortless. It means that your efforts are well positioned to produce the desired results. First, your goals are rooted in truth, so they're wisely set. Second, you maintain loving connections to keep you motivated. And third, your actions are focused and productive.

Flow isn't a passive state. It doesn't mean letting go and simply allowing your life to happen to you, as if you're gently floating down a stream being pulled along by the current. That isn't intelligent behavior. If you live like that, you'll eventually get washed out to sea. Animals in nature stay busy when necessary; otherwise they die. Your own cells also work hard to keep you alive; they remain active even while you sleep. Flow is a state of action.

You aren't here to live in denial of your desires, to settle for an easy life devoid of purpose and conviction. The state of flow results from conscious thought and action in the direction of your dreams. Learn to satisfy your desires and fulfill your dreams instead of pretending they don't matter to you.

Truth, love, and power are immensely practical principles. When applied diligently, they yield tangible results. These are the same principles that inspire all meaningful human accomplishment. Consider the first time men landed on the moon. The necessary knowledge and engineering was grounded in scientific truth. The people involved were deeply passionate about their work; and focused, disciplined action was required to make the mission a success. If even one of these principles was absent, the mission could not have succeeded. Consider any serious human achievement, including your own, and you'll see truth, love, and power staring back at you.

When you maintain the state of flow—real flow that is, not the fairy-tale version—it will feel as if there's powerful energy working through you, lovingly supporting you, and driving you onward. You know without a doubt that you're on the right track as you make progress toward something meaningful and important. What inspires you most isn't the achievement of any particular goal; it's the endless flow of creative self-expression. You fall in love with the journey itself.

A feeling of peaceful centeredness is a natural by-product of intel-ligent living. This doesn't mean you stop experiencing negative emo-tions; instead, it means that deep down, you know you're doing the best you can. Knowing you're on the right path will reduce your feel-ings of doubt, worry, and stress; and a deep sense of inner peace will arise in their place.

It's comforting to know that truth, love, and power are the only guiding principles you really need. You don't need to live by a com-plicated set of rules, laws, or values. Embracing these principles can greatly simplify your life by helping you shed the conditioning forces that have shaped your life in the past but that no longer serve you today. In order to make intelligent decisions, you need only steer yourself in the direction of truth, love, and power. The better your alignment, the more intelligent you become, and the more inner and outer peace you experience.

Peace arises naturally from the principle-centered path. You don't need to achieve any specific external results to be at peace; you just need to be pointed in the right direction. Picture yourself driving home in your car. You've driven home many times before, and there's a certain inevitability about the process. You know that if you just keep heading in the right direction and making the correct turns, you'll eventually reach your destination. A principle-centered life produces similar results. You know in advance that reaching your goals is basi-cally a done deal. And because of this, it becomes more important that you enjoy the journey instead of obsessing over the end result.

Beauty

We naturally recognize intelligence as beautiful. As you witness how elegantly the principles of truth, love, and power operate in your life, you may even consider it a spiritual experience. It's almost like discovering a new law of mathematics or physics. Suddenly you start seeing it everywhere as part of the underlying structure of reality.

When you see an object fall to the ground, you may not under-stand the laws of physics. When you insert a battery into a child's toy, you may not know how electricity works. And when you pet a dog, you may not understand biology. Whether you're aware of them or not, ever-present laws still operate at all times. Similarly, when you successfully achieve a goal you've set, fall in love with someone, or learn a new skill, you're following the underlying laws of personal growth. You're aligning yourself with the principles of truth, love, and power, whether you realize it or not.

Beneath the surface chaos of reality, there are many governing patterns to be found. As you become aware of these patterns, life becomes incredibly fascinating. A rich diversity of emergent behavior often arises from seemingly simple rules. Truth, love, and power are not terribly complicated concepts. You probably had a good intuitive grasp of them before you even read this book, although I hope that I've helped enrich your understanding. You might even consider these ideas to be common sense at first glance, but what you may not have understood is the incredible richness that can be derived from these concepts and how elegantly they interact with each other.

It's common sense to predict that an apple will fall if you drop it. The real trick is figuring out how and why it falls. Once you learn that, seeing an object fall to the ground is no longer such a routine experience. Now it becomes a thing of beauty. Similarly, you'll begin to observe the beauty of all personal growth challenges when you see them through the lenses of truth, love, and power.

Notice that every principle governs both thought and action. You can think accurate thoughts and speak truthful words. You can think loving thoughts and also express love outwardly. You can focus your mind on the inside and take disciplined action on the outside. Each principle has internal and external aspects; the principles apply to your private thoughts as well as to your public actions.

Begin to see reality through the lenses of truth, love, and power, starting with your own life. Notice how these principles govern your career, your health, your relationships, and more. Observe how a lack of truth creates problems for you, how a lack of love causes you to feel disconnected and alone, and how a lack of power makes you feel helpless and victimized. Discover how much easier your life becomes and how much happier you feel when you align yourself with truth, love, and power. Use the principles to make your life a thing of beauty.

How to Live Intelligently

Intelligent behavior results from an integrated process of perception, thought, and action. For behavior to be intelligent, each part of this process must be aligned with truth, love, and power. And in order to behave intelligently, you must first know that you're intelligent because this quality is self-aware. Second, you must actively connect with aspects of yourself, with other people, and with objects and activities in order to learn from them and inspire new ideas. And third, you must act upon your ideas to explore, experience, and share them. These steps usually run concurrently, and it can be very beneficial to practice them deliberately.

Here are several exercises you can use to live more intelligently, thereby increasing your alignment with truth, love, and power.

Conscious Assessment

Perhaps the most direct way to live more intelligently is to assess your current alignment with the seven principles. You can ask these questions with your entire life in mind, but you'll probably get better results if you pick a certain area such as your health, career, or relationships. You can write your answers in your personal journal or simply answer them aloud.

1. Truth

- Am I truthful with myself and others, or do I feel compelled to lie about anything?

- What do I predict will happen if I continue on my current course?

- Are my predictions reasonable and accurate, or am I too optimistic or pessimistic?

- Do I fully accept the truth of my situation, or am I living in denial?

- What do I need to learn next, and what's the best way to learn it?

- What can I do right now to become more truthful?

2. Love

- Do I take time to connect with myself and others, or do I feel disconnected and alone?

- Do I express my true self when I communicate, or do I project a false image?

- Do I love and accept myself and others unconditionally?

- Do I seek out compatible new relationships?

- How can I exercise and improve my social skills?

- What can I do right now to become more loving?

3. Power

- Do I accept complete responsibility for everything in my life?

- What do I really want, and what am I willing to do to get it?

- Am I focusing on what's most important to me, or am I distracting myself?

- Am I putting in the time to do what needs to be done?

- How can I continue to build my self-discipline?

- What can I do right now to become more powerful?

4. Oneness

- Do I recognize the truth that we're all connected, like individual cells in a larger body?

- Can I empathically tune in to the joy and sorrow of others?

- Do I treat others with compassion and fairness?

- Am I making a meaningful contribution to the world?

- Do I think and act with a sense of unity?

- What can I do right now to experience more oneness?

5. Authority

- Do I take command of my life, or do I blindly follow others?

- Are my actions effective, producing the results I want?

- Do I persist in the face of obstacles and setbacks, or do I give up too easily?

- Am I confident that I'll achieve the goals I set for myself?

- How can I spend my time on what's truly important and avoid wasting time on trivialities?

- What can I do right now to increase my authority?

6. Courage

- Do I live boldly and courageously; or do I succumb to fear, timidity, and cowardice?

- Where is the path with a heart, and what can I do to honor that path right now?

- Do I take the initiative, or am I stuck in a waiting mode?

- Do I courageously pursue the most direct course; or do I follow a slower, more manipulative route?

- How can I train and educate myself to overcome my fear?

- What can I do right now to exercise my courage?

7. Intelligence

- Do I live in alignment with truth, love, and power?

- Are my interactions with others authentic or phony?

- Do I have the right message and the medium for creative self-expression?

- Do I enjoy the state of flow by taking intelligent action?

- How can I improve myself today?

- What can I do right now to express my intelligence?

These questions will help you assess how close you're getting to a principle-centered life. Don't be discouraged if many of your answers seem negative. Simply accept where you are right now, and think about the next steps you can take to increase your alignment.

Growth Blitzing

A growth blitz is a way to quickly increase your alignment with every principle. The concept is simple, and you can make it as easy or as challenging as you want. The more challenging you make it, the greater the risk of failure, but the greater your gains will be if you succeed.

For each of the seven principles, set a specific growth target. Decide to make a small improvement in each area. Since the principles are mutually reinforcing, a small gain in one area will help you improve in all other areas. For example, if you can become just a little more accurate in your thinking (truth), the effectiveness of your actions (power) will improve as well.

Here are some suggestions for growth targets you might set for each principle. You only need one target per principle, but you can choose multiple targets if you're confident that you can handle it.

1. Truth

- Confess to a lie or secret you've been concealing (*easy:* confess to a stranger over the Internet; *hard:* confess to someone you've been lying to).

- Write down your most realistic prediction for what you think your life will look like five years from today; then ask someone else to make a similar prediction for you, and compare your answers.

- Read a book on a topic you know virtually nothing about.

- Invite an intelligent friend to debate you on a subject where you suspect you may hold erroneous or inaccurate beliefs.

- Begin a 30-day media fast.

2. Love

- Send someone a handwritten card or letter just to connect. E-mail doesn't count!

- Start a conversation with a total stranger, and try to figure out what's most important to that person.

- Find a creative way to say "I love you" or "I care about you" to someone who's never heard it from you before.

- Give someone an unexpected gift to let this person know he or she is appreciated by you.

- Invite someone over for dinner who's never been to your house before.

3. Power

- Write a fresh list of goals for every area of your life. Use the chapter titles from Part II of this book as your guide.

- Set aside at least one hour to work on your single most

important project. Refuse to do anything else until the time has elapsed. For a more challenging version, make it three or four hours.

• Name something you've always wanted to do that you could accomplish in less than a day if you were totally committed; then go out and do it.

• Plan and schedule your next day from the time you awaken to the time you go to bed. At the end of the day, give yourself a 1 to 10 score for how well you stuck to the schedule. Try to beat that score by at least one point the next time you attempt this exercise.

• Play a competitive game with someone, and bet the other person that you'll win. Make the bet for something more interesting than money.

4. Oneness

• Perform an act of kindness for a stranger.

• Share a painful story from your past by posting it on the Internet so that others may benefit from the lessons you learned.

• Identify an area from your life where you've been unfair to someone, and take immediate action to remedy the situation.

• Spend a couple of hours hiking alone in nature. Quiet your thoughts and pay as much attention to your senses as possible.

• Initiate an e-mail exchange with someone who lives in another country, and find out what you have in common.

5. Authority

- Cancel an activity that you realize no longer serves you.

- Volunteer to be in charge of a group or family project, and see it through to completion by delegating tasks to others.

- Conduct a personal experiment you've always wanted to try, such as a new diet, a new sleeping pattern, or a new way of interacting with others.

- For one day, wear an outfit that no one seems to like but you.

- Teach someone else how to perform a task you're very good at.

6. Courage

- Make a new request of someone who recently rejected you.

- Identify an opportunity that you know is worthwhile but that you've been afraid to pursue, and go for it anyway.

- Walk up to someone and state in no uncertain terms exactly what you want from that person.

- Make an advance commitment to a specific course of action that makes facing one of your fears unavoidable.

- Do one thing today that scares you.

7. Intelligence

- Call someone you know, and do your best to communicate as authentically as possible during the entire call.

- Take out a piece of paper and draw something that represents the real you.

- Identify a recent setback you've experienced, and devise a creative plan to work around it.

- Visit a museum and look for expressions of truth, love, and power in every exhibit.

- Brainstorm a list of 20 new ideas you can use to improve your life.

Growth blitzing helps you achieve balanced improvements because you're paying respect to all seven principles. You'll find that some principles are very easy for you, while others are much more difficult. You control the pacing of these exercises, but one week is a reasonable time frame for completing one action from each principle. That's one action per day for seven days. If you want a real challenge, try doing all seven in a single day. Also consider doing your growth blitz with a partner or group, so you can hold each other accountable.

Cultivate an Intelligent Microcosm

Instead of trying to improve the preexisting parts of your life, this exercise challenges you to add a new activity where you'll do your best to stay aligned with truth, love, and power from the very beginning. So instead of correcting old problems, your goal in this case is to avoid introducing problems of misalignment in the first place.

Suppose you meet someone new. This person doesn't know you yet, so you don't have any previous baggage together. You're free to get this relationship right from day one. Try to be as open and honest with this person as you possibly can. Skip the superficial chatter, and aim for deep conversations about subjects that truly matter to you. Take the initiative, and invite this person to participate in interesting activities with you. See how quickly you can develop a genuine bond of trust.

You can apply the same principles whenever you begin a new hobby or activity. For example, if you decide to take up gardening, educate yourself by reading gardening books, connect with others through gardening clubs or Websites, and take action to plant your own garden. Whenever you add another activity to your life, treat it as a small universe that comes pre-aligned with truth, love, and power, even though the rest of your life may be far more chaotic.

Don't expect perfection. When you make mistakes—and you surely will—forgive yourself and move on. Do the best you can, and let that be enough. Your intelligent microcosm will serve as a powerful motivator to bring the rest of your life into principle-centered alignment.

✦ ✦

The principles of truth, love, and power form the essence of human intelligence. We become more intelligent by increasing our alignment with these universal principles. This alignment doesn't happen by accident. It can only be achieved by conscious choice. Every step we take in the direction of truth, love, and power is a step toward greater intelligence.

These principles may seem a bit abstract, and you may still have some doubts as to whether they can actually work in the real world. Don't panic! In Part II of this book, you'll learn how to apply these fundamental principles to all areas of your life to generate practical, down-to-earth results.

PART II

Habits

Spirituality

Career

Relationships

Money

Health

Practical
Application

Chapter 8

HABITS

Spirituality   Career

Relationships   Money

Health

"Good habits, which bring our lower passions and appetites under automatic control, leave our natures free to explore the larger experiences of life."

— RALPH W. SOCKMAN

In any given moment, you have the freedom to consciously decide how you want to spend your time. You can center yourself in the present moment, remain completely aware of everything you do, and make very deliberate movements. Hold up your hand and look at it. Move your arm and wiggle your fingers. Consciously command your muscles to move the way you want them to. Notice that your physical actions are under your conscious control.

There was a time in your life when this was impossible for you. When you were a baby, your arms would flap around wildly. You couldn't get them to go where you wanted; in fact, you didn't even know what they were. But eventually you solved the problem of how to control your hands and arms. You still benefit from that early learning experience today.

Habits are memorized solutions. When your mind figures out how to get something done, it saves the solution, which is reinforced whenever you apply it. Driving a car, eating a meal, and reading written text are all memorized solutions. It took you a lot of effort to learn these skills, but today you can replay these known patterns instead of starting from scratch every time.

Habits are your mind's approach to time management. It would be extremely inefficient for you to consciously decide how to spend every minute of every day. Your conscious mind has better things to do than solve the same problems over and over, so it delegates known problems to your subconscious mind in order to recall and apply the memorized solutions.

Whenever you delegate problems to your subconscious mind, your conscious mind is free to focus on higher-level functions. For example, since I learned how to type when I was a teenager, I don't have to worry about consciously directing my fingers to compose each individual word. My subconscious has already stored those patterns, which have been reinforced with decades of typing experience. I normally type thousands of words every week, so my subconscious has memorized various patterns for turning my thoughts into words, phrases, and sentences. This allows me to focus my conscious mind on the high-level concepts I want to communicate, and my subconscious will help me express those thoughts as text. Without this powerful collection of habits working for me, it would be very difficult for me to efficiently convey my thoughts in writing.

Unfortunately, your innate habit-forming powers have some significant drawbacks. Sometimes your subconscious mind will memorize inefficient, inaccurate, or ineffective solutions. You may learn that smoking is a good way to handle stress or that complaining is the best way to garner sympathy and attention. In order to align yourself with truth, love, and power, you must eventually uproot and replace habits that have serious negative side effects.

In this chapter, you'll begin to consciously evaluate your current habits, identify positive changes you'd like to make, and learn practical techniques to make permanent shifts. This will not be easy. Even when you know what to do and how to do it, changing ingrained habits can be very difficult. The comprehensive approach presented herein will give you a definite edge in this area, but ultimately your success will be determined by your alignment with the seven principles.

Habits and Truth

To apply truth to your habits, take a moment to assess the habits you're already running. What are your best habits? What are your worst? Do you have any addictions? Do these habits serve you well or hold you back? Do they help you align with truth, or do you feel compelled to lie about them? What habits are you hiding? What habits are you most proud of?

Grab a piece of paper and brainstorm two lists: a list of your positive habits and another list of your negative habits. How do you know if a habit is positive or negative? Use your mind's predictive powers to imagine what long-term, cumulative effect each one will have if you maintain it for the rest of your life. How will it benefit you? What will it cost you? What does the long-term outlook suggest? If you could snap your fingers and change this habit immediately, would you do so? Be brutally honest with yourself. Then accept any unpleasant truths you discover, even if you feel powerless to change them.

Now brainstorm a third list: all the new habits you'd like to implement. Which new habits would enhance your life? Would you like to become an early riser, go vegetarian, or exercise daily? What would your life be like if you gave up television, newspapers, and random Web surfing? What would happen if you only checked e-mail once a day and used the time you saved to pursue a new hobby? What positive new habits would you love to adopt—if only it were possible to do so? If you successfully adopt these habits today, what will your life look like ten years from now?

Review your three lists again, and ask yourself if you're willing to accept the long-term consequences of your current habits. Are you willing to live with the outcomes you predict, or would you like to improve them by making some changes? Is the status quo good enough for you, or can you do better?

Bringing truth to your habits is an important step, but nothing will change if you don't take action. You must accept the greater truth that if you don't consciously and deliberately alter your habits, you'll continue reinforcing your existing patterns by default, and your predicted outcomes will likely come to pass. If you wish to improve upon those results, you must do whatever it takes to change your habits now, even if you expect the process to be brutally difficult. Facing a significant short-term challenge today is vastly superior to decades of regret.

Habits and Love

A common mistake people make when seeking to change entrenched habits is assuming that they must tackle such challenges alone and in private. That simply isn't true. The principle of love reminds you to take advantage of your ability to connect. Enlist the help of others to dramatically increase your chances of success. Don't let pride get in the way of results. Reach out and ask for help!

It's a virtual certainty that other people have already navigated the changes you wish to make in your life. Instead of painstakingly figuring out your own solutions from scratch, take advantage of the collective wisdom of others. Seek out role models who've already achieved what you desire, and request advice or mentoring. Look for good books on the subject, and apply what you learn from them. Ask for help and support from friends and family. Find someone to coach you through the process of change, even if you have to pay for their time.

Don't feel as though you're imposing on others by asking them for help. They're always free to say no or to request a fair exchange of value in return, but often they'll be delighted to help you for free. With just a few minutes of effort on their part, other people can offer you advice that may save you months of wasted effort. Most folks find it very rewarding to provide basic help when requested, especially when they know you'll apply their suggestions.

You can take this a step further by using the power of communion. Consider joining a group of like-minded people who share compatible goals, especially a group that meets at least weekly. Learn from others who are farther along the same path you want to travel. You'll be overwhelmed by how supportive and encouraging complete strangers can be when you connect with them through such groups.

Strong addictions are rarely overcome without outside help. One of the best solutions is to find someone who has already overcome your addiction, and ask them to mentor you through the process of quitting. People who've successfully made such a change know how difficult it is and are often happy to assist others through the process. This is the basis of many organization such as Alcoholics Anonymous, a society of almost two million people who work together to overcome alcohol addiction.

In a similar vein, ask yourself if there are any incompatible connections you need to release. Do you have a circle of cynical friends who complain incessantly, encouraging you to adopt an equally disempowering attitude? Do you enjoy smoke breaks with your co-workers, making it harder for you to quit? Is your roommate a complete slob, preventing you from being more organized? We'll explore such relationship challenges in more detail in Chapter 12, but for now it's important to recognize that the ongoing influence of your social circle will often be the deciding factor when it comes to habit change.

Make a habit of intentionally reaching out and connecting with others. Break the limiting pattern of trying to do everything solo. Join a club or attend social events just for the experience of connecting with new people and expanding your social network. This habit will benefit you in ways you can scarcely imagine, filling your life with empowering friends you'd never have met otherwise.

Habits and Power

Power is perhaps the most important principle when it comes to habit change. In order to change your habits, you must focus on your desired outcome and exert a serious effort. The more disciplined you become, the easier it is to change your habits.

Remember that you're responsible for how your life turns out. Whether your habits make you or break you, you're the one who must deal with the long-term consequences. Since habits wield power over your results, you must wield power over your habits.

In the game of chess, it's generally a bad idea to try to attack your opponent's king right out of the gate unless your opponent is a complete beginner. If you want to win, you must be smarter than that. Chess has an early game, a middle game, and an endgame. In the early game, you want to get off to a strong start and try to gain a slight advantage. In the middle game, you employ tactics to capture your opponent's pieces and put yourself in a superior position. It's only in the endgame that you go after the king directly, and even then you may need to continue weakening your opponent for a while before you're ready to declare checkmate.

Changing habits is a lot like playing chess. If you go for a direct frontal assault right out of the gate, your attacks will be easily deflected, and your efforts will only make you look silly. Don't try to tackle an entrenched habit head-on by powering through it. Focus your early game efforts on making indirect moves. Aim to put yourself in a superior position by attacking the habit's supporting structure. Change the circumstances to stop reinforcing your old patterns, and assemble the proper scaffolding to support your new desired behaviors.

In the early game, you're merely setting up your pieces, but you aren't trying to change the habit yet. Buy some books about the change you want to make, ask for advice from others who've already made similar changes, and see if you can find someone to mentor you. Join a support group if possible. Do whatever you can to create the right conditions for future success.

In the middle game, you'll employ specific tactics to give yourself an advantage. If you've played the early game properly, you should already know what those tactics are. You may come up with your own tactics, of course, but you'll probably learn most of them from other people. For example, if you want to change your eating habits and lose weight, specific methods may include measuring food portions, keeping a food journal, buying extra fruits and vegetables, ridding your house of junk food, learning healthy recipes, keeping the television turned off at mealtimes, finding a diet buddy, joining a weight-loss group, buying a new scale, posting pictures of thin people to motivate you, avoiding situations where you tend to overeat, charting your progress, and so on. You'll implement many of these tactics in advance—before you even begin your new diet—so that when you're ready to start, you're already in a superior position.

Once you reach the endgame, it's time to go after your target directly. If you've done the preparation work of the early and middle games, you'll be ready for the final thrust. This is where you put your power to the test. Can you make the desired change stick? Can you break the old pattern and implement the new one?

Here are two powerful methods for achieving victory in the endgame of habit change: *30-day trials* and *stair-stepping.*

30-Day Trials

I learned about 30-day trials during my years as a software developer. Developers who sell their software over the Internet frequently offer free 30-day trial versions so that potential customers can try the software risk free before deciding whether they want to buy it. By the end of the trial period, many people will purchase the software because they've become accustomed to using it. Try-before-you-buy is a very effective sales technique.

You can use a similar strategy to condition a new habit or behavior. The most difficult part of any new habit is making it through the first month, especially the first several days. Once you've made it through those first 30 days, it's much easier to keep going because you've overcome inertia.

When we think about changing a habit permanently, we often psych ourselves out before we begin. Thinking we must give something up for a lifetime is too overwhelming to even consider. Enter the 30-day trial. Instead of committing to a permanent change, your goal is to make a smaller temporary commitment. Test your new habit for only 30 days. After that you're free to quit and return to your old ways. It's only one month out of your life. That isn't so bad, is it?

Exercise daily for 30 days. Give up TV for 30 days. Get up at 5 A.M. every day for 30 days. Think of each 30-day trial as a fun and interesting challenge. You're merely conducting a test to see if you like it. A 30-day trial still requires some discipline and persistence, but not nearly as much as a permanent change because you can always see the light at the end of the tunnel. You have a guaranteed escape route if things don't work out. Any sacrifice or deprivation you endure is temporary. You're completely free to return to your old ways on Day 31.

What happens when you actually complete a 30-day trial? First, you'll have gone far enough to establish your new behavior as a habit, making it easier to continue if you so desire. Second, you'll break your previous pattern in this area, so your old habits won't exert as much of a pull on your behavior. Third, you'll have 30 days of success behind you, so you'll already have proven to yourself you can do this. And fourth, you will have enjoyed 30 days' worth of results, and if those results are positive, you'll be more motivated to continue the habit.

At the end of your 30-day trial, your ability to continue in your new habit is much greater than it was at the start of your trial. If you're ready to make the habit permanent, you may find it fairly easy to keep going, since momentum is now on your side. If you don't feel ready to make that kind of commitment, though, you can extend your trial to 60 or 90 days. The longer your trial period, the easier it will be to lock in the new habit.

Another possibility is that you'll reach the end of your 30 days and decide you don't want to continue the new habit. Remember that this is just a trial, so you're not obligated to "buy" if you don't like it. In that case you're free to drop the habit and try something else. No harm, no foul.

If you find your 30-day trial too difficult, scale it back a little. Try five or ten days for your first trial. Then take a break and go for a longer experiment when you feel ready. You can also scale back the challenge level. For example, instead of trying to give up coffee for 30 days, try limiting your intake to no more than one cup a day for 30 days. Feel free to adapt the concept to fit your level of discipline. Allow yourself to be challenged but not overwhelmed.

I've enjoyed great success with 30-day trials, as have many other people who've applied this technique. One of my first successes was in 1993, when I became curious about what it would be like to be a vegetarian. I was in college at the time; and my typical diet consisted of burgers, tacos, and pepperoni pizza. I thought it would be interesting to try eating a vegetarian diet for 30 days. I'd learned about vegetarianism in a nutrition class, and I wanted to know what it was really like. I honestly had no intention of continuing beyond the 30 days. I was curious but definitely not committed.

Within the first week of going vegetarian, I noticed I had a lot more energy, I could concentrate better, and my thoughts seemed crisper and less foggy. The transition was easier than I expected, and I never felt deprived. At the end of the 30 days, I liked the results so much that I just kept going. I never really decided to become a vegetarian, but the habit stuck.

Four years later, in 1997, I decided to try eating a pure vegan diet for 30 days, which meant cutting out eggs and dairy, too. That change produced even better results, so again it was a no-brainer to keep going. I haven't eaten any animal products since.

These trials are best suited to daily habits. I haven't found them as effective for actions taken less frequently, such as weekly activities. However, if you can turn such habits into daily actions, you can still conduct a 30-day trial and then reduce the frequency after the experiment is finished.

Here are some specific ideas for applying 30-day trials:

- Avoid watching TV. You can always record your favorite shows and watch them at the end of the trial if you're afraid you'll miss something.

- Give up online forums and idle Web surfing.

- Shower or bathe every day, and groom yourself to look your best.

- Every day, introduce yourself to someone you don't know.

- Go out every evening and do something different each time.

- Clean and organize your home or office for 30 minutes a day.

- Trade massages with your partner on alternating days, so you each get 15 massages.

- Break addictions such as cigarettes, soda, junk food, coffee, pornography, and the like.

- Get up at 5 A.M. every morning. (This was one of the best trials I ever did.)

- Read for an hour a day. This is an incredibly empowering habit.

- Learn ten new vocabulary words each day.

- Meditate once or twice a day.

- Keep a daily journal.

Can you run multiple 30-day trials at once? That depends on you. Many people have great success implementing multiple habits simultaneously, while others prefer to focus on one habit at a time. I recommend limiting your first 30-day trial to three new habits maximum, and it's best if the habits are mutually supportive, such as diet and exercise changes. When people try to adopt four or more habits at the same time, they often become overwhelmed and give up on all of them within the first week.

You can make your trials more enjoyable by involving family or friends. This will give you an instant support group, and it can be a positive bonding experience as well. My family and I once did a 30-day trial with no TV. It worked well because we spent time talking to each other, playing games together, and going on family outings.

The 30-day trial is a powerful but simple technique. When you commit to doing something every single day for 30 days straight, it's much easier to bypass internal resistance and accept the challenge willingly. Pick a new habit you'd like to experience or an old pattern you'd like to break, and get started on Day 1 today.

Stair-Stepping

Stair-stepping is a simple method for gradually changing habits. Instead of making a big change all at once, you aim to take one small step in the right direction. Once you've gotten comfortable with that change, take another small step. Continue taking baby steps one at a time until you eventually reach your goal.

For example, if you want to stop drinking coffee, first take note of how much coffee you currently consume. Then set an initial goal to reduce your daily intake by 25 percent. So if you drink four cups of coffee a day, you'll either drop it to three cups a day or you'll drink four cups that are only three-quarters full. Maintain that new level for a week before taking the next step. At that point, reduce your intake to 50 percent of your original level, and do that for another week. Then drop it to just 25 percent of the original level, again maintaining it for a week. And finally you're ready to eliminate coffee completely. If a 25 percent change is too much for you to handle, start with a 10 percent change.

You can use stair-stepping for a wide range of habits. I know several people who've used this method to quit smoking, dropping their cigarette consumption by a small amount every week until they were down to one cigarette per day (and sometimes down to one cigarette every two or three days) before finally quitting for good. Another person used this method to become an early riser, setting his alarm clock just five minutes earlier each day until he reached his goal.

✦ ✦

Changing habits can be very challenging, so you probably won't conquer every habit on your first try. As in the game of chess, even the best players eventually meet their match. When you fail at one of your habit challenges, go back and review the moves you made in the early game, middle game, and endgame, and see if you can figure out where you went wrong. Did you fail to prepare well enough in the early game? Were your middle-game tactics poorly executed? Did you blunder the endgame by making an avoidable mistake? What lessons can you apply to improve your play for next time?

Habits and Oneness

You don't live in a void. For better or worse, your habits impact the lives of others. Take a moment to consider the social consequences of your actions. Do your habits help others align themselves with truth, love, and power, or does your behavior lead people astray? Your actions have a conditioning effect on other people, subtly influencing them to adopt similar behaviors. This is especially true of children, who frequently look to adults for guidance.

Oneness teaches us that we're all role models. As we interact with others, we teach them how to behave, whether we realize it or not. Our interconnectedness means that individual habits can't be considered in isolation. One person's bad habits can create serious consequences for others, and sometimes those consequences are severe, as in the case of a drunk-driving accident. Consequently, we must not only be responsible to ourselves, but also to the community in which we live.

Finally, use habits to reinforce oneness itself. Instead of living in an isolated cocoon, make a habit of contributing to others. Find something you can do on a regular basis to give value to total strangers, not just your family and friends. Consider doing volunteer work, or find a way to contribute through your career. For example, I created my Website to share personal growth ideas with people around the world. It's extremely rewarding to receive daily feedback from those who benefit from my work, even though most of them have never met me.

Some people also recommend tithing, which means giving a tenth of your money away to worthwhile causes (*tithe* means "tenth"). If you decide to tithe, just be aware that giving money is no substitute for direct involvement.

Cultivate at least one habit to deepen your experience of oneness. Make a habit of going for long walks in nature. Enjoy prolonged physical contact with someone close to you. Offer hugs instead of handshakes. Smile at strangers you pass on the street. If you make habits of these simple actions, you'll rarely feel disconnected and alone.

Habits and Authority

Remember that you're the commander-in-chief of your life. You must decide which habits you'll keep and which you'll abandon. Conduct personal experiments to discover which habits produce the best results for you. Which habits increase your effectiveness? Which ones get in your way?

Here's a list of 66 habits that can help boost your personal effectiveness. Scan these items to see if any of them appeal to you. Then use 30-day trials and/or stair-stepping to make the changes you desire.

1. **Daily goals.** Set targets for each day in advance. Decide what you'll do; then do it. Without a clear focus, it's too easy to succumb to distractions.

2. **Worst first.** To defeat procrastination, learn to tackle your most unpleasant task first thing in the morning instead of delaying it until later. This small victory will set the tone for a very productive day.

3. **Peak times.** Identify your peak cycles of productivity, and schedule your most important tasks for those times. Work on minor tasks during your nonpeak times.

4. **No-comm zones.** Allocate uninterruptible blocks of time for solo work where you must concentrate. Schedule light, interruptible tasks for your open-communication periods and more challenging projects for your communication-blackout periods.

5. **Mini-milestones.** When you begin a task, identify the target you must reach before you can stop working. For example, when writing a book, you could decide not to get up until you've written at least 1,000 words. Hit your target no matter what.

6. **Timeboxing.** Give yourself a fixed time period—30 minutes works well—to make a dent in a task. Don't worry about how far you get. Just put in the time.

7. **Batching.** Batch similar tasks such as phone calls or errands together, and knock them out in a single session.

8. **Early bird.** Get up early in the morning, perhaps at 5 A.M., and go straight to work on your most important task. You can often get more done before 8 A.M. than most people do in a full day.

9. **Pyramid.** Spend 15 to 30 minutes doing easy tasks to warm up. Then tackle your most difficult project for several hours. Finally, end with another 15 to 30 minutes of easy tasks to transition out of work mode.

10. **Tempo.** Deliberately pick up the pace and try to move a little faster than usual. Walk faster. Read faster. Type faster. . . . Go home sooner.

11. **Neat freak.** Reduce stress by cultivating a relaxing, clutter-free home and office.

12. **Agendas.** Provide clear written agendas to meeting participants in advance. This greatly improves meeting focus and efficiency. Use agendas for important phone calls, too.

13. **Pareto.** The Pareto principle is the 80-20 rule, which states that 80 percent of the value of a task comes from 20 percent of the effort. Focus your energy on that critical 20 percent, and don't overengineer the noncritical 80 percent.

14. **Ready-fire-aim.** Bust procrastination by taking action immediately after setting a goal, even if the action isn't perfectly planned. You can always adjust your course along the way.

15. **Minuteman.** Once you have the information you need to make a decision, start a timer and give yourself just 60 seconds to make the actual decision. Take a whole minute to vacillate and second-guess yourself all you want, but come out the other end with a clear choice. Once your decision is made, take some kind of action to set it in motion.

16. **Deadline.** Set a deadline for task completion, and use it as a focal point to stay on track.

17. **Promise.** Tell others of your commitments so that they'll hold you accountable.

18. **Punctuality.** Always arrive early for appointments. Punctuality enhances authority.

19. **Gap reading.** Read books and articles while waiting for an appointment or standing in line.

20. **Resonance.** Visualize your goal as already accomplished. Put yourself into a state of actually being there. Make it real in your mind and you'll soon see it in your reality.

21. **Prizes.** Give yourself frequent rewards for achievement. See a movie, schedule a professional massage, or spend a day at an amusement park.

22. **Priority.** Separate the truly important tasks from the merely urgent. Allocate blocks of time to work on critical tasks, those which are important but rarely urgent, such as physical exercise, writing a book, and finding a relationship partner.

23. **Continuum.** At the end of your workday, identify the first task you'll address tomorrow and set out the materials in advance. The next morning, begin working on that task immediately.

24. **Slice and dice.** Break complex projects into smaller, well-defined tasks. Then focus on completing just one of those tasks.

25. **Single-handling.** Once you begin a task, stick with it until it's 100 percent complete. Don't switch tasks in the middle. When distractions come up, write them down to be dealt with later.

26. **Randomization.** Pick a totally random piece of a larger project, and complete it. Pay one random bill. Make one phone call. Then select another random piece and repeat.

27. **Insanely bad.** Defeat perfectionism by completing your task in an intentionally terrible fashion, knowing you never need to share the results with anyone. Write a blog post about the taste of salt, design a hideously

dysfunctional Website, or create a business plan that guarantees a first-year bankruptcy. With a truly horrendous first draft, there's nowhere to go but up.

28. **Delegation.** Convince someone else to do a task for you. Offer a fair trade or reasonable payment.

29. **Cross-pollination.** Learn new skills that are unrelated to your work. Train in martial arts, study a foreign language, or learn to play chess. You'll often encounter ideas in one field that can boost your performance in another.

30. **Intuition.** Go with your gut instinct. It's probably right.

31. **Optimization.** Identify the processes you use most often, and write them down step-by-step. Rework them on paper for greater efficiency, then implement and test your improved processes. Sometimes we can't see what's right in front of us until we examine it under a microscope.

32. **Super slow.** Commit yourself to working on a particularly hideous project for just one session a week, 15 minutes total. Declutter one small shelf. Purge ten clothing items you don't need. Write a few paragraphs. Then stop and wait another week.

33. **Dailies.** Schedule a specific time each day for working on a particular task or habit. One hour a day could leave you with a healthier body, a finished book, or an income-generating Website a year later.

34. **Add-ons.** Build a new habit by tacking a task onto one of your existing habits. Water the plants after you eat lunch. Send thank-you notes after you check e-mail.

35. **Plug-ins.** Inject one task into the middle of another. Read while eating lunch. Return phone calls while commuting. Listen to audio programs while grocery shopping.

36. **Gratitude.** When someone does you a good turn, send a thank-you card. That's a real card, not an e-card. This is rare and memorable, and the people you thank will be eager to bring you more opportunities.

37. **Training.** Train up your skill in various productivity habits. Increase your typing speed to at least 60 words per minute. Learn to speed-read. Improve your communication skills.

38. **Denial.** Just say no to noncritical requests for your time. If people get upset with you, let them.

39. **Recapturing.** Reclaim other people's wasted time for yourself. Visualize your goals during dull speeches. Write out your grocery list during pointless meetings.

40. **Mastermind.** Explain your most challenging problems to several other people, and invite all the advice, feedback, and constructive criticism you can handle.

41. **Twenty.** On a piece of paper, write down 20 creative ideas for improving your effectiveness.

42. **Challenger.** Deliberately make the task harder since challenging tasks are more engaging and motivating than boring ones. Perform physical chores such as filing or cleaning with your nondominant hand. Compose poetic e-mails to clear your inbox.

43. **Asylum.** Complete an otherwise tedious task in an unusual or crazy manner to keep it fun and interesting.

Make routine phone calls using fake foreign accents. Take notes in crayon.

44. **Music.** Experiment to discover how music may boost your effectiveness. Try trance or rock music for e-mail, classical or New Age music for projects, and total silence for high-concentration creative work.

45. **Miracle worker.** Estimate how long a task will take to complete. Then start a timer, and push yourself to complete it in half that time.

46. **Paying it forward.** When an undesirable task is delegated to you, re-delegate it to someone else.

47. **Bouncer.** When a seemingly pointless task is delegated to you, bounce it back to the person who assigned it to you, and challenge them to justify its operational necessity.

48. **Opt out.** Quit clubs, projects, and subscriptions that consume more of your time than they're worth.

49. **Decaffeinating.** Say no to caffeine, suffer through the withdrawal period, and let your natural creative self re-emerge.

50. **Conscious procrastination.** Delay noncritical tasks as long as you possibly can. Many of them will die and won't need to be done at all.

51. **TV-free.** Turn off the TV, especially the news, and recapture many usable hours.

52. **Timer.** Time and log all your tasks for an entire day, preferably for an entire week. The simple act of monitoring your time usage can boost your effectiveness tremendously.

53. **Valor.** Identify the item on your task list that scares you the most. Muster all the courage you can and tackle it immediately.

54. **Nonconformist.** Run errands at unpopular times to avoid crowds. Shop just before stores close or shortly after they open. Take advantage of 24-hour outlets.

55. **Agoraphobia.** Shop online whenever possible. Get the best selection, consult reviews, and purchase items within minutes.

56. **Reminder.** Add birthday and holiday reminders to your calendar a month or two ahead of their actual dates. Buy gifts then instead of at the last minute.

57. **Do it now!** Recite this phrase over and over until you're so sick of it that you cave in and get to work.

58. **Coach.** Hire a personal coach to stay motivated, focused, and accountable.

59. **Inspiration.** Read books and articles, listen to audio programs, and attend seminars to absorb fresh ideas and inspiration.

60. **Gym rat.** Exercise daily. Boost your metabolism, concentration, and mental clarity in 30 minutes a day.

61. **Troll hunt.** Banish the negative "trolls" from your life; and associate with positive, happy people instead. Mindsets are contagious. Be loyal to truth, love, and power, not to your pity posse.

62. **Evil eye.** Practice your best evil eye in a mirror, and use it liberally on anyone who enters your space to interrupt your most important tasks.

63. **Politician.** Throw money at your problems until they eventually succumb. How many of your problems can be solved more easily if you define them in financial terms? Can you justify the cost of hiring an assistant, a babysitter, or a cleaning service?

64. **Modeling.** Find people who are already getting the results you want; interview them; and adopt their attitudes, beliefs, and behavior.

65. **Proactivity.** Even if others disagree with you, take action anyway, and deal with the consequences later. It's easier to request forgiveness than permission.

66. **Real life.** Give online activities (such as gaming, reading blogs, or posting on forums and message boards) a rest, and reinvest that time into your real life, which, if you're a gamer, is probably suffocating beneath a pile of dead, smelly orcs.

All habits are not equal, so take the time to form important ones that can make a real difference in your life and those of others. For example, the habit of journaling helps me solve problems and gain new insights, and the habit of blogging allows me to share what I've learned with other people. In both cases I'm typing on my computer, but blogging is the more impactful habit. Often the simplest way to make a habit more significant and meaningful is to find a way to share it with others.

Habits and Courage

Use a variation of the heart-centered question to evaluate your habits. Which habits put you on the path with a heart? Which ones lead you astray? Don't wait for good habits to install themselves or for bad habits to die on their own. You must take the initiative and create the changes you desire. Cultivate behaviors that keep you on the heart-centered path, and drop habits that don't have a heart.

To build your courage, make a habit of doing something that scares you. In my Toastmasters club, we do impromptu speaking at every meeting. Someone will ask a random question such as "If you could change anything about yourself, what would it be and why?" Then you must immediately get up and give a one- to two-minute speech on that topic in front of the group. Your goal isn't to give a perfect presentation off the top of your head. Instead, the idea is to build confidence speaking in front of people. When you can summon the courage to speak in front of a group with no preparation, it makes prepared speaking that much easier. The courage you build in one area of your life will also spill over into other areas.

Don't allow the courage requirement to dissuade you from forming powerful new habits, especially those that involve interacting with other people. Follow the path with a heart, even when it compels you to face tremendous personal challenges. Honor your deepest connections, and let your conscience be your guide.

Habits and Intelligence

Consciously cultivate the most authentic habits you can. For each habit you consider, ask yourself: *Is this really me? Is this consistent with the person I most want to be?* If any part of your life feels phony and inauthentic to you, it needs to be replaced with a more genuine alternative. This won't be easy, but it is correct.

Your ultimate goal in this area is to create a set of mutually supportive habits that synergistically increase your alignment with truth, love, and power. Good habits enable you to remain in a positive flow state while you focus on creative self-expression. You consciously make the high-level decisions, and your habits take care of the low-level details. When your habits work together so congruently, the result is both beautiful and elegant. You may never reach this ideal within your lifetime, but every step you take in this direction is worthwhile.

One of my best decisions ever was to make a daily habit of working on my personal growth. First I started reading self-help books and listening to audio programs; then I began conducting my own growth experiments. Later, I formed an online community to explore personal growth with other people. Although I experienced failures and setbacks along the way, the habit of trying to improve myself just a little bit each day has been incredibly rewarding.

Success in this area has nothing to do with external accomplishments. True success is being able to look at yourself in the mirror and be completely at peace with what you see. When your habits are aligned with truth, love, and power, the guy in the glass is your friend.

✦ ✦

Expect to invest a lot of time and energy working on your habits. Most of your personal growth efforts will likely be directed at breaking old patterns or forming new ones. Your habits put your results on autopilot, so you need to ensure that those results are aligned with what you want. What sense does it make to pursue your greatest dreams if your daily habits will only sabotage you? If you want to live more consciously, you must consciously cultivate good habits.

Despite the difficult challenges you'll face in this area, working on it gives you tremendous leverage. One new habit can permanently alter the course of your life for the better. In the final analysis, the rewards justify the required effort. Good habits will support you well in all areas of your life, including your health, your relationships, and obviously your . . .

Chapter 9

"Work is love made visible."

— KAHLIL GIBRAN

Think of your career as your primary outlet for creative self-expression. Your career may take the form of an income-generating job you perform or a business you manage, but it doesn't have to. Your career is your occupation; at a very basic level, it's simply what you do to occupy your time. Of course if you're going to live consciously, this choice becomes a rather important one.

Your career has two components: your medium and your message. Most people think of their careers in terms of the medium, which is the specific method you use to express yourself. For example, you could say that I'm a writer, speaker, or blogger, since those represent some of the media outlets I use to express myself. Most job titles are defined in terms of expressive media, including doctors, lawyers, police officers, teachers, pilots, and so on.

The message of your career is at least as important as the medium. Your medium is *how* you express yourself, but your message is *what* you express. My message is about consciously growing as a human being, but I can express that same message through different media. I can write about it, speak about it, or even make a movie about it if I wanted to. Someone else could use these same media to express an entirely different message. For example, a doctor's message could be about healing, compassion, scientific discovery, education, vitality, or a variety of other possibilities. Just because two people share a similar medium doesn't mean that they share the same message.

Very often people identify themselves with the medium of their careers. This is a huge mistake. Your medium is merely a shell; it cannot define you as a person. You can expect that your career medium will change over time, but your message will be much more stable. Your message is who you are, while your medium is simply how you choose to express yourself.

Years ago, I chose to express myself through the medium of game development. Today I prefer writing and speaking. Many years from now, I may be doing something entirely different, but my underlying message of conscious growth is unlikely to change much. Similarly, your true career path is about your message, not your medium.

In this chapter, you'll explore career development in great detail, paying attention to both your medium and your message. To have a fulfilling career, you must identify your core message and adopt an appropriate medium for expressing it. Unless you're already ridiculously passionate about your current situation, there's a good chance that your medium is a poor match for your message. If you simply fell into your current line of work, you may need to make significant changes to realign yourself with truth, love, and power. Correcting such problems won't be easy, but you should know by now that I won't let you settle for less than you deserve.

Career and Truth

What do you perceive when you look at your current career? What do your most honest predictions reveal about your path? Did you choose this path, or did you simply fall into it? Is your career aligned with the truth of who you really are? If you were starting over from scratch today, would you choose this same line of work again? Do you have any regrets about the paths you didn't choose?

To align your career with truth, you must ask these tough questions and answer them as honestly as possible. Accept your answers even if you don't like what you see. You're always free to make different choices from this point onward, but in order to do so, you must unconditionally accept where you are. Never pretend to love a career that you know is wrong for you.

Truth is an essential part of career development. This means being true to yourself as well as being down-to-earth and practical. One practical consideration is that you must generate sufficient income to meet your needs. While it's certainly possible to earn income outside your main career, for most people a career serves as the main source of income. Doing what you love won't be very sustainable if you can't pay your bills.

Another practical consideration is selecting a medium that fits your message. It can be very challenging to get this right on your first try. However, the good news is that you aren't limited to just one attempt. You're free to shift your medium over time as you become more aligned with the truth of who you are.

When I was involved in computer-game development, my inner message was still about growth and improvement, although I wasn't as aware of it as I am today. I became interested in writing games because I was attracted to the challenge of such work. There were so many fascinating things to learn, such as graphics programming, animation, input processing, sound engineering, collision detection, path finding, game logic, artificial intelligence, and more. Working in this field was a tremendous growth experience and kept me busy for several years. I don't regret it at all.

One of the first computer games I released was a shoot-'em-up game called *BrainWave,* which employed some simple artificial-intelligence techniques, so the enemy characters would gradually adapt to your firing patterns and become smarter as you played. The longer you played, the more challenging the game became.

As I progressed further along this career path, I became less interested in shooting games, and I later developed a nonviolent puzzle game called *Dweep*. I designed the game to give players a serious mental workout, in many ways similar to playing chess. I felt an unusually strong connection with that game because I put so much of myself into it. In truth, I was trying to express my passion for personal growth through the medium of game development. That particular medium gave me plenty of expressive power, but it wasn't an ideal fit for my message. Most people who buy computer games are seeking entertainment, but I wanted to do more than just entertain people.

While I was running my games business, I started writing articles on the side to help out other independent software developers. At first I wrote about technical skills and sales techniques, but soon I shifted to personal development topics such as goal setting and productivity. I loved sharing what I learned, and it was a joy to receive feedback from people who applied my ideas to improve their results. At the time, however, I was still blind to the underlying pattern. I had stumbled upon the medium of writing, but it wasn't until several years later that I seriously considered it as a career path. I'd always thought of myself as a software guy, not a writer; but the new medium of writing was a much better fit for my message. In the time it took me to develop a single computer game, I could produce more than 100 articles on a variety of different topics.

I don't know of a good method for you to discover the perfect career medium on your very first try. However, I don't think that's really the point. Your career path is an ongoing journey, and it probably won't be an entirely linear one. Finding the right medium for your message is a continual process of refinement. Your choice of medium will evolve over time as you bring yourself into greater alignment with truth, love, and power. As you discover what's most important to you in life, you'll make better, more congruent choices. Don't worry about trying to be perfect. Simply make the best decision you can, and then put it into action. If you make a bad choice, you'll find out soon enough.

The most important element of choosing the right medium is whether it's a good fit for your inner message. It's important to stay true to that message, even if you must endure a substantial pay cut. In order to transition from game development to personal development, I allowed my income to drop significantly, and my family made some sacrifices to support my decision as we cut back on expenses.

Regardless of financial concerns, it was the right decision, and within a few years my income was higher than ever. It's perfectly okay to go through a short-term plunge in your finances when you undergo a career transition. If the new medium is a better fit for you than the old one, then you should be able to earn even more income once you build sufficient skills.

Never allow considerations such as security, money, or fame to get in the way of truth. Real security doesn't come from your job or position; it can only come from your alignment with truth, love, and power. You'll explore money in more detail in Chapter 10, but for now just consider that the best way to optimize your income is to find a career medium that allows you to share your most important message. By sharing your message with others, you provide exactly the kind of value that can generate abundant income. And as for fame, if you do become famous, then let it arise from your alignment with truth, love, and power, not because of a false image you've concocted.

Truth will help you pick an appropriate medium for your message, but it won't necessarily help you identify the message itself. For that you need to apply other principles, especially the principle of love.

Career and Love

The principle of love relates heavily to the message of your career. When you discover your core message, it will connect with you on a very deep level, and the emotional release of that connection can literally move you to tears.

Here's a simple yet powerful process you can use to discover your core message, also known as your life purpose. This process has produced major breakthroughs for many who've tried it. Find a place where you can be alone and won't be interrupted, then complete the following steps:

1. Take out a sheet of paper or open up a blank word-processing document where you can type. I recommend the latter because it's faster.

2. Write at the top: *What is my true purpose in life?*

3. Write down an answer (any answer) that pops into your head. It doesn't have to be a complete sentence. A short phrase is fine. If you're feeling nihilistic, begin with the answer: "I don't have a purpose," or "Life is meaning-less," and take it from there.

4. Repeat Step 3 until you write the answer that makes you cry. This is your core message.

How long will it take to converge on the final answer? That varies tremendously from person to person. It largely depends on how closely you're aligned with truth, love, and power. Usually it takes at least 15 to 20 minutes to clear your mind of all the false answers that will arise from your memory. When the true answer finally arrives, it will feel like it's coming from a different source entirely. For most people, this takes 30 to 60 minutes and more than 100 false answers. Some people come up with the right answer almost immediately. Others have to return to this exercise repeatedly for several days in a row before finding the answer that really strikes them at a deep level.

At some point during the process (typically after about 50 to 100 answers), you may want to quit because you just can't see the right answer emerging. You may feel the urge to get up and do something else. That's normal. Push through this resistance and just keep writing. The discomfort will eventually pass.

You may discover a few answers that give you a mini-surge of emotion, but they don't quite make you cry. Highlight those answers as you go along so you can come back to them to generate new permutations. Each one reveals a piece of your message. When you start getting these kinds of answers, it means you're getting warm. Keep going.

When I did this exercise, it took me about 25 minutes, and I reached my final answer at Step 106. Partial pieces of the answer (mini-surges) appeared at Steps 17, 39, and 53; and the bulk of it fell into place and was refined through Steps 100 to 106. I began feeling impatient and irritated around Steps 55 to 60. At Step 80 I took a two-minute break to close my eyes, relax, clear my mind, and focus on the intention for the answer to come to me. This was helpful: the answers I generated next were much clearer. I've made only minor changes to this purpose statement since then. Here's the current version:

To live consciously and courageously;
To enjoy, increase, and share peace, energy, passion, and abundance;
To resonate with love and compassion;
To awaken the great spirits within others;
And to fully embrace this present moment.

This may or may not mean anything to you, but it has a deep emotional impact on me every time I read it. When you find your unique answer to the question of why you're here, it will resonate within you very strongly. The words will have a special energy for you, and you'll feel that energy whenever you read them.

If you're inclined to ask why this process works, just put that question aside until after you've successfully completed it. Once you've done that, you'll probably have your own answer. Most likely, if you ask ten different people who've completed it why it works, you'll get ten different reasons, all filtered through their belief systems, each containing an element of truth.

Many people have sent me their purpose statements upon completing this exercise, and they always strike me as beautiful. Discovering your core message is only the first step, however. Once you know your message, you must use the principle of truth to find a proper medium to express that message (see the "Career and Truth" section earlier in this chapter). Then you must apply the principle of power to turn your medium and your message into action.

Career and Power

You are completely responsible for your own career path, so it makes sense to build a career you want instead of settling for what you don't want. Your current situation is the result of your previous choices, so if you aren't happy with it, remember that you're always free to make new choices. The only one who can keep you trapped is you.

Avoid the common mistake of settling for a career that disempowers you. If you find yourself in a situation where your contribution is neither valued nor respected, get up and leave. Go where your talents are appreciated. Otherwise you're simply abusing yourself.

You deserve to have an empowering career, but that won't happen until you fully commit to it. The obstacles and setbacks you encounter aren't intended to keep you from reaching your ultimate goal. They're merely part of the training course you must complete in order to prove you're strong enough to hold on to your dream once you reach it. Demonstrate by your actions that you're 100 percent committed and the obstacles will tend to recede on their own.

Reasonable career choices will depend on your knowledge, skills, and talents; and it's up to you to proactively develop those abilities. You may have been born with few advantages, but you're perfectly capable of growing beyond the limits of your upbringing. If you didn't receive a good education, then educate yourself now. If you're starting off broke or in debt, then accept that as your reality, and work your way out of it with disciplined effort. If you're surrounded by people who denigrate and criticize you for wanting more, leave them behind and build a new social group that will support you. Stay loyal to truth, love, and power and you'll attract others of a similar nature.

Don't waste time making excuses because that will only disempower you. If you want to grow beyond your current situation, you can't pretend to be powerless. No matter how many obstacles stand in your way, you can still use your power to knock them down one by one. If it takes years to reach your goal, then so be it. The time is going to pass anyway, so you might as well put it to good use. Years from now you'll either be where you want to be . . . or you won't. You can either invest your time in growth or do the time in a cage.

Career and Oneness

Your career choice isn't merely an individual matter. Your choices in this area affect us all. Oneness encourages you to consider your career impact on an even deeper level. What can you do to make a positive difference in the world? What are you here to contribute? Will your contributions be physical, mental, social, scientific, artistic, moral, or something else?

Your career is your primary outlet for contribution. Do your current choices honor the fact that we're all connected, or do you live entirely for yourself at the expense of others? It isn't enough to do no harm. You must commit to doing good.

These decisions impact everyone around you. When you contribute through your career, you encourage others to do the same. As you honor the principle of oneness, you help others develop a sense of it as well. That commitment elevates us individually and collectively.

Reject any career path that causes you to treat other people as dollar signs, prospects, or annoyances instead of genuine human beings. Refuse to accept work that dehumanizes you or anyone else. Recognize that if you work for a company whose values are out of alignment with truth, love, and power, then you are out of alignment as well; and you're responsible for the consequences. Hold yourself to a higher standard of social responsibility, even if it requires making some sacrifices for the greater good.

Career and Authority

Use your career to do work that truly matters to you. Be the commander-in-chief of your life, not the grunt. Don't labor just to pay your bills, to satisfy your boss, or to make someone else rich. Work for the ongoing betterment of yourself and others.

A consequence of living a principle-centered life is that you'll naturally attract and accept more responsibility, eventually rising into a leadership role. This may include the external trappings of authority such as a management position, but it may also manifest as a less formal ability to influence others. Either way, such principle-centered leadership is well deserved. It's intelligent for all of us to be guided by those who are truthful, loving, and powerful. Those who succumb to falsehood, apathy, or timidity don't make good leaders.

There are many leadership styles, but all effective leadership must be centered in the principles. We respect leaders who speak truthfully and authentically, even if we don't always agree with their decisions. We connect with leaders who show compassion, caring, and kindness. And we're empowered by leaders who demonstrate focus, effort, and discipline in doing the important work that needs to be done.

Building a successful career is both a privilege and a responsibility. The more authority you bring to your career, the more you can do to serve others, and the greater your impact will be. This is an honor to be accepted and embraced by those who are ready for it.

Career and Courage

Where is the career path with a heart—the path that terrifies you, the path the stirs your soul, the path you secretly fantasize about? That's the path that honors the real you. That's the path that keeps you aligned with truth, love, and power. If you aren't doing something that scares you and challenges you, you're playing the game of life too timidly, missing golden opportunities that could make a real difference. If your career path doesn't require courage, you're in the wrong career.

If you avoid all risk, you only weaken yourself. If you follow the heart-centered path, you can expect to take risks from time to time. Some will turn out in your favor; some won't. If your decisions are made intelligently, however, the cumulative effect will almost certainly be positive, in many cases to an enormous degree.

I've taken many calculated career risks in my life. Sometimes I was afraid, but when I believed I was right, I summoned the courage to act in spite of fear. Many of those risks didn't pay off. Some of them left me broke or deep in debt. However, some turned out far better than expected, such as the decision to switch careers from game development to personal development. On balance, if you put all my failures and successes together, the long-term results look pretty good. I'm very happy with where I am today, and I'm willing to continue taking intelligent risks as my career continues to unfold. I know that in order to keep growing on my particular path, more courage will be required. Instead of running from fear, I've learned that I must turn to face it.

Risk taking isn't gambling. In my hometown of Las Vegas, people visit the casinos to place bets where the odds are clearly stacked against them. Barring exceptional luck, the longer they play, the more money they lose. Mathematically speaking, when you see a game where the odds are against you, the ideal number of bets you should make to maximize your return is zero.

However, when you take calculated risks, you're making bets where you expect the odds to be in your favor. Even so, these risks won't always pan out. Sometimes you may place a big bet and lose, and the loss will set you back for several months or longer. But how many of those bets can you afford to make in your lifetime? You can probably make dozens of attempts or more. Even if you have only a slight edge, eventually you'll win enough times to more than cover your losses. Mathematically speaking, when you see a game where the odds are in your favor, the ideal number of bets you should make to maximize your return is infinite. Place as many as you possibly can; in the long run, the more bets you make, the more you win.

Another factor to consider is that when you lose a bet in most casino games, the odds remain unchanged when you place your next bet. Each effort is independent of the one before it. This isn't true, however, when you take courageous career risks. Every time you lose, you learn. The more you lose, the more you learn, thereby skewing the odds in your favor with each subsequent bet.

The main reason the odds of success in many competitive endeavors seem low is that there's so much "churn" at the bottom. New people constantly enter the field, give up within the first few months, and get replaced by more newcomers. They try it, they fail, and they move on. They lack the courage to persist when the going gets tough. But if you just stick with it long enough, you'll soon bypass the slush pile and get into the long run where the odds keep getting better because you're gaining valuable experience and wisdom.

I often notice people starting new home-based Internet businesses with great enthusiasm. But six months later, they've given up and have abandoned their Websites. I try to spread the word that six months is nothing. You need to put in at least a couple of solid years to get past the bottom rungs. StevePavlina.com earned a whopping $167 during its entire first six months of operation, and I was working on it full-time. That's about 17 cents per hour—not exactly what you'd call an unqualified success. It would have been easy to give up under those conditions, and most people would have done exactly that. But I kept on learning, making improvements as I went along, and the calculated risk eventually paid off.

When it comes to taking career risks, you must understand that in the long run, you control the odds. By taking the initiative again and again, you'll eventually figure out what you need to know in order to succeed. When people ask me what their odds of success are in some endeavor such as blogging or online business, my response is: "If you train in martial arts, what are the odds of becoming a black belt?" Does it make any difference what percentage of white belts eventually become black belts? Maybe that answer matters to a statistician, but it shouldn't make any difference to you. All that matters is whether you're committed to becoming a black belt. You decide whether you make it or not.

If you want to build an outstanding career, you have to develop your failure tolerance. You must be brave enough to take calculated risks and accept the inevitable setbacks that occur without going into a tailspin of depression. Some of your bets will lose, including the ones that are 99 percent in your favor. It can be very disappointing when that happens, but it's all part of the game. It takes courage to play a game when you know you're eventually going to suffer a loss. Don't let a few failures get you down. Just keep making the best decisions you can.

It's okay to risk going broke when you're convinced that the risk-reward ratio is reasonable and you're willing to deal with the worst possible outcome. Going broke is really no big deal. I've done it a few times myself; and to my surprise, I discovered there was no stop sign after running out of money, so I just kept going and rebuilt from scratch. A lack of money can't stop you if you're determined. Are you courageous enough to risk going broke to pursue your dreams?

Don't play the career game for cash. If you think money is the top prize, you'll get suckered in by all kinds of get-rich-quick schemes, and you'll make a lot of dumb bets. Even when you win the money you seek, you still lose because you miss the mark. The real prize is fulfillment. This means putting yourself in a position where you're doing work you love, building your strengths and talents, enjoying abundant income, and making a meaningful contribution to others. Now that's a prize worth having.

Don't settle for cowardly career choices. Don't wimp out on your dreams. Exercise your courage to go after the prize of true fulfillment, which is so much greater than the illusion of security. Don't get so attached to material possessions that you're afraid to risk them for what really matters. When you die, all your stuff will be left behind anyway; it's really not that important. What matters is how much conscious growth you experience while you're here since that's the only thing you can possibly keep after you die.

Career and Intelligence

To build an authentic career, you need to find the path that keeps you aligned with truth, love, and power. This requires paying attention to the following four questions:

1. *Body (needs):* What *must* I do?
2. *Mind (abilities):* What *can* I do?
3. *Heart (desire):* What do I *want* to do?
4. *Spirit (contribution):* What *should* I do?

An authentic career is found in the place where all four of these questions produce the same answer. This is the career that meets your needs, leverages your abilities, fulfills your desires, and makes a positive contribution to others. This means that your body, mind, heart, and spirit are aligned with truth, love, and power.

Consider your current career in light of the questions above. Are you successfully balancing all four of these areas, or did you only get some of them right? Does your career generate sufficient income to meet your needs without causing you to sink into debt? Does it leverage your strengths and talents? Do you love the work you do each day? Are you doing work that truly matters to you?

Motivation is strongest when these four areas are in harmony. If any area is lacking, it will drag down the other three. When I ran my computer-games business, I loved the work I was doing, and I was certainly leveraging my strengths. But for the first several years I didn't do a good job of meeting my needs, and I wasn't making much of a contribution either. Eventually, I found a way to generate sufficient income, but the spirit side of the business was always lagging behind. That one deficiency curtailed my enjoyment of the work, prevented me from building my skills as much as I could have, and held me back from greater financial success. What seemed like a 7 on a scale of 1 to 10 was gradually revealing itself as a 1.

When I shifted my career to personal development, I was still doing work I loved, I was still leveraging my strengths, and I began making a contribution that felt good to me, but I wasn't able to meet my needs right away. That last element did come later, however, and the result has been absolutely wonderful.

It may take significant effort to build an authentic career, but it's definitely worthwhile. When you have all four areas working synergistically together, the combined effect is truly amazing. Instead of meeting your needs, you experience true abundance. Instead of applying your knowledge to your tasks, you unlock your true genius. Instead of tolerating your daily routine, you work in a state of joy. And instead of just putting in the time, you fill your days with a sense of purpose.

What if you know these four areas are out of balance? If you can't immediately target all four, where should you begin? Of all of them, the heart area is the best place to start because it gives rise to all the rest. There's some truth to the notion that if you do what you love, the money will follow. It's not quite that simple in practice, but the basic idea is correct. If you simply persist in doing what you enjoy, you'll eventually get good at it. Once you reach a decent skill level, you'll be able to share the value you create with others, and many people will appreciate it. Then if you simply ask for fair value in return, you can begin to generate income from your work. This process may take many years to unfold, but it will lead you to a very positive place, and it all starts with doing what you love.

Consider the alternatives. When you aim to meet your needs above all else, it's easy to fall into the trap of doing soulless work to earn a decent income. The longer you follow that path, the more skill you build at something you don't enjoy. As you gain experience and seniority in that line of work, your income may continue to rise. But you aren't happy, and you probably aren't contributing in a way that fulfills you. The longer you follow this path, the deeper a hole you dig for yourself. The secondary gain of your income substitutes for the true fulfillment you really crave. If you find yourself in this situation, I'm sorry to tell you that the best way out is to allow yourself to crash. Bring truth, love, and power back into your life and you'll realize that no amount of external success can compensate for betraying the guy in the glass. Your true self cannot be bought at any price.

Another problematic alternative arises when you do your best to give to the world but fail to attend to the other three areas. I call this *lightworker syndrome.* Such people tend to be very loving and compassionate, but they don't put forth the effort to develop the skills that would make a significant contribution possible. They're very much aligned with love, but their power is way too weak, and this holds back their ability to contribute. They have to keep putting their grand mission on hold in order to scrape together enough money to pay the rent. If you want to change the world, then choose an approach that will be effective. You won't do anyone much good if you can't meet your basic needs.

The last alternative is to make your top priority the development of your talents and skills, but this can also be a dead end. You may wind up getting really good at something you simply don't enjoy or that fails to meet your needs, and this disconnects you from your true self. I think it's a huge mistake for parents to pressure their children to go into a certain line of work such as medicine or law just because it's what the parents want. The world doesn't need more unhappy, unfulfilled doctors and lawyers.

There are no substitutes for true happiness. It's better to do what you love, homeless and broke, working from a park bench, than to sell your soul for millions of dollars. The good news, however, is that if you follow the heart-centered path, you probably won't be broke for long. You'll be doing work that provides value for others, which is precisely how you generate income in the first place.

✦ ✦

In order to create a fulfilling career, you must make conscious career decisions. You can't simply play follow the follower (as opposed to follow the leader), traipsing down a path that others are following just as blindly. Don't compromise. If you find yourself on a path without a heart, get off of it as quickly as you can. Other people may protest loudly, but a few years later, you'll notice that something rather funny happens. The same people who hated you for leaving will turn around and ask your advice on how they can do what you did. The reason people get angry in such situations is that you force them to face the unpleasant truths they've been avoiding as well. You'll be an inspiration for others who wished they had your courage. This is true even if the strongest resistance comes from your own family members.

Don't get down on yourself if you can't discover your ideal career right away. Just keep making the most conscious decisions you can and you'll eventually get there. The heart-centered path is a lifetime journey, not a fixed destination.

Now it's time to turn our attention to one of the least understood areas of personal development, the subject of . . .

✦ ✦ ✦ ✦

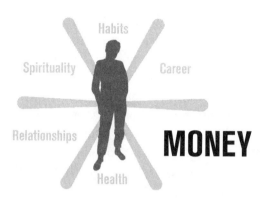

Chapter 10

"It is not easy for men to rise whose
qualities are thwarted by poverty."

— JUVENAL

It's undeniable that money plays an important role in our lives,
but what exactly is that role? Is money a harmful distraction, or can it
actually help us live more consciously? Is it better to give or to receive?
Is poverty more enlightened than wealth?

Even among highly conscious individuals, money can be a con-
tentious, polarizing topic. Social conditioning overloads us with so
many conflicting views on the subject that it's no wonder people are
confused. Confusion about money causes us to compartmentalize the
financial part of our lives. Money becomes a thing unto itself with its
own rules and formulas. We literally treat it as something that must

be cordoned off and sealed in a vault, isolated from other parts of our lives lest it somehow infect us with its inhuman properties.

Like most people, I grew up with incongruent beliefs about money. On the one hand, I saw evidence that money was good. Intellectually, material wealth seemed important, for money clearly bestows certain advantages. It can purchase food, clothing, shelter, transportation, education, technology, entertainment, medicine, and so on. Given the way our society currently functions, if you have money, you have solutions. It surely won't solve all your problems, and it can create new problems of its own, but on balance it's safe to say that money is a powerful problem-solving tool. Inspirational radio personality Earl Nightingale said it best: "Nothing can take the place of money in the area in which money works."

On the other hand, there were some things I didn't like about money. Intuitively, it felt hollow and meaningless to me. I didn't like that it was used as a gatekeeper for certain *privileges* such as proper medical care, healthy food, or decent educational resources. I was also disturbed that some people behave dishonorably to attain it. While I was sometimes impressed by the achievements of the world's titans of wealth, many of them acquired their money through means I couldn't stomach.

Have you been struggling with similar internal conflicts? If so, you're certainly not alone because this battle is largely the result of social conditioning. We have some influences telling us that money is very important, while others tell us it isn't. Notice what happens during the holiday season. Advertisers tell us to spend, spend, spend. They suggest that the more money we spend, the happier our holidays will be. On the other hand, we might watch a classic movie such as *It's a Wonderful Life* that tells us we need to keep money in perspective and that relationships are far more important. Mixed signals abound.

Social conditioning about money affects how we relate to each other as well. What prejudgments do you make about people based on their financial status? What assumptions would you make about a millionaire? About someone who's totally broke? How would you feel dating someone who earned ten times as much as you do? How about one-tenth as much as you earn?

These mixed associations lead many conscious people to conclude that money itself is the problem. Perhaps it's better to live without it altogether or at least to minimize its role in our lives. If money is truly a distraction from conscious living, wouldn't the most conscious choice be to shun money altogether? Should you give up all your worldly possessions and go live in a cave somewhere?

Despite what you may have been conditioned to believe, the simple truth is that there are no special rules for money. It obeys the principles of truth, love, and power the same as any other part of your life, and it's a mistake to try to isolate yourself from the world's financial realities. In this chapter, I'll offer you a holistic way of thinking about money, one that should satisfy your intuitive feelings as well as your logical mind.

Money and Truth

What is money? Money is a social resource—the primary social resource. Money has no inherent value of its own, but we assign it value through social agreement. If you have $100, you can withdraw $100 of value from society by spending that money. The reason this works is that we agree by consensus that $100 has a certain value. If we all agreed that money was worthless, it would have no value whatsoever.

Because it's a social resource, money isn't a perfect medium of exchange. The value of anything, including money itself, is determined by social consensus. That may be the agreement of only two people, such as when you buy an item from another person. Or it may be the consensus of a large group, such as when you buy or sell stock in public companies.

Although there are serious consequences to doing so, you're free to opt out of the social contract of money. Most people would find that totally impractical, but the option is available. However, if you still want to take advantage of social resources, you'll need to create your own social contracts on a case-by-case basis. This could include barter or other forms of exchange, or it could involve leveraging relationships to meet your social needs.

For most of us, the social contract of money is far too advantageous to ignore. While the monetary system certainly isn't perfect, it's more efficient than the alternatives. By assigning a monetary value to our social exchanges and by making it easy to transfer money from one person to another, trades can be performed with relative ease. Buying groceries, working at a job, or connecting to the Internet are all examples of social trades, and by consensus all of them are reducible to money. Even money itself can be assigned a price, as anyone in debt can readily attest.

Money is essentially social credit. It's an IOU from society, enabling you to extract a certain amount of social value whenever you spend it. The more money you have, the more society owes you, and the more value you can extract.

Let's now consider the truth about what it means to earn money. Since money is a social resource, earning money means acquiring more of that resource. When you spend, you convert money to value; but when you earn, you convert value to money.

One way to earn money is to sell possessions. Take an item and sell it to someone else who wants it and you'll receive money for it. Another option is to acquire items at one price and turn around and sell them for more than your costs. Companies dig up resources all over the planet and sell them for a profit. For individuals, this approach might take the form of buying objects, stocks, or bonds at one price and selling them at a higher price. Sometimes value is added in the process (which may just be added convenience); other times money is earned through market inefficiencies, whereby one party in a transaction profits from an unbalanced exchange that extracts more value than it provides.

Perhaps the most common way to earn money is to sell your time. Get a job and trade hours for dollars. The greater your ability to deliver social value through your labors, the greater your earning potential becomes. The difference between earning $25 per hour versus $250 per hour is that the latter work has much greater social value. This isn't anyone's fault; the difference is due to the social consensus about the value of certain work. Take note of the difference between absolute value and social value. Top competitive athletes may not perform useful societal work in an absolute sense, but their compensation is based on the collectively agreed upon social value of their performance, which currently runs very high.

Another way to earn money is to build a system that earns money for you, such as a business. This is my personal favorite, since it provides much more leverage than selling time. It's also less risky in the long run, since owning and controlling an income-generating system is more secure than having a job where you can be fired or laid off.

You can also earn money by selling money itself. By investing in assets, you can earn interest, dividends, or appreciation in the form of capital gains.

Of course, a final option for making money is to steal it. Historically, this has been a popular option, but I won't give it serious consideration here.

So far, this is really just common sense, but it's amazing how easy it is to lose sight of the simple truth that money is a human invention to facilitate the exchange of value. To shun money as something evil or unnecessary is a huge mistake. When properly aligned with truth, love, and power, it becomes a valuable tool of conscious living—one that's too important to ignore. If you want to live consciously, you must learn to use money intelligently.

Money and Love

The principle of love advises us to tune in and connect with the concept of money on a deeper level, so let's do exactly that and see what the process reveals.

There are two basic ways to earn money:

1. Make a meaningful social contribution, and receive payment commensurate with the social value of your contribution.

2. Take advantage of market inefficiencies to extract money without contributing any substantial value.

The first option includes getting a job and performing useful work, running a business that provides valuable products or services, reselling items with value added, or investing in any of these outlets. The second option includes gambling, begging, criminal activities, buying and reselling items with no added value, or investing in any of these.

Here's another way of labeling these two strategies:

1. Contribute
2. Mooch

Unless you've somehow opted out of the monetary system, you're using one or both of these earnings strategies right now. However, one of them will likely be dominant in your life. Either you're creating genuine social value and being fairly compensated for it, or you're mooching off the value created by others.

Note that contribution is essential for the monetary system to survive and thrive, but mooching is not. The only way moochers can survive is by extracting value from contributors. But ultimately someone must contribute, or there can be no value for the moochers to extract. Unless you've found a way to be completely self-sufficient, you're always extracting some value from society, such as your food, clothing, and shelter. The question is whether you're feeding fair value back into the system to compensate for what you're pulling out.

Some degree of mooching is to be expected. Children mooch off their parents. Those who are unable to contribute mooch off those who can. Whenever we enjoy the fruits of someone else's labor without paying for it, we're mooching. We all mooch off the hard work of our ancestors. But eventually we must decide whether we'll continue down that path or begin making a genuine contribution.

Obviously, your life will include some contribution and some mooching, but what's your primary income-generating strategy? Do you contribute real social value, or do you mooch off the value of other contributors? Take note that if you work for a larger organization, you share in their income-generating strategy as well. Are you working for a moocher or a contributor? The big picture can't be ignored.

The Moocher Mind-set

Opting in to mooch mode means you're extracting more social value than you're contributing. Your focus is on getting as opposed to giving, so you take more out of the system than you give back. The moocher mind-set suggests you can always rely on others to pick up your slack. It's the attitude of unearned entitlement. Since you still need to extract value such as food, clothing, and shelter—value others must provide for you—you live at the expense of others. Your burden may be shouldered by a willing individual such as a parent, or it may be shared by society at large; either way you survive by suckling the social teat.

Sometimes mooching becomes so habitual that it's easy to overlook. Many people who think of themselves as working in contribution-based careers harbor an underlying moocher mind-set. They aim to extract more social value than they actually contribute. This includes the attorney who records more billable hours than were actually worked, the CFO who fudges the numbers to inflate a company's stock price, and the employee who performs personal tasks while on the clock. Such actions are unbecoming of genuine contributors.

Another name for the moocher mind-set is the scarcity mind-set. Since you aren't creating value of your own, the money you extract must come from someone else. It's a zero-sum game. Whatever you gain, someone else must lose.

The moocher mind-set makes the attainment of financial abundance very difficult because in order to succeed financially with this worldview, you must embrace certain values that most folks would consider negative. Your gain is someone else's loss, so getting rich requires taking advantage of people. In order to gain by mooching, someone else must cover your extraction with real value. The more wealth you accumulate, the more you take from others, and the more you force others to pick up your slack. Consequently, mooching is essentially the same thing as theft.

Most people can't handle the thought of becoming wealthy at the expense of others, so the moocher mind-set frequently gives rise to self-sabotage. If you fall into this pattern, you'll experience a love/

hate relationship with money. On the one hand, you may want more money, but on the other hand, you'll probably feel disinclined to do what it takes to get it, since you know that the more wealth you acquire through such means, the more someone else has to pay for it.

For example, if you make a living as a professional poker player, then you know that the more you earn, the more money others must lose, and somewhere down the line, someone must provide real value to cover the cash you're extracting. This isn't the best motivation for a highly conscious person to achieve financial abundance. In order to make money this way, you must disconnect from your true self and put up walls that disconnect you from others.

Some people bypass this problem of financial self-sabotage by lowering their consciousness and turning away from the principle of love. They learn to make money while numbing themselves to the full consequences of how they're earning it. They invent justifications to explain their actions while shrinking their awareness in order to avoid connecting with the truth. For example, a car salesman may generate extra commissions by overpricing cars for unwary customers, but in so doing, the salesman denies himself the opportunity to form honest, loving connections with those customers. By embracing the moocher mind-set, he falls out of alignment with the principle of love.

A small percentage of people are able to adopt the moocher mind-set without lowering their awareness. They skew the principle of love in the direction of self-love, essentially rejecting the principle of oneness along with its virtues of empathy, compassion, honesty, fairness, contribution, and unity. This is the mind-set of career criminals who intentionally harm others for personal gain. Although I don't personally recommend it, I will admit that it is possible to consciously choose this path. Fully exploring this option is outside the scope of this book, but if you care to learn more about it in order to come to a more conscious choice regarding your own path, please visit the Archives page at **www.StevePavlina.com/blog/archives**, and scan for articles that include the word *darkworker* in the title.

Unless you're able to completely suppress your conscience, the moocher mind-set makes financial abundance incompatible with conscious living. This is the mind-set that leads you to ask: *How can I get more money?* instead of *How can I contribute more value?* The more conscious and loving you become, the more you'll hesitate to increase your income through such means, since your gain is someone else's loss. Consequently, those who adopt the moocher mind-set often succumb to financial self-sabotage. The solution is either to suppress your conscience or to drop the moocher mind-set and lovingly embrace . . .

The Contributor Mind-set

Now let's consider the contributor mind-set, which recognizes that the best way to make money is to provide fair value in exchange. Create genuine social value and receive payment commensurate with that value. Due to market inefficiencies, sometimes you'll be underpaid and sometimes you'll be overpaid, but the basic idea is that you earn money by contributing.

If you want to earn income as a contributor, you must impart social value, not personal value. Many would-be contributors get stuck on this concept. Personal value is whatever you say it is. You're free to decide what has value for you personally, and it doesn't matter if anyone agrees with you. Social value, however, is determined by social consensus. If you believe that your work has tremendous value, but virtually no one else does, then your work may have high personal value but little or no social worth. Let me repeat the key point: your income depends on the social value of your work, not the personal value.

If you want to generate income from your efforts, you must create social value. There's no getting around that. No social value means no income. If your skills and efforts aren't aligned with the creation of genuine social worth, you won't be able to generate much income as a contributor.

This isn't an unfair system. Since money is a social resource backed by collective value, it makes sense that you won't get paid much for providing something of little or no importance to the group. The saying "Find a need and fill it" rings true.

My Website, for example, provides a fair degree of social value. Whether you or I value it as individuals is financially irrelevant. It successfully generates income because the overall social consensus is that the site's content is valuable. That makes it possible for the site to generate abundant income. If it offered no social value, there'd be no financial potential.

Another name for the contributor mind-set is the abundance mind-set, which says that wealth can be created from ideas and action. Your personal gain is a reflection of the social value you've contributed. If you want to earn a high income, you must contribute substantial social value. The more social value you provide, the more money you can earn. This is a win-win mind-set because you're putting value into the system for the benefit of others.

Under the contributor mind-set, you receive money as payment for your social service. The money you earn is society's way of saying: "In exchange for your valued contribution, you are hereby granted the right to extract equivalent value from society at a time of your choosing." This is a beautiful thing!

The only real limit on your income is how much social value you can create. If you want to earn more money, develop your skills and talents to facilitate the creation of lots of social value. Focus on giving, and the getting will largely take care of itself. The systems to reward social service are already in place, so all you need to do is plug your service into the existing marketplace.

Generating income from social contribution is a very positive experience. Consequently, it won't lower your consciousness like the moocher mind-set. With the contributor mind-set, wealth and consciousness aren't in conflict. In fact, they synergize extremely well together, especially if you reinvest some of your income into expanding your contribution.

If you adopt the contributor mind-set, just be aware that members of the moocher mind-set will sometimes mistakenly count you among them. As you work to increase your social contribution and thereby earn a higher income, moochers will project their values onto you, concluding that you must be taking advantage of others for personal gain just as they are. Don't let moochers dissuade you from your path. Let your inspiration come from the desire to provide even more social value. Don't withhold your work just because others misinterpret your motives.

Under the contributor model, you always have the option of making pro bono contributions (that is, you can create social value and give it away for free). You don't have to be paid if you don't want to. I like having this option because it means I can make my work accessible to those who can't afford it. My Website represents a tremendous personal investment of time and energy, so it certainly isn't free from my point of view. But because I'm very good at leveraging technology to keep my operating costs low, it's practical for me to provide abundant content without charging for it.

I encourage you to consciously choose the contributor mind-set because it's aligned with love, while the moocher mind-set clearly is not. Don't sacrifice your humanity for money. Never treat a human being like a dollar sign. No amount of money is worth the price of such horrendous disconnection. Sharing genuine value with others is an act of love, one that can earn you plenty of money while simultaneously increasing your connectedness and consciousness. So the good news is that you can generate as much wealth as you desire without lowering your consciousness, but only if you focus your energies on the contribution side.

Money and Power

The principle of power says that you're responsible for your own financial situation. If you dislike your current circumstances and want something better, it's up to you to make it happen. You can yield control of your financial destiny to others, but final responsibility always rests with you. You're the one who must live with the results you experience.

Self-help literature often recommends that we set clear financial goals. We're told to decide in advance how much money we want to earn and how much we want to have in the bank. I've often set such goals for myself. Sometimes I achieved them; many times I didn't. Eventually I learned a more important lesson: in order for our financial goals to be sound, they must reflect our truest, deepest desires. A goal is worthless if it doesn't empower you.

When I gave it some serious thought, I realized that I just didn't care about making specific amounts of money. A million dollars has no real meaning to me. By putting so much emphasis on certain sums, I was giving my power *to* money instead of wielding power *over* it. Money was becoming my master instead of my servant. So instead of focusing on specific financial goals, I decided to aim directly for what I thought money would give me. I thought it would provide me with the freedom to travel, so I set travel goals instead. I thought money would get me a nicer house, so I set a goal to have a nicer house instead. I thought being wealthy would allow me to make a bigger contribution, so I set a goal to make a bigger contribution instead. Ironically, when I stopped treating money as an end unto itself, I had more of it flowing through my life than ever before.

The truth is that you don't need any specific sum of money in the bank or a specific level of income to achieve your goals. There are countless ways to do so, and many of them require little or no money. People who are dead broke have traveled around the world. Why not you? When you decide in advance that a lack of funds is an obstacle to achieving your goals, you disempower yourself. If you want something badly enough, target it directly. Your path may lead you to earn and spend money to get there, or it may not. Don't automatically assume that money is necessary to achieve a particular goal; this narrows your options and stunts your creativity.

Since money is a medium of exchange, it only has power when it flows. A number in a bank account is utterly worthless. Money's value lies in the exchange, not in its possession. When you earn it, you create value. When you spend it, you gain access to value created by others, thereby enabling them to create more value as well. It's wise to save a portion of your income, but know that saved money must eventually flow back out again, if not during your lifetime then certainly afterward.

Money and Oneness

The best way to earn money is through honest contribution. Do what you feel is best for everyone, not just yourself. Align your financial results with the highest good of all. Ask yourself: *Would anyone be deeply saddened if I stopped contributing? Would anyone cry if I went out of business?* If the answer is no, it's a safe bet you're on the wrong path.

Contributing social value is the primary strategy for making money consciously, but by itself it isn't enough to guarantee success. The problem with focusing on social value is that your personal values may not be aligned with the social consensus. When you attempt to provide social value without achieving congruence with your personal values, your motivation will be weak. You won't be inspired because you'll be doing what you feel you *should* do, not what you *want* to do. Alternatively, when you attempt to satisfy your personal values without providing any real social value, you get the starving-artist syndrome: you may be inspired by work you love doing, but it won't pay the bills.

The solution is to work within the area of overlap between your personal values and social values. This will enable you to do what you love while creating something that others treasure as well. Don't force yourself to choose between your integrity and your income—demand that both be satisfied.

Social and personal values will fluctuate over time, so be prepared to adapt. During the first few years I ran my computer-games business, it aligned perfectly with my personal values but not with social values. I loved the work, but I wasn't making any money. After several years, I reached a point of balance, where I was enjoying the work and making a nice living from it. Farther down the road, my personal values shifted: creating games no longer inspired me even though the work still had social value. Eventually I changed careers.

Personal development work currently has high social value, and it also aligns beautifully with my personal values. Consequently, I can generate substantial income in this field and be very fulfilled at the same time. Don't underestimate the importance of alignment between personal and social values. Both are essential if you want to make money consciously.

Unless you're really inflexible, it shouldn't be exceedingly difficult to envision a way for you to contribute that also aligns with your personal beliefs. This is a problem that can be solved if you put some thought into it. Often the simplest way to create value for others is by sharing what you love to do. I love working on my own growth, but that doesn't do much for others. However, when I share what I'm doing and teach people what I've learned, that *does* create social value. And when I do so via the Internet and share my work with millions of people around the world, the value I can provide is massively multiplied. Once you have a solution that works for you, you'll be in a position to generate abundant income while serving the greater good. Don't expect this to be easy, but it is certainly worth the effort.

Money and Fairness

Conscious income generation must also be aligned with the virtue of fairness, which arises from oneness. To make a sustainable contribution, it's important that you're fairly compensated for the value you produce. If you contribute, you deserve to be paid. This mind-set keeps the body healthy, as well as the individual cells. Fairness is a more intelligent value than either greed or self-sacrifice.

It took me a long time to realize that in the area of money, fairness must be the governing principle. For much of my adult life, I fell on the self-sacrificing side, believing that it was noble to give without expecting anything in return. After many years of hard work, I had little to show for my efforts. I'd give away my value, and others would gladly take it because I offered it freely or very cheaply. I went bankrupt doing this, and that hurt my capacity to give.

Meanwhile, I'd see others who clearly fell on the greed side. They'd get ahead financially by taking advantage of people, but this had a terribly dehumanizing effect on them. I knew I could never go that route no matter how tempting it appeared—but I couldn't help but notice that they were earning a lot more money than I was. I often pondered how much more I could contribute if I wasn't struggling financially and could at least pay all my bills. I figured there had to be a third alternative. That alternative is fairness, and it arises naturally from the principle of oneness.

I admit I continue to err on the self-sacrificing side a little too often—this is an area where I still have much growing to do. Such values were ingrained in me from a young age, but I now realize that being too self-sacrificing is a huge mistake and runs contrary to the principle of oneness. With each passing year, it becomes ever more obvious that in order for my contribution to be sustainable, I must receive a fair level of financial support for the benefits I provide. To sacrifice myself to help others without receiving fair value in return is to enter into an abusive relationship.

Whenever an organization adopts unfair compensation practices, the effect is dehumanizing. If you find yourself working in such a system, you're not only submitting to abuse, but you're also contributing to the abuse of others. Please don't do that. If you're being treated unfairly, it's up to you to bring your life back into alignment with truth, love, and power.

Money and Authority

How can you generate enough value to achieve the level of income you desire? You're in command, so this is your decision to make. If your current approach isn't effective, you may need to experiment to find something that works. Keep asking yourself these two questions: *How can I create and deliver more value? How can I increase my capacity for value creation?* Then use your power to act on the truths you discover.

When we start out in life, most of us have few skills that can be used to create social value. With our bodies we can perform unskilled physical labor, but that doesn't provide much value because it's too common and readily replaceable. In order to generate significant value, we must invest in ourselves by developing our talents and skills. If you want to earn more money, you must train yourself to create and deliver more social value. You can certainly take advantage of educational resources, but never forget that you're responsible for your own learning. If insufficient education is holding you back financially, it's up to you to remedy that situation. Keep developing your skills to the point where you're capable of making a meaningful contribution; then develop them some more. You may be in a weak position right now, but that's no excuse because you're perfectly capable of making small improvements each day, and incremental improvements lead to major changes. If you start on such a path today, you won't even be able to fathom where you'll be in five years.

In order to provide the social value I'm capable of delivering today, I had to invest thousands of hours in self-development and education. While many of my peers slacked off in high school, I enrolled in challenging honors classes and put in the effort required to earn straight A's, and I studied computer programming on the side. After graduating from college, I continued reading hundreds of books on a variety of topics, and I attended seminars and workshops to continue my education. The way I see it, school is never out. If you want to put yourself in a position of creating substantial value, you must commit to being a lifelong student.

If you're thinking that most people will never make such a commitment, you're absolutely right. Developing socially valuable skills is hard work, but those who put in the time are rewarded handsomely for their efforts, not only financially but also by the intrinsic rewards of creative self-expression.

Be sure that your self-education is practical. It's entirely possible to build skills that are of great interest to you but that no one will pay for. There's nothing wrong with acquiring interesting knowledge that has little or no financial value—just don't whine and complain that no one will open their wallets for you.

Strive to become an authority in the area of overlap between your personal interests and social demand and you'll have an easier time earning money. When I was a teenager, I loved playing video games. Maybe I could have been a game tester, but such jobs typically pay close to minimum wage so that didn't seem like a great option. However, I also thought it would be fun to create games. This provided more social value, so consequently I was able to generate a decent income from those efforts, even while I was still in school.

If you can't find the area of overlap between what you enjoy and what people are willing to pay for, try harder. Don't settle for one or the other. Persist, and you'll eventually find a way to have both. If you can generate a great income from doing what you love, you'll love your work even more. I can tell you from experience that it's a lot more fun to work with plenty of money coming in than it is to labor on while sinking into debt.

Money and Courage

Don't expect someone else to know what your skills and talents are worth. If you let others determine your salary, it's a safe bet you're being underpaid. You must take the initiative and ask for what you want. If the price you ask is fair and reasonable and if there's genuine social demand for the value you can provide, someone will surely pay you for your efforts.

Don't be timid or wimpy when it comes to asking for money. That's a sign that you don't believe in your value. If you really can't provide what you're claiming you can, then don't ask to be paid until you're ready. But if you know you can contribute genuine value, summon the courage to ask for fair compensation in exchange. Be direct, but be able to build a solid case for why you deserve it.

Use the heart question to help guide you toward principle-centered income-generating opportunities. Ask yourself: *Does this path have a heart?* If the answer is no, then let it go and invest your time and energy elsewhere. Have the courage to put human beings first, money second. Honor what your conscience tells you. If it feels wrong, it *is* wrong. Even if it feels neutral, it's still wrong. Never chase soulless profits.

Even when you're on the heart-centered path, you'll need courage to stay there. Sometimes you'll need to defend against dishonorable attacks. It's unfortunate when that becomes necessary, but it happens. I'm happy to say that having been in business for most of my adult life, I've never sued anyone. However, there have certainly been times when I found it necessary to defend myself, such as when hackers and spammers attacked my Website. Even when you do your best to genuinely help people, you may need to deal with those who have no qualms about trampling on others for their own personal gain. If you know you're on the path with a heart, don't let such problems dissuade you from continuing. Do your best to recover and keep moving forward.

Sometimes you'll be surprised by the support that comes your way when you demonstrate your commitment to putting people first. On multiple occasions, hackers have e-mailed me to let me know about a security flaw in my Website configuration, including offering advice on how to fix it. Instead of using their skills to harm my site, they actually helped protect it. I've found that the more I align my work with truth, love, and power, the more goodwill I generate, and the more I receive support from unexpected sources. When you commit yourself to the heart-centered path, it will often seem as though the universe backs you up.

Money and Intelligence

Intelligence is the ultimate source of wealth. You can provide tremendous value to others by cultivating your own creative self-expression, thereby generating all the income you desire. Instead of trying to *get* money, focus your efforts on creating and delivering value to others, and plenty of resources will flow back to you in return. True wealth comes from within.

By making intelligent choices, you should be able to increase your capacity to provide social value, thereby increasing your income. This requires that you optimize for long-term value creation instead of short-term profit. Bypass the low-hanging fruit and go after the big opportunities, the ones that inspire and challenge you to grow.

If you feel that you must behave inauthentically in order to earn income, you're getting off track. Don't dehumanize yourself and others by pretending to be something you're not. If you express yourself creatively and genuinely, you'll be able to provide value for others and meet your needs at the same time.

Every week I receive offers (usually from other entrepreneurs) that could potentially make me a lot of money, but that would require me to do something that isn't aligned with truth, love, and power. For example, I could boost my monthly income by thousands of extra dollars if I recommended products that I know deep down won't help anyone. The product promoters even provide their own endorsement letters, so all I have to do is slap my name on them and send them off. I always decline such offers without a second thought. Unfortunately, there are many people in the business world who assume that the whole point of being in business is to make as much money as possible. That's a very misguided philosophy. The point of business is to create and deliver value for the benefit of all, not to extract it at someone else's expense.

What about tithing? Is it wise to donate a percentage of your income to charity? I've been making monthly charitable contributions for years, but it isn't a significant portion of my income, and I don't consider it a big deal. If there was a charity doing something I thought was so important that I should donate a substantial amount of my own money to it, I'd be doing that work myself. Right now, I can see that my best outlet for contribution is through my own business as opposed to paying a charity to perform such work on my behalf. But I still donate some money where I feel it can be put to good use in a way that's different from what I'm already doing.

When you get your financial house in good order, you'll have excess capacity to take on projects that aren't motivated by profit. My Website hosts popular discussion forums that attract thousands of participants from around the world. I charge nothing to access them, even though it costs me time and money to maintain them. From a purely financial standpoint, the forums are a flop; however, they provide a valuable public service, and participants often tell me how much the forums have helped them. I'm happy to continue providing this service, and even though it isn't much of an income generator, I consider it a success because it contributes to the business purpose of helping people grow.

If you give more value than you receive while ensuring you're being treated fairly and not falling into a pattern of self-sacrifice, the excess value you provide will overflow into public goodwill. Superior service gets noticed because it's so rare. People will gladly recommend you to their family, friends, and co-workers, thereby bringing you a steady stream of new opportunities. This is true whether you're self-employed or you work for someone else.

It's intelligent to give more than you receive, since this is precisely what generates growth. This is how I built up my Website traffic from scratch. I produced and gave away the equivalent of 20 books worth of original content without charging a dime for it. All of that value generated massive referrals. The content was certainly good enough that I *could* have charged money for it, but I deliberately decided to overload the goodwill side in order to maximize the growth rate. There's no reason you can't use a similar strategy yourself. Push harder on the service side, and you'll soon find people lining up to pay you.

✦ ✦

If you want to earn money without lowering your consciousness, you must align your income with truth, love, and power. If you're making a valuable social contribution, then by any reasonable standard of fairness, you should be paid for it. This won't happen automatically though. You must consciously cultivate such conditions while doing your best to follow the heart-centered path.

I used to think I needed a certain amount of money to feel totally secure. But now I realize that no amount can provide security. We live in a world of rapid and accelerating change. Even if you stockpile a huge amount of cash, you don't really know if it will be worth anything down the road. It may be lost or stolen, or the currency itself could fail. The only true security is intelligence—our ever-increasing ability to stay aligned with truth, love, and power. This isn't merely an individual issue; it's a collective one. As human beings, our only real safety lies in our intelligence, but fortunately that's all we need.

As strange as it may seem, I found that the easiest way for me to feel financially secure was to make peace with the possibility of ending up broke and penniless. Because the future contains so many unknown variables, I can't reliably predict where I'll end up. I don't even know how long I'll live. So I must accept that no matter what I do, the final outcome of my life remains uncertain. I was eventually able to make peace with this by realizing that the best I can do is to make intelligent choices here and now, choices I believe are aligned with truth, love, and power. I can demand no more of myself than that.

I never really expect to retire, since I'd rather die onstage, so to speak. But if I reach the point where I've used myself up, and I have no money left to take care of my basic needs, I would hope that someone somewhere has received enough value from my work to help me through my final days. But even if that doesn't happen, I can still be at peace by knowing that I lived consciously. If for some reason my life ends in hardship, so be it. It will have been worth the price.

Of course, the irony is that once I let go of my attachment to specific financial outcomes and realized I could accept the worst-case scenarios, all the energy that was preoccupied with fear, worry, and concern began flowing into my work, thereby enabling me to generate more income than I'd ever seen before. Perhaps the best path to wealth is to release your fear of being poor. Realize that life is still worth living, regardless of how much money you have.

Do your best to create and share your value with others, and you'll help create a richer and more abundant world for all of us. And if you want to enjoy the full richness of the human experience, be sure to take good care of your . . .

Chapter 11

HEALTH

"The body too has its rights; and it will have them. They cannot be trampled upon or slighted without peril. The body ought to be the soul's best friend, and cordial, dutiful helpmate. Many of the studious, however, have neglected to make it so; whence a large part of the miseries of authorship. Some good men have treated it as an enemy; and then it has become a fiend, and has plagued them."

— AUGUSTUS WILLIAM HARE AND JULIUS CHARLES HARE

Do you treat your physical body as your soul's best friend or as a fiend that plagues you? Is it a temple or a tomb? Your body is your avatar (the image that represents you) in the physical universe. It's the character you control, and you're the consciousness that controls it. It's subject to the laws of the physical universe, but your consciousness isn't so limited. Your body is the channel through which you express yourself in physical form. It's your paintbrush on the canvas of physicality. Consequently, its health is important. If your body is in poor health, its brush strokes will be flawed. But when it's vitally alive and full of energy, it contributes to masterful art as the purest extension of your thoughts.

When I'm in poor health, I'm keenly aware of my body. I grasp the importance of health most clearly when I'm lying in bed with an illness. I keep thinking, *I want to be well again.* However, when I'm in good health, I scarcely notice my body. It becomes an almost invisible extension of my consciousness.

The challenge of achieving and maintaining good health can appear confusing on the surface. Many experts recommend complex rules for what to eat, how to eat, and when to eat it. Whenever there seems to be a consensus on a subject, someone will come out with a new book espousing the opposite approach. As you'll soon see, however, the universal principles of truth, love, and power can help you cut through this confusion, enabling you to develop sound health practices that will serve you well for life.

Health and Truth

Overweight doctors write new diet books. Supplement manufacturers publish health magazines. Drug companies sponsor television news programs. Uncovering the truth about health can be difficult if you've been overexposed to disguised marketing messages that favor sales over truth. Health-product marketers often seem to follow Mark Twain's classic advice: "Get your facts first, and then you can distort them as much as you please."

My goal here isn't to convince you to adopt my personal beliefs about health. Instead, I want to give you the means to think intelligently about the matter for yourself. Consequently, I won't overload you with statistics because that would be entirely pointless. I can track down the data to build any case I want, but you'd never know if you could trust that I was sharing the whole truth with you. If I was really manipulative, I could even use distorted facts and figures to try to convince you to buy a special line of overpriced supplements, the kind that enrich only two things: your urine and the manufacturer's pocketbook. I'm not a trained research scientist, and most likely you aren't one either, so let's skip the chest-pounding stats battle and consider a more sensible approach.

Take a moment to clear your head of everything you think you know about health. As Bruce Lee would say, "Empty your cup." Let's return to the first principles, starting with your basic perceptions. Set aside the uncertainty of what you think you should be doing, and examine what your senses are telling you right now.

Take a good look at your body. Get naked and evaluate yourself in a mirror if possible. What do you see? Do you appear overweight or underweight? What parts of your body do you like best? What do you wish you could change? What color are your eyes? How would you describe your hair? Notice your external perceptions as well as your internal reactions to them.

How do you feel? Are you alert and energetic or foggy and slug-gish? Do you feel light or heavy? How often do you get sick? Do you sleep restfully at night and awaken refreshed, or is your sleep disturbed and restless? Are you relaxed or stressed? Is your emotional state positive or negative? What kinds of foods do you eat and in what quantities? How do you feel about your diet? Do you perceive that it's healthy, or are there problems you already know about? Do you have any unhealthy addictions? Do you consume drugs such as caffeine, nicotine, or alcohol?

How would you rate your overall physical fitness on a scale of 1 to 10? How would you evaluate your aerobic capacity, strength, flexibility, and endurance? What kind of exercise do you do and how often? What physical recreation do you currently enjoy? Are you able to function well, or do you suffer from any physical problems? Do you have the physical vitality you desire?

Be completely honest with yourself. What do your perceptions reveal about your physical body and your current state of health? If you want even more information, ask for a friend or family member's perceptions of your physical body as well, or consider getting a full medical checkup.

Now turn your attention to your predictions. You never know if these will be accurate, but you can certainly make reasonable guesses based on your current patterns. In order to be totally honest with yourself, use a third-person perspective. Imagine that an objective, unbiased observer carefully examines all the details of your physical life. What will that person predict for your physical future? Is the expected outcome positive or negative? Is your health improving or declining? Where are your current habits taking you? Is this what you want? If you're feeling brave, ask a friend or family member to make these predictions for you as well; then compare this person's forecast to your own. This will help compensate for your internal biases and bring more truth to your situation.

In the past, you may have resisted your most honest perceptions and predictions, especially if you didn't like what you saw, but this time do your best to accept everything as completely as you can. Accept where you are right now and what you have to work with. Accept the body you've been given, despite its flaws. For better or worse, this is the vehicle you'll be using for the rest of your physical life.

There are some things I really like about my body. I like that I have blue eyes. I like that I'm left-handed, even though it can sometimes be annoying to live in a right-handed world. I like that I'm six feet tall, which is just tall enough to get a good view when standing in a crowd but not so tall as to require ducking while walking through a doorway. I like that I have plenty of strength and endurance. I like that my body isn't particularly hairy, that I know how to juggle, and that I don't get sick very often.

There are also some things about my body I dislike. I don't like being nearsighted, and I don't like having to shave every day. My teeth are discolored from when I wore braces as a child. My body isn't very flexible, and my posture could use improvement. I've been colorblind since birth, so I've never seen a sunset the way other people see it. And of course, half of my thoughts seem to originate from below my waist.

We all have our unique physical issues to deal with. Some of those may be within our power to change, while others may not have practical solutions. Regardless of the specific details of each situation, the path to better health begins with identifying and accepting what we already know to be true.

Health and Love

Use the principle of love to deepen your connection between your mind and your body. Quiet your mind, turn your attention inward, and just listen. What do you hear? Does your body report any problems that need action? Do you feel any subtle emotions arising? What does your intuition tell you?

The principle of love helps you connect with the foods that are most naturally attractive to you. Pay attention to which ones feel intuitively right and which feel intuitively wrong. How do you feel about an apple? A hot dog? A bowl of rice? A stalk of broccoli? Do some items feel healthy to you while others don't? Could you improve your health simply by doing a better job of honoring what your intuition is already telling you? Are you treating your body in a loving manner?

I feel most connected to foods that sprout from the earth itself, especially fresh fruits and vegetables. Items that emerge from a factory or a slaughterhouse feel intuitively wrong to me. I feel more loving and connected when I eat natural plant foods.

When I think about eating animals, however, I feel disconnected from empathy and love. I'm forced to connect with the reality of rotting, decaying flesh. I know that a living being has been violently killed before its natural life span is up, usually after being imprisoned its whole life under conditions any human would consider torturous. I know that slaughterhouses experience massive employee turnover because few human beings can stomach such work for long. I know that enormous amounts of resources must be expended and tons of waste produced in order to deliver animal foods to my plate. I see major incongruencies and unfairness, with some animals being valued as loving human companions while others are treated as edible substances, merely because of differences in taste and profitability. I see a living being that's been reduced to a dollar sign.

The only way I can justify eating animal foods is to disregard my intuition and dismiss my conscience. Since I've committed myself to conscious living, I cannot possibly do this. I've eaten no animal flesh since 1993 and no animal-derived products since 1997. I wish I could say that these realizations were the catalyst for those changes, but the truth is that I conducted a 30-day trial of eating no animal foods purely out of curiosity, and my awareness of the consequences of my food choices increased during and after the experiment to the point where I could never go back.

When I eat processed, packaged foods, I feel more foggy and disconnected. I see lifeless chemicals that may fuel my body but can never fully nourish me. I know such foods are marketed and sold based on their profitability, not their health properties, so these products don't feel loving to me. I see falsehood promoted as truth, fragmentation presented as wholeness, and weakness pitched as strength. Eating large quantities of such foods lowers my consciousness and makes me less of who I am.

What do you feel when you tune in to the foods you eat? Your impressions may be completely different from mine, and that's perfectly fine. Listen to your own feelings, not the echoes of other people's opinions. What does your intuition tell you?

Next, tune in and connect with your physical-activity patterns. What does your intuition say about your current exercise habits, work activities, and stress levels? Do you really need an expert to tell you where you can improve, or does your intuition reveal the first steps on the path of positive growth? Are you treating your body in a loving manner?

Of the foods you eat and the activities you experience, which ones are most compatible with the real you? Which ones are incompatible? Does killing and eating living creatures feel good to you, or does it turn you off? How do you feel about fruits, vegetables, grains, and legumes? Are you more naturally drawn to whole or processed foods? Can you feel the difference between loving and unloving choices? How do you feel about various forms of physical exercise? What do you perceive when you think about the physical elements of your daily routine, including your work?

Applying the principle of love to explore your deepest feelings isn't easy. Nevertheless, if you wish to grow into a more conscious human being, you must follow those answers wherever they lead. Don't deny what you know in your heart to be true. It's okay if you lack the strength to change right now. It's better to smoke a cigarette or down a glass of alcohol consciously, with full awareness that it's wrong for you, than to lower your consciousness and disconnect from your intuitive feelings.

Health and Power

You can probably guess that I'm going to tell you that your health is your responsibility, and of course you're right. In a world that isn't fully committed to health, the most natural and beneficial practices are often considered extreme. Favor a salad instead of a steak and you're labeled a health *nut*. Make a habit of daily exercise and you've become a fitness *freak*. Stop eating manufactured foods and you're a *fanatical* purist. The truth is that if the average person wouldn't consider your current health practices extreme, you probably aren't very healthy. In the United States, average people die of heart disease, cancer, or stroke, all of which are heavily influenced by lifestyle choices. *Average* is slow suicide.

In order to be healthy today, you must exercise your self-discipline to overcome the drag of social conditioning. Summon the maturity to make intelligent choices for yourself, regardless of what throngs of sick people encourage you to do.

Set physical goals that inspire you. Being slightly healthier than average is still unhealthy, so aim higher. What do you really want in this area? Do you want to be free of disease, to be physically strong, and to overflow with physical energy and vitality? Poor health limits your power; good health increases it.

Use progressive training to make incremental improvements in your health habits. Don't try to achieve perfection on your first try. Surely you can identify one small positive change to make. Kick off a 30-day trial today to implement that new habit. If you don't like it, you can always revert back. Remember that it's only 30 days. Diet and exercise are habitual activities and will have a major impact on your long-term health results. Use your self-discipline to practice the best habits you can today; then let them run on autopilot.

Health and Oneness

Turn the principle of oneness within and realize that the health of your body depends on the health of your cells, and vice versa. Your body and your cells are completely interdependent. Neither can survive and thrive without the other. Your body and mind are intimately connected as well. Buddha said, "To keep the body in good health is a duty" because good health is necessary to keep our minds strong and clear.

You'll have to decide whether to extend the principle of oneness beyond the human race. Will you apply this principle to other living creatures as well? For me, that extension feels right. If I'm totally honest with myself, I must admit that turning animals into food violates my sense of empathy and compassion, causing me to fall out of alignment with oneness. When I look at a puppy and a piglet, it doesn't seem fair to me that one is treated as a beloved pet while the other becomes a meal. Consequently, I favor fresh fruit as the largest part of my diet because eating fruit doesn't harm the plant that spawns it. The seeds can also be planted to grow even more fruit. Interestingly, I've found that shifting my diet in the direction of greater empathy and compassion for all creatures has yielded many health benefits as well. (If you care to read about my specific experiences in this area, please see the article "Why Vegan?" at **www.StevePavlina.com/vegan.**)

Turn oneness outward and realize that you influence others by your example. Your personal health habits affect us all. Have you ever felt more motivated to exercise after watching a top athlete? Did reading a book written by a *health nut* ever inspire you to improve your diet? Are you aware that you have a similar effect on everyone you interact with? By your example, you teach others how to live. What kind of example are you currently setting?

Team up with other health nuts, fitness freaks, and fanatical purists (that is, sane people) to work toward good health together. Loosen your ties to relationships that reinforce negative health habits, and favor those that encourage more positive ones. Treat your social circle as an extension of your own body.

In 1998, I trained for the Los Angeles marathon by going on many long runs along the beach. Unfortunately, when I went to sign up for the actual race, I discovered to my chagrin that the event was going to be held on my wedding day. When I informed Erin of this dilemma, the evil eye she proffered made it fairly clear that I'd have to miss the race and get married instead.

I still wanted to run the marathon, however, so I tried again the following year. This time I joined the L.A. Roadrunners, a popular marathon-training group that ran along Venice Beach every weekend. I loved the group runs and enjoyed them much more than training solo. One of my sisters also joined the group with me, so we were able to run together and enjoy many long talks. You can have quite a conversation during a 20-mile run.

However, fate struck again. I suffered a knee injury during the final week before the race and had to miss it. I wasn't willing to give up though, so the next year I trained again and successfully completed the marathon, but this time I went back to solo training. That was much less enjoyable, and I really missed the Roadrunners. The lesson I learned was that I enjoyed exercise more when I used it as a way to connect with like-minded people.

Many cities have fitness-oriented groups where people come together to work on their physical goals. Try a basic Internet search to see what's available near you. You may discover as I did that training with others is far more motivating than going it alone.

Despite its obviously personal nature, health isn't something to be considered in isolation. When one of us is sick, we all suffer for it in some small way. Because of the interconnected nature of human society, there's a practical limit as to how far an individual can race ahead in the quest for greater health. It's folly to ignore our interconnectedness.

For example, how will you escape the negative health effects of global pollution when all of the fresh water on earth is polluted with synthetic chemicals? It isn't enough to pursue health for yourself alone. If you want to be as healthy as possible, you must help others make healthier choices as well. As your individual health journey unfolds, share what you learn along the way to help others grow and improve. We're all in this together.

Health and Authority

Regardless of your current health knowledge or lack thereof, you're in command of your physical destiny. While you can certainly consult with experts, the only true health guru in your life is you. Your well-being is yours to manage. You can delegate control but never responsibility.

What passes for modern health care is still fairly primitive, sloppy, and error-prone, especially when compared to other technical disciplines. If you go to a doctor to report a health problem, there's a fair chance you'll be misdiagnosed, and you may be treated based on that. Even if you get a correct diagnosis, your treatment is likely to be qualified with words like *should, hopefully,* and *side effects.* Ask your doctor why the problem occurred and how to prevent it from happening again, and you may hear: "We aren't exactly sure."

If my auto mechanic ever said to me, "Your car should be drivable now, Mr. Pavlina. Of course, there may be some side effects, including shakiness, sudden deceleration, and fluid leakage, but hopefully it won't be too bad," I'd be inclined to take my business elsewhere.

Alternative health care isn't immune to such problems either, and we still end up with should's and maybe's. I'm not suggesting these problems are the fault of health practitioners. I'm sure they're doing the best they can. Nevertheless, these are issues we can't ignore.

What are your very best long-term health options? I don't know. I'm not you. If I were to explain to you in exact detail what works for me, it wouldn't mean you'd get the same results. Even if I could tell you what produces positive results for the average person, is that any guarantee it will work for you as well? When you consider your unique blend of genetic, environmental, and personality factors, how close to average are you, anyway?

The simple truth is that when it comes to the health of your own body, the only authority you can really trust is yourself, and even then you must still be careful to watch out for blocks like false beliefs and media conditioning. If I give you any particular advice in this area that doesn't resonate with you, you should reject it and trust your own judgment instead. That last sentence becomes rather dizzying if you consider that the statement also applies to itself, but I think you get the point I'm trying to make. You're the authority here, and you should only trust my advice to the degree that it's congruent with your own common sense.

If you can't blindly believe so-called experts, how can you possibly become a competent health authority? First, you can look closely at your own perceptions and predictions. Second, you can tune in and connect more deeply with the choices you've been making to see what your intuition has to say. And third, you can fill in the gaps with personal testing and experimentation. Sometimes when you aren't sure if a choice is right for you, the only way to learn the truth is to dive in and test it for a while.

I've had great success using 30-day trials for physical experimentation. That's how I became vegetarian and later vegan. It's also how I became an early riser, regularly waking up at 5 A.M. each morning, including weekends. In each case, I wasn't sure if the change was right for me, so I conducted a short-term trial to find out. Usually the results were conclusive one way or the other, and it was a no-brainer to either make the change permanent or drop it completely.

Sometimes my trial results were mixed. For example, in January 2008, I conducted a 30-day trial of a low-fat raw-foods diet. I ate nothing but raw fruits, vegetables, nuts, and seeds with only 10 percent of my calories coming from fat. I recorded daily logs of everything I ate in exacting detail and shared them on my Website as I went along (the final summary can be found at **www.StevePavlina.com/ raw**, if you're curious). Although that experiment didn't turn out as I expected, I still learned a great deal from it. It was by far the hardest 30-day trial I ever did, but one thing that motivated me to keep going was knowing that I wasn't just doing it for myself. I was also creating an enduring resource for others. Even though the trial didn't work out perfectly, it gave me enough information and experience to successfully become a raw foodist two months later. Of course, I'll continue to share updates on my Website as my diet keeps evolving.

Personal experimentation is a powerful tool for self-discovery. Try different diets. Test a variety of exercise routines. Experiment with sleep patterns. Find out what works best for you via direct trial and error.

There's always a risk when conducting such exercises, but blindly following social norms is inherently risky anyway. Remember that you're ultimately responsible for your own health decisions.

If you do conduct your own experiments, consider this additional advice. First, keep a training log to record your results, at least weekly if not daily. Your logs may prove extremely useful to you down the road, perhaps even years later, so be as honest as you can in your reporting. Second, consider sharing your records publicly, such as via a blog. This allows others to learn from your experiences as well. When I conducted my raw-food trial, I received a tremendous amount of encouragement, coaching, and practical advice from experienced raw foodists who could see exactly what I was eating day by day. This helped me stay on track and avoid some potential pitfalls during my trial. I really wish I'd kept daily logs of my earlier vegetarian and vegan 30-day trials, since I'd love to look back and see what I was eating then. Those notes would have been great resources to share publicly for the benefit of others, especially since my results were so positive.

When you get overwhelmingly positive results from a temporary experiment, make it permanent and lock in your gains. Allow this new habit to raise your baseline. If you continue making such personal upgrades year after year, you'll probably encounter some setbacks now and then; but in the long run, it's reasonable to expect that your health will see substantial improvements. For me, the biggest benefits have been mental rather than physical. Largely because of the health changes I made during the previous 15 years, my thinking is crisper and sharper than it's ever been, and I can concentrate very deeply while tuning out distractions. This benefits me personally as well as those I serve.

Your path to better health may follow a different route from mine, but the nice thing about universal principles is that they're independent of individual circumstances. You can use the same process I did to become the authority of your own body, even if you ultimately decide to manage yours differently from how I manage mine.

Health and Courage

Strive to adopt a health and fitness plan with a heart. Don't be intimidated by challenging physical goals. A weak mind creates a weak body. Turn the pursuit of health into a lifelong adventure. If a goal doesn't scare you a little, it probably isn't worth pursuing. Would you like to run a marathon or triathlon? Do you think mountain climbing could be a fun experience? Does earning a black belt in martial arts appeal to you? Take a break from the monotonous treadmill and do something physical that inspires you. Live the way you think a healthy and vital human being should.

Take the initiative to prevent health problems. Use diet and exercise to stave off disease and keep your body strong and energetic. Don't wait for a crisis to strike before taking action to improve your health. Receiving traditional medical treatment should be considered a last resort when preventive measures fail. It makes little sense for your primary health care to be provided by those who profit from your prolonged illness.

Keep your fitness routine simple and direct. Don't overcomplicate your life with fancy or expensive exercise equipment; and don't mistake manufactured supplements, powders, and shakes for a healthy, natural diet. Here's a simple rule of thumb that will save you a lot of money: if it comes in a can, bottle, or canister, you don't need it.

For many years, my sole exercise routine was to get up before dawn and go running outside for 25 to 45 minutes. I did that nearly every morning and enjoyed abundant physical energy and alertness throughout the day. On January 1, 1997, I made a New Year's resolution to exercise for at least 25 minutes every single day for the entire year. When it rained, I ran in the rain. When I was too tired, too sick, or didn't get home until after midnight, I still went out and exercised. I successfully completed that challenge without skipping a single day, soundly shredding all my previous excuses for not exercising. If you're worried about getting sick, take heart that regular exercise will strengthen your immune system considerably.

A little water falling from the sky is hardly an excuse to avoid exercising. In fact, it can be quite exhilarating. I once did a 12-mile training run with the L.A. Roadrunners under conditions of heavy rain and fierce wind. People driving past us honked their horns and waved encouraging gestures, probably impressed and amused by all the fitness freaks sloshing down Ocean Avenue. I don't recall the details of most of those old training runs, but I remember that particular one very vividly, even though it happened nine years ago. Two hours in the rain was a worthwhile trade for such a salient, fun memory. Incidentally, when I finally ran the L.A. Marathon, it rained continuously for the first two hours of the race.

It's better to apply your courage to the prevention of disease and the enjoyment of good health as opposed to being forced to face a major illness. But if you find yourself going the latter route, realize that the best health habits for reversing disease are the same ones that prevent it, and the habits that cause disease are the same ones that prolong it. It may take a lot of heart to break your most ingrained negative habits and recover from a serious illness, and there's no guarantee of success; but if you value your life, it's worth the effort to do what you can to restore your health and enjoy a few more days here.

Health and Intelligence

Intelligent health habits create long-term sustainability, enabling you to focus more time and energy on what's truly important to you. When you put good habits on autopilot, you don't have to fuss over your health as much. You can simply use your body as a vehicle for creative self-expression, knowing that your background habits are successfully maintaining—and even improving—your health.

While it can be very challenging to install good habits, once they're running strong, the effort to maintain them should be minimal. In fact, you should generally expect a net gain from your best health habits, even in the short term. For example, regular aerobic exercise allows me to feel refreshed with significantly less sleep, so the habit more than pays for itself. Snacking on fresh fruit throughout the day is also very efficient. Peeling and eating a few bananas is virtually effortless, and the payoff is increased energy and alertness without any drowsiness. A collection of healthy habits creates an ongoing sense of positive flow.

The human body is an exquisitely beautiful wonder to behold, but it's more important to be healthy on the inside than to look like a supermodel on the outside. When it comes to body image, your most authentic choice is to accept and love yourself as you are, including those parts you may not consider attractive. Do your best to ignore the social conditioning that says you have to look a certain way. If you look like a toad, there are plenty of color-blind people who will take you for a princely frog.

✦ ✦

All of your experiences in the physical universe come through your physical body. It's your primary vehicle of interaction here, so it makes sense to take proper care of it. Strive to get the most from the make and model you currently inhabit. Build up some excess capacity so that you can flow through your days feeling alert and energized instead of tired and sickly. Even if your health isn't perfect, take a moment to appreciate whatever level of well-being you *do* have. Learn to feel grateful just for being alive in a physical form on this wonderful planet.

Maybe someday we'll be ready to upgrade these squishy husks to nearly indestructible android bodies, or perhaps we'll simply transfer our conscious minds into a collective singularity, but at the time of this writing, that day hasn't arrived. Consequently, I recommend that you maintain your current hardware for the long haul, instead of running it into the ground.

Of course, one of the best reasons to be healthy is that good health will expand your capacity to build and enjoy loving . . .

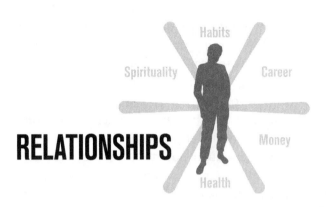

Chapter 12

Habits

Spirituality

Career

RELATIONSHIPS

Money

Health

"The worst solitude is to be destitute of sincere friendship."
— SIR FRANCIS BACON

Human relationships are a tremendous source of learning and growth. Our greatest rewards in life originate there, as do our most challenging problems. Relationships can be complicated and confusing at times, but as you'll soon learn, the principles of truth, love, and power bring an elegant simplicity to the picture, helping us build conscious, loving connections.

We have a rich menu of intimate relationship possibilities to choose from. Some people prefer to be completely monogamous, opting for a single romantic partner until finally separated by death. Others prefer serial monogamy, experiencing a variety of partners in succession.

Still others enjoy polyamorous relationships, favoring multiple partners at the same time. And finally, some opt for celibacy and channel their romantic energies elsewhere. Some people are straight, others gay, and some bisexual. There are no right or wrong answers here. You have the freedom to direct the course of your relationships however you see fit, with the caveat that your partners willingly choose to share those experiences with you.

Since some of the ideas in this chapter run afoul of mainstream social conditioning, you may encounter parts you disagree with, and that's fine. Aside from demonstrating how to apply the seven universal principles to your relationships, I don't aim to convince you to change your particular values to match my own. I do, however, want to challenge you to question your assumptions about relationships and make your own conscious choices, even though your preferences may differ wildly from mine.

Our lives are filled with a myriad of basic relationship forms: family members, friends, acquaintances, co-workers, intimate partners, adversaries, and strangers. Regardless of your current situation, the principles of truth, love, and power can help you improve all of these. In this chapter I'll mainly focus on intimate relationships, but the concepts apply to all other human connections.

Relationships and Truth

Let's begin with a basic assessment of your current circumstances. What do your perceptions tell you? What's the truth?

How do you feel about your current relationships? Are you happy or dissatisfied? Do you feel connected to the people around you, or are you disconnected and lonely? Are your relationships rooted in truth, or have they been infected by falsehood? Do the people in your life know you for who you are, or do you only reveal a shadow of your true self? Do your relationships empower or disempower you? Do you have what you want, or is something still missing?

Be honest in assessing your own role. What do you contribute to the people closest to you? What do you have to offer a partner? Do others benefit by having you in their lives, or do you take advantage of them without providing much in return?

Look beyond the external forms of your relationships, and seek the real truth about them. For example, a marriage can be a label to describe a legal partnership, or it can represent a deep interpersonal bond between two people. What do you see when you look behind the labels? What's the true nature of your relationships?

Observe the breadth and depth of your current relationships. Do you have a constant influx of new people coming into your life? How many people would claim to know you if asked? How deep are your bonds? Which people would consider you a close friend or an intimate partner? Would you like to have more connections in your life? Would you like to deepen any of your existing connections?

As you assess your current situation, keep in mind that your relationships exist only in your mind. Your perceptions define them. In order to accurately assess your current status, you must look within. Accept your thoughts as they come, and don't be surprised if your feelings about certain relationships are ambivalent or unclear.

Now turn your attention to your predictions. Where do you honestly see your current relationships heading? Which ones are growing closer, and which are drifting apart? Where is your momentum taking you? What does your present situation tell you about your future?

Obviously there's too much uncertainty in human relationships to be perfectly accurate in making predictions, but all you need to do here is make reasonable guesses. Your honest expectations, even if they may turn out to be inaccurate, still contain a great deal of truth because they reveal your beliefs. Your beliefs will affect your actions, thereby causing future changes in the direction of your relationships. Therefore, it's important to become aware of your honest predictions because such awareness gives you the power to consciously change what isn't working.

Pay special attention to your feelings, since they contain their own predictive intelligence. Positive emotions represent positive predictions, and negative emotions reveal negative predictions. Sometimes you may feel like a relationship is declining even when everything seems great on the surface. Then you may have a discussion with your partner and discover that there are important overlooked problems you need to work through together.

There are times when I have a bad feeling about my relationship with Erin. On the surface, everything might seem fine, and I can't think of anything that's wrong, but from time to time, I'll get this nagging feeling that there's an invisible wall growing between us. If I try to dismiss such notions, they only persist. When I tell Erin how I'm feeling and we talk through it, invariably it turns out that unresolved issues have been creeping into our lives, causing hidden resentment to build. When we bring those problems to the surface, even if we don't solve them right away, the feeling of closeness returns once again. Usually, we end up feeling closer than ever.

I've thus learned to place a great deal of trust in my feelings when it comes to relationships. When something feels wrong to me, I know the best thing I can do is go to the other person and explain that something doesn't seem right so that we can work together to sort it out. When you bring truth to your relationships, you build closeness and trust.

Falsehood is clearly damaging, but so is inattention. If you stop deliberately injecting fresh truth into your relationships on a regular basis, distance is created by default. Truth isn't merely the absence of lying; truth is an essential relationship activity.

Accept whatever truths you discover about your relationships, even if you feel trapped in your current situation. Don't succumb to denial. If you feel depressed and lonely, accept those feelings. If you feel your marriage is headed for divorce, accept your honest predictions. If you feel completely stuck and powerless to change, accept that. Never close your eyes to the truth. If you want to grow beyond your current limitations, you must first learn to stop resisting where you are.

Finally, it's important to accept the true nature of human relationships. All of them are guaranteed to be temporary. No matter how strong your bonds are, they'll all eventually end in separation or loss. No relationship can possibly endure, at least not in physical form. Allow your awareness of this truth to give you a deeper appreciation of the people in your life. When you accept that your relationships are temporary, they'll become more precious to you, and you'll be less likely to take other people for granted.

Relationships and Love

You build and expand your relationships by deciding to connect with other people and allowing them to connect with you. The most basic way this happens is through direct communication. The more you communicate with your fellow human beings, the more connected you become. These links allow you to enjoy the emotional side of love as you develop feelings of closeness and caring.

Erin and I have an extremely close relationship because we spend a great deal of time talking to each other. When we first met in 1994, we'd spend hours on the phone discussing anything and everything that was important to us, and this habit of connecting through conversation has been with us ever since. I love that Erin brings a unique perspective to every subject, and I value her opinions and insights. I know that she feels the same about me as well.

Communication is only the beginning, however, since human relationships have the potential to move from connection to communion. Even with frequent interpersonal communication, there's a risk of falling into a rut and hitting a plateau. Exchanges that are lacking in truth, love, or power eventually grow stale, but when all three elements are present, the blocks to deeper levels of connection and closeness are removed.

If you consider your default manner of communication, you'll probably find that it's unbalanced. Most likely you favor one or two channels instead of using all three. For example, I have a habit of leaning too much on truth and power. I love exploring new truths, and I especially enjoy empowering and challenging people to take action. My weakness is that my communication can be lacking in empathy and compassion. Erin, on the other hand, is very good at communicating with truth and love; however, she has a harder time motivating people to action because she sometimes overlooks the power channel.

Think about some of the people in your life and see if you can identify their dominant communication channels. Which people favor truth, wanting to talk about facts and exchange information? Who reaches out mostly with love, wanting to discuss anything and everything just for the sake of connecting? Who communicates with power, trying to drive people to action and make changes? You'll see some aspects of truth, love, and power in all communication, but most people tend to lean heavily on one or two channels.

What mix of truth, love, and power do you use to connect with others? Realize that your weakest channel will be the source of many of your communication problems. You can actually achieve significant growth in your relationships by learning to use your weakest channel when communicating in addition to your strengths.

Learning to communicate with love was a tremendous challenge for me. I was raised by two left-brained parents, my father being an aerospace software manager and my mother a college math professor. The dominant communication channels in our home were truth and power, with love trailing far behind. I don't recall phrases such as "I love you" being spoken much at all, and hugging was an uncommon occurrence. Consequently, by the time I reached adulthood, my communication was predominantly rooted in truth and power. My ability to connect with empathy and compassion was weak; in fact, seeing others connect with love often made me uncomfortable.

Erin, on the other hand, was raised in a home where love and truth dominated, and power was nearly absent. Her family was very caring and affectionate and enjoyed spending time together. Erin and her siblings were invited to participate in family decisions, including planning vacations. However, she grew up in a fairly undisciplined environment that lacked strong guidance, and this caused numerous power problems for her later in life. For example, as a young adult, she found herself in an abusive relationship; and it took her years to summon the will to finally leave, fearing for her safety as she did.

When Erin and I began our relationship, the channel of truth was our dominant means of connecting. We were both very curious people and could talk exhaustively about many different subjects. Consequently, we became very close in a short period of time, and we absolutely loved each other's company. As our relationship evolved, we helped each other grow tremendously.

When I first met Erin, she was working part-time as a secretary while attending graduate school. I brought a new level of power to her life, encouraging her to quit her uninspiring job and to identify and pursue her dreams. Instead of using my power to dominate and control her, my alignment with truth enabled me to use my power to do what was truly best for her. As Erin will readily attest, my influence helped her connect with her power in a way she'd never done before, and she's been extremely happy with the results.

Erin had a similar effect on me by teaching me to get in touch with my heart. I'd never met such an openly loving and compassionate person before. We met a few months after I graduated from college, a time when I was more interested in computers than human beings. Because she was aligned with truth, I recognized that her loving side was totally genuine. She easily slid past my shields and brought out my natural compassion and empathy in a way I'd never have thought possible. It was Erin's influence that eventually motivated me to switch my career from game development to personal development. If we hadn't met, there's no way I'd be doing work focused on helping people grow.

In order to connect, we need a base level of compatibility. There has to be some overlap in communication styles with which to form a link. If there's insufficient overlap, a close connection simply won't take root. In order to grow, however, we need some differences in our strategies. Otherwise we quickly hit a plateau in our ability to connect. Our similarities bring us together, but our differences help us grow.

Now that you're aware of the importance of truth, love, and power, you can consciously direct the evolution of your relationships, and you can also diagnose problems. If I go to Erin and tell her I'm feeling disconnected, her face brightens because she knows she can help me. The same happens when she comes to me and asks for my help in setting a new direction or deciding which projects she should focus on next. These efforts not only help us grow as individuals; they also deepen our intimate connection.

If you're in a relationship right now, can you identify your primary area of compatibility? Do you connect on truth, sharing information and learning from each other? Do you connect on love, expressing affection and enjoying each other's company? Or do you connect on power, encouraging and supporting each other to achieve your dreams? While all three may be present to some degree, which strategy is the most dominant?

The practical application here is that when you know your dominant connection strategy, you can use it deliberately to regain your closeness whenever you start feeling a little distant from each other. Similarly, you can use your differences to intentionally help each other grow. Through our relationships we can consciously increase our alignment with truth, love, and power.

Relationships and Power

The best relationships serve to increase your power rather than diminish it. The point of entering into a relationship is to increase your alignment with truth, love, and power, thereby experiencing greater wholeness. If a connection pulls you further out of alignment, it isn't worth maintaining. The longer you cling to disempowering relationships, the weaker you become. Your best relationships will help you meet your needs, fulfill your desires, gain clarity, and feel more connected. They'll add value to your life in ways that are important to you.

If you succumb to relationships that weaken you or make you feel trapped, you're giving your power away. It's your responsibility to remedy such situations, regardless of the circumstances. Realize that you can choose to leave at any time. There may be negative consequences to doing so, such as loss of income if you leave an abusive partner, but such problems are temporary. When you drop disempowering relationships, you can expect to regain your power soon enough. Unfortunately, the very nature of abusive connections is that they undermine you to the point that it's hard to even imagine being strong again. If you find yourself in a situation that weakens you and you don't choose to leave, then you're choosing to stay, which means you're choosing to abuse yourself.

A conscious relationship requires effort and commitment on both sides. One person can't carry the whole thing alone. If you're spending more time fighting resistance instead of sharing love, you're better off letting go. Put yourself in a position to enjoy something more mutually rewarding, and don't settle for less than you're worth. Empowering yourself isn't a selfish act. When you hold your relationships to the standard of empowerment, you grow stronger, and your strength flows out to the people around you as well.

What do you do if your most disempowering relationships are with your own family members? There's no honor in remaining loyal to someone who disempowers you. When you weaken yourself like that, you do the same to the people around you as well, dragging everyone else down with you. Don't force yourself and others to suffer from a misguided sense of loyalty. If you're a very loyal person, then give your commitment to those who actually deserve it; don't blindly yield it to those who claim it as their birthright.

What do you really want from your relationships? What character qualities do you find most attractive in others? While you're always free to connect with anyone at any time, it's important to set standards for deeper levels of bonding. Allow yourself to form friendships and even intimate partnerships with people who empower you and increase your alignment with truth, love, and power. Filter out those who would only lead you astray.

When it comes to long-term relationships, I choose my friends and associates carefully. I favor friends with high personal standards, people who are already strongly aligned with truth, love, and power. I don't form very close bonds with those who are dishonest, unintelligent, unaware, apathetic, abusive, unfocused, undisciplined, or irresponsible. My work puts me in direct contact with a wide variety of individuals, and I'm happy to help everyone when I can, but I only develop deeper relationships with the ones who meet my personal criteria.

On the other hand, when someone *does* meet my standards for friendship, we may move from being casual acquaintances to close friends very quickly. The single most important factor I look for is a commitment to conscious growth. I'm immediately drawn to such people and find it easy to connect with them. Their particular position is largely irrelevant to me. I don't care if they're teenagers or seniors, Christian or Buddhist, rich or poor. Our mutual interest in growth becomes a compatible point of friendship, while our differences allow us to learn from each other.

Before I had such standards, I found my relationships much less fulfilling. I still had an easy time making friends, but too often I'd bring people into my life who drew me further out of alignment with truth, love, and power. For example, during my late teens, I got sucked into the college drinking scene. I went from never consuming alcohol to getting totally drunk on a weekly basis. At one party, I drank the equivalent of 14 shots and woke up the next morning with virtually no memory of the previous night. I had to ask my friends what happened. Apparently, I threw up on someone, passed out in my own vomit, and eventually staggered down the hall back to my dorm room and fell asleep. When I drifted apart from those friends, I never had problems with alcohol again. Today if I say to Erin, "Hey, let's get drunk tonight," she'll just laugh at me because she finds alcohol completely unappealing, and she knows I feel the same way.

It's been said that you can predict your future by looking at the people with whom you spend the most time. That isn't far from the truth. Your relationships will have a tremendous influence on your self-development. If you find yourself using all your power and self-discipline to resist the negative influence of your own friends, you're fighting a losing battle. Use your power to break off such relationships, and surround yourself with people who naturally empower you. As a general rule, whenever you find yourself stuck in a disempowering environment, don't fight the situation. Just get up and leave. If you still wish to address the problems of that environment afterward, you'll be in a stronger position to do so from the outside looking in.

I know there are times when it can be difficult in the extreme to leave a disempowering relationship. The degree of challenge doesn't change the solution, however. You'll actually free up tremendous energy when you stop struggling against the currents and start thinking about how to escape such a negative situation. Even while you re-main physically stuck, you'll feel more empowered as soon as you begin turning in the right direction. That's because it's your alignment with power that makes you truly stronger, and this alignment can be achieved regardless of external circumstances. Power is a direction, not a position.

The best thing you can do to empower others is to empower yourself. You'll do a lot more good for others when you keep yourself strong. Weakening yourself helps no one. In order for the whole body to be strong, the individual cells must take good care of themselves.

Be careful to avoid relinquishing your power to your relationships. In order to achieve an empowering level of *interdependence,* you must retain a reasonable degree of *independence.* If you find yourself unable to make decisions as an individual and must defer to someone else to make all the important choices, you're giving away your power and shirking your responsibility to live your own life. As Kahlil Gibran wrote in *The Prophet:* "Let there be spaces in your togetherness."

If you want to attract high-caliber partners, the best thing you can do is to improve your own alignment with truth, love, and power. If you find yourself constantly attracting the wrong kinds of people—or if you have trouble attracting anyone at all—it's because you're out of alignment with these fundamental principles. If you think the solution is to apply phony techniques to charm the right person, then you're succumbing to falsehood and deception, which will only backfire on you. If you want to attract someone honest, work on your own hon-esty. If you want someone loving and caring, seek to deepen those qualities in yourself. If you want someone bold and adventurous, work on your courage.

While there's a wide variety of personality traits people find attrac-tive, the principles of truth, love, and power are universal attractors. No sane person wants a relationship filled with lies and deception. No one wants an apathetic or uncaring partner. And no one intentionally enters an abusive relationship. Despite our differences, we're all attracted to the same fundamental qualities in each other. We all desire relationships centered in truth, love, and power. The more you develop these within yourself, the more universally attractive you'll become.

Relationships and Oneness

When we want to reach out and develop new relationships, we need to remember that everyone else is already connected to us. We're all individual cells in the same body, and the notion that we're all separate and distinct beings is nothing but an illusion. Technically we don't have to build relationships with other people from scratch. We need only tune in to the fundamental connection that's already there.

Erin and I have both found that when we adopt the mind-set of oneness, we attract compatible new people into our lives with relative ease. We often form new relationships through synchronistic encounters. An unusual or unlikely series of events leads us to the right people at the right times, and we get the eerie feeling we were somehow destined to meet. In fact, this is precisely how Erin and I met. We both attended the same college at the same time, but we didn't meet until a chance encounter after graduation. We had so many interests in common that it seemed like we were meant to be together.

More recently, Erin and I spent several days in Sedona, Arizona. We walked into a touristy-looking shop, picked up a strong vibe from a woman we'd never met, and started up a conversation. Thirty minutes later we'd become friends and said good-bye with hugs. A week later, this woman sent us a gift in the mail to thank us for some guidance we gave her. For Erin and me, this has become an increasingly common occurrence. Before I experienced the mind-set of oneness, I could never walk into some random store and expect to be hugging someone I'd never met before. Be prepared for fascinating social experiences as your alignment with oneness increases.

I think the reason this mind-set is so effective is that when you assume a preexisting connection, people tend to pick up on your openness and respond in kind. Apparently, the best way to break the ice with someone is to assume there never was any ice to begin with. This is especially true of those who are very conscious and self-aware. Such people naturally respond to friendly overtures from like-minded individuals, and hurtful rejections are rare. If you approach someone from a mind-set of oneness and are rejected harshly, it's a safe bet the other person isn't aligned with this principle and would therefore be incompatible with you anyway. The nice thing about oneness is that it naturally attracts others who feel the same and filters out those who don't. The more you resonate with oneness, the more oneness-oriented relationships you'll attract, thereby further reinforcing your experience.

Social conditioning teaches you to focus on the risk of rejection when approaching someone you've never met. Oneness teaches you to focus on the opportunities for connection. A rejection is a sign of incompatibility, so it can't really be considered a bad outcome. On the other hand, once a positive connection is made, there's the possibility that both people will be utterly transformed for the better. This can hardly be considered a risk; rather, it's the kind of bet that's worth making repeatedly.

In addition to initiating new connections, be open to receiving advances from others. When someone makes an overture, respond with empathy and kindness. Be inviting and friendly. If you realize the connection isn't right for you, let the other person down easily. When you find it necessary to turn people down, be careful not to disempower them. Be honest but gentle. On the other hand, if you sense a compatible connection off the bat, lower your shields, allow your feelings to guide you, and let the relationship develop as it may.

Many committed relationships succumb to cheating or divorce because one or both partners end up feeling disconnected for too long. They allow themselves to connect with their primary relationship partner but not with anyone else. Such misguided loyalty becomes a controlling trap that knocks people out of alignment with oneness. This creates strong cravings for more genuine connections, forcing people either to settle for isolation or to seek new intimacy outside the primary relationship. A belief that such connections are wrong makes the problem worse, causing people to lie about their affairs, thus creating even more distance from oneness.

When you're in a close relationship, respect the fact that your partner isn't your property. Don't cling to other people so tightly that you cut them off from being able to connect with anyone but you. In order to maximize your opportunities for conscious growth, you must be open to forming new connections with a variety of people, especially when you're in a committed relationship.

Social conditioning tends to fail us in this area. We're encouraged to find and marry a single partner, focusing our deepest levels of physical and emotional intimacy on only one person. However, simple observation tells us that relationships of this nature usually fail, ending in separation, divorce, or estrangement. Even when the legal marriage doesn't terminate and cohabitation continues, the bond often stagnates and fails to satisfy either person's long-term emotional needs.

Committed relationships require placing a high value on your partner's overall well-being. This includes honoring the need to connect with other people, sometimes casually and other times more intimately. If your primary relationship prevents you from connecting deeply with others, you have a cage, not a conscious partnership.

Relationships and Authority

You're in charge of your own destiny. While chance encounters may play an important role in your life, you'll get the best results by consciously deciding what you want and taking action to get there. Taking command of your relationships doesn't mean controlling or dominating other people. It simply means holding yourself in high enough esteem to know you deserve to experience the connections you desire.

Because of the inherently personal nature of this area of life, you can't simply delegate it to someone else. If you want to be effective at connecting with others, you must strive to become your own relationship authority.

For my part, I found it very difficult to develop my interpersonal skills. I was fairly shy growing up. In kindergarten, I was the kid you'd find playing alone in the sandbox, preferring to connect with sand toys than with other children. I staunchly avoided anything that forced me to exert myself socially. I attended a private all-boys high school, which was wonderful for me academically but held me back from developing my ability to interact with the opposite sex. During my teen years, I felt more at home in the orderly digital world of computers than in the chaotic company of human beings. Consequently, as my technical skills surged ahead, my social skills fell even further behind.

When I started my game-development business after college, I navigated the technical hurdles with relative ease, but I was frequently blindsided by the human element. I repeatedly chose to do business with the wrong people at the wrong times because I was a poor judge of character. With a great deal of help from Erin, I gradually developed better interpersonal intelligence, and my people skills improved by leaps and bounds. Looking back, I can scarcely believe some of the mistakes I made, but I was simply too ignorant to know any better. The change I experienced was so great that I actually shifted from introvert to extrovert on a standard personality test.

Some people say you can fake social confidence by putting yourself in the right frame of mind. As I mentioned in Chapter 5, I think the *fake it till you make it* strategy is a big mistake. It's better to put in the time to build real social skills instead of falsely pretending to be something you're not.

While you can certainly improve your relationship skills through trial and error, I think it's easier to enlist the help of a mentor; however, this will only work if you respect and apply your mentor's advice. When I was in college, I hired a personal coach for several months. I only wanted him to help me improve my academic productivity, but he kept trying to help me with my social skills. He knew that I was lacking in that area due to a personality assessment I completed before our first coaching call. He kept giving me assignments such as "Go out and smile at ten people today." But since I wasn't committed to making such changes, I ignored his advice and eventually ended the coaching relationship. When I met Erin, however, I was in a more receptive state of mind, so I was able to apply her ideas with less resistance.

Finding a social mentor shouldn't be too difficult. Just identify someone you know who seems to have an easy time connecting with people, someone whose interpersonal skills are more developed than yours. Tell that person that you wish to improve your social skills; and ask for pointers, advice, and perhaps an ongoing coaching relationship. My experience is that most folks are flattered by such requests, often finding it a fun challenge to try to turn a wallflower into a social butterfly. If for some reason you don't know anyone who can coach you, feel free to ask for advice in the Social & Relationships discussion forum on my Website (**www.StevePavlina.com/forums**), and I'm sure you'll get plenty of suggestions for where to begin.

Interpersonal skills ultimately must be developed through action. It isn't enough to search the Web or read books on how to connect with people. At some point you must put your ideas into practice. The more firsthand experience you gain, the more comfortable you'll feel, and the more your natural self will emerge.

Relationships and Courage

Courage plays a variety of important roles in human relationships. First, you need courage to initiate new connections and overcome the fear of rejection. Second, you need courage to intimately connect with people. Third, you need courage to face the truth about relationships that have gone awry. And finally, you need courage to end those relationships that no longer serve you.

If you want to bring new relationships into your life, don't wait for others to come to you. You must take the initiative. In the long run, waiting causes too many missed opportunities and leads to regret. If you're hesitant to initiate contact, use the progressive-training method from Chapter 6 to gradually build your courage, or recruit a social mentor as discussed in the previous section.

When meeting someone new, my favorite opening line is simply: "Hi, I'm Steve." I prefer to be direct and straightforward instead of using a disingenuous approach. If I get a cold response, I move on. Someone who'd respond with aloofness to a friendly overture isn't going to be compatible with me anyway, so there's no need for me to push such people to connect. I'd rather engage with someone who's naturally open and friendly instead of trying to reel in a cold fish.

Dealing with rejection and occasional embarrassment is a small price to pay for the rich rewards of human relationships. Your imagination may transform such fear into a fire-breathing dragon, but in reality, it's nothing but a puny imp guarding a massive treasure, easily defeated once you finally decide to face it down. The biggest risks are missing out on laughs you never shared, people you never helped, and the potential partner you sentenced to solitude. That's way too high a price for avoiding a little harmless rejection or embarrassment. In the long run, you probably won't regret the connections you made that didn't work out; you'll regret the ones you never made, forever wondering what might have been.

From time to time, stop and ask the heart question with respect to your relationships: *Does this relationship have a heart?* Then consciously decide which ones you want to maintain, which you want to deepen, and which you want to break off. Don't settle for a life filled with shallow, empty interaction. Go for deep connections, and ensure your life is filled with plenty of heart.

One of the most difficult challenges involves confronting a relationship that has gone sour. Negative emotions such as sadness, resentment, anger, guilt, and worry make the risk seem much greater. If you find yourself facing such a situation, trust the principles of truth, love, and power to guide you. Have a heart-to-heart talk with your partner, and honestly share your thoughts and feelings. When you do so, focus on sharing the truth of what you feel instead of jumping to conclusions or placing blame. To ensure you're speaking the truth, use first-person sentences: *I feel . . . I believe . . . I'm concerned that . . .* This normally creates much less resistance in the other person than second-person sentences: *You said . . . You made me . . . You always . . .*

When discussing relationship problems with your partner, don't hold back. Speak your truth, regardless of what you think the consequences will be. Don't be surprised if the other person responds defensively at first. Just keep talking and listening, and do your best to work through the defensiveness. Make it clear that you're seeking truth, and ask your partner to share a similar commitment.

There have been multiple times in my relationship with Erin when I thought we were close to breaking up. It seemed like too many problems had infected our marriage, creating a noticeable disconnect between us and causing our relationship to fall out of alignment with truth, love, and power.

But when we finally sat down together and talked things through, sometimes for hours at a time, we reached a new level of closeness and intimacy. In order to deepen the relationship, we had to be willing to risk losing it. We had to trust that aligning ourselves with truth, love, and power would lead to the best outcome for both of us. So far, that approach has always brought us closer.

You may find that aligning yourself with truth, love, and power requires that you end a relationship. If your partner is leading you away from a principle-centered life and is unwilling or incapable of correcting that problem, you're better off leaving. Free yourself to enjoy a new connection that increases your alignment with truth, love, and power. When you end a relationship, be direct, honest, compassionate, and strong. Speak your truth, and let the cards fall where they will. There's no dishonor in ending something (including a long-term marriage) that doesn't fulfill you. You have every right to pursue your own happiness.

Don't confuse the question of whether or not you should leave with your prospects for a new relationship. If it's clear that your current situation is leading you astray, end it. Once you're on your own again, you'll have the opportunity to attract a new partner. It's unlikely that you'll be able to accurately assess your chances of entering a new relationship while you're still clinging to your old one. Everyone around you will perceive you as unavailable, so you won't be able to get a clear sense of where you stand until you've already moved on.

Since all human relationships are impermanent, live with the awareness that every one of your current connections will eventually end. Take the time to appreciate them while they last, and don't take them for granted. Even when a relationship ends in death, it can still continue in your thoughts. The memories of loving relationships can become your most sacred treasures.

Relationships and Intelligence

Do your best to build authentic relationships with other people. They won't ever turn out perfectly, but perfection isn't necessary. The wheels on your car aren't perfect circles, but they still roll just fine. Similarly, none of your relationships will be perfectly aligned with truth, love, and power, but they can still provide incredible growth experiences.

One of the best things you can do to attract new people into your life is to focus on your own creative self-expression. By expressing yourself authentically, you draw others to you, making it easier to form compatible new relationships.

When I express myself through my writing and speaking, I receive a lot of feedback. After a speech, people come up to me and introduce themselves. After I post each new article on my Website, people e-mail me their thoughts about it. These initial contacts have led to the formation of many new relationships, which then flow back into my creative output. New contacts inspire new article ideas, often by directly telling me their suggestions, and fresh creative output draws a steady stream of people into my life. Ultimately, this creates a positive cycle of flow.

Most of the growth you experience as a human being will come from your interactions with other people. Sometimes that growth will be straightforward and predictable, such as that from a teacher-student relationship. Other times it will take many twists and turns, such as that from the relationship between two intimate lovers. In all its various forms, human relationships are a beauty to behold, well worth the price of admission.

Sharing your life with others is one of the best parts of being human, but it doesn't come without risk. Unlike other aspects of personal development, the stakes are higher with relationships because your mistakes could potentially hurt someone deeply. There's no getting around that risk completely, but the decision to align yourself with truth, love, and power will help guide you through the major stumbling blocks. When you make mistakes, do your best to forgive yourself, forgive others, and move on.

Congratulations for making it this far! In our final chapter together, we'll expand our horizons to take personal development beyond the physical plane and into the realm of . . .

✦ ✦ ✦ ✦

Chapter 13

SPIRITUALITY

> *"History does not record anywhere at any time a religion that has any rational basis. Religion is a crutch for people not strong enough to stand up to the unknown without help. But, like dandruff, most people do have a religion and spend time and money on it and seem to derive considerable pleasure from fiddling with it."*
>
> — ROBERT HEINLEIN

For the purposes of this chapter, the word *spirituality* refers to your collection of beliefs about reality, including your understanding of how reality works, as well as your personal role in the universe. Whether you participate in a popular religion or take an independent path, whether you believe in divine creation or adhere to strict physical objectivity, your beliefs about reality define the overall context of your life. In this sense, all of us are spiritual beings because we all have certain beliefs about reality. Even to believe nothing can still be considered part of a spiritual belief system.

Your spiritual growth is an integral part of the process of human development. The principles of truth, love, and power don't dictate a specific spiritual philosophy, so there's plenty of freedom to explore a variety of beliefs. However, the principles do establish that the highest ideal for your spiritual philosophy is intelligence. If your beliefs don't fulfill the requirements of intelligence at the very least, they can't be considered spiritually sound because they'd be in violation of universal principles. If a spiritual philosophy succumbs to falsehood, if it disconnects you from life, or if it weakens you, it runs afoul of the principles and will only lead you astray.

Social conditioning teaches us to have strong attachments to our spiritual beliefs to the point of integrating such beliefs into our identities. We say, "I *am* a Christian," or "I *am* an agnostic," as if such philosophies define us as human beings and can't be changed. In this chapter, I'll challenge you to look at your spiritual beliefs through the lenses of truth, love, and power. My goal isn't to convince you to follow any particular practice but rather to help you bring greater conscious awareness to your current spiritual life.

Spirituality and Truth

A sound spiritual philosophy must be firmly rooted in truth. This requires that we strive to perceive reality as accurately as possible. How exactly can we achieve accuracy when trying to perceive the true nature of reality? We can't just use our eyes and ears to look up the meaning of life.

A practical solution to this dilemma is to view reality through multiple belief systems in order to seek the big picture. Your beliefs act as lenses that cause you to focus on different aspects of reality. A Muslim, a Buddhist, and an agnostic may all view the world differently, yet there are clearly areas where their perceptions overlap. When we dismiss the incongruencies, we find there are areas of consensus. What's most notable is that the commonalities consist of the universal principles of truth, love, and power. To the degree that various spiritual philosophies agree with each other, they all encourage their practitioners to seek greater alignment with truth, love, and power. In the areas where they don't agree, you'll typically find falsehood, disconnection, and disempowerment. Despite the wide range of spiritual belief systems, it's wonderful to see that the common denominator is that we all inherently value these three fundamental principles.

Stereo vision is one of our more fascinating human abilities. Our eyeballs capture 2-D snapshots of our environment, and our brains and visual circuitry rapidly combine them into 3-D images. Even though each eye perceives reality in two dimensions, by combining the data from both eyes in a specific way, we perceive our visual fields in apparent 3-D. This image is richer than either of its 2-D components. You could also say it's a more useful representation of reality than the raw, preprocessed data taken in by our eyes. The combined input from all of our physical senses creates a rich web of sensory information. Consequently, when we go out to dinner with friends, the sights, sounds, smells, tastes, and textures of the evening create an experience that's greater than the sum of its parts.

Spiritually, we also have access to a rich set of input. Unfortunately, most of us are taught to devote our attention to a small subset of that input and tune out the rest as irrelevant or misleading. This spiritual blindness creates functional problems for us. Such problems manifest in many forms, including depression, loneliness, hopelessness, and meaninglessness.

Just as your physical senses act as lenses through which you perceive different subsets of reality, your spiritual senses also act as cognitive filtering mechanisms. These filters allow you to focus on bits and pieces of preprocessed information which may or may not be useful to you. The more spiritual sensory data you can access and comprehend, the richer your spiritual life will be, and the more accurately it will model truth.

Your spiritual sensory equipment includes:

- First-, second-, and third-person viewpoints (I/we, you, it/they)

- Subjective (consciousness is primary) and objective (physical world is primary) viewpoints

- Intuition and gut instincts

- Feelings and emotions

- Logic and reason

- Dreams and visions

- Religious and philosophical beliefs (Christianity, Buddhism, atheism, skepticism, Darwinism, romanticism, and the like)

- Cultural, social, political, and economic beliefs (stereo-types, gender roles, fashion preferences, citizenship)

- Functional beliefs (how to earn a living, what to eat, how to communicate)

- Personal beliefs (goals, values, expectations)

Suppose you're cooking dinner for yourself. You can use your eyes to measure the ingredients, your ears to listen for the timer beeping, your nose to inhale the aromas, and your tongue to taste the result. If you wanted to do so, you could rely solely upon just one or two of your senses to prepare a meal, but you'd probably find it more difficult to achieve a good outcome.

Similarly, when we confront the key spiritual questions of our lives, such as *Who am I?* and *What is my purpose in life?* we can consult the full spectrum of sensory channels available to us, or we can limit our input to a small subset of those channels. In general, when we limit our input too severely, we end up making things harder than necessary, much like trying to prepare a meal while wearing a blindfold and earplugs. This is what happens when we say, "I'm only going to consider this single spiritual point of view because it's the one and only truth."

Our perceptions are the lenses through which we view reality, but they aren't reality itself. What we perceive is invariably preprocessed to one degree or another. We aren't consciously aware of individual photons of light or oscillating atmospheric compression waves. We simply observe a photograph or a song. Whenever this kind of sensory compression occurs, a tremendous amount of raw data is irrecoverably lost. Each of our senses compresses and repackages the field of perceivable data in different ways, and it's this heavily processed output that finally reaches our conscious awareness.

Our beliefs and other cognitive filters give us similar glimpses into reality, but they also provide us with highly compressed and processed afterimages of the underlying data. For example, suppose you attempt to perceive nonphysical entities. What will you consciously experience? Through the lens of Christianity, you may connect with angels and saints via the mechanism of prayer. Through a Native American lens, you may perform a vision quest to consult with ancestral spirits or animal guides. Through an atheistic or skeptical lens, you may perceive nothing at all or perhaps something very fuzzy and inconclusive. Through a psychic or mediumistic lens, you may conduct a two-way conversation with a spirit guide or deceased person. What's actually there, however, is none of these things. You don't consciously perceive reality as it truly is because the raw data would overwhelm your cognitive abilities. Instead, you must attend to the highly compressed versions.

Even though each channel of input has limited expressiveness, if you can access a diverse enough set of channels, each one compressed and filtered in different ways, you can develop a more accurate and complete picture of reality. Each belief system you consider provides another way of viewing the same underlying data, thus helping you develop a better understanding of the whole.

Just as we can augment our physical senses with technology such as night-vision goggles or radio antennae, we can also significantly improve our spiritual senses. Exploring different belief systems and considering unfamiliar perspectives allows us to create new data filters that we can then add to our collection of cognitive tools. These filters process the same underlying reality as our standard physical senses, but they present that information in different ways, often revealing important patterns that our previous filters overlooked.

Our eyes may be able to see well enough, but they perceive more information when augmented with a microscope, telescope, or oscilloscope. Similarly, a single belief system such as atheism or Christianity provides some insight into a greater reality beyond the physical, but any singular filter is full of informational holes, gaps, and incongruencies. Think of these problems as compression errors. However, if you consider the viewpoints of a half-dozen belief systems, the big picture finally begins to take shape.

How do you know which particular lenses will provide the most relevant information for a certain situation? You figure it out in the same way you learn to use your physical senses. Do you ever make the awkward mistake of trying to get to know someone by tasting them? Perhaps you did when you were a baby, but most likely you favor your eyes and ears for that now. Through trial and error, you learned which senses are most appropriate for each situation.

We still make sensory mistakes, however. Sometimes we become fixated on the wrong input channels. Have you ever caught yourself ogling someone you're attracted to, not remembering a word that was said? Or have you ever put too much emphasis on your taste buds, shoveling food into your mouth while your eyes couldn't help but notice how overweight you were becoming? Despite these occasional failures, however, it's still the case that life is much richer with a variety of sensory channels instead of just one.

By learning to consider reality from multiple perspectives, you'll overcome many of the limitations of individual belief systems. You'll gradually shed false beliefs that distort your perceptions, you'll fill in gaps in your understanding, and you'll come into greater alignment with truth.

Spirituality and Love

A love-centered spiritual practice should help you become more connected with yourself and others. While some spiritual seekers eschew the modern world and withdraw into solitude, there's no reason you must adopt such a lifestyle. It's possible to pursue spiritual development in isolation, but the principle of love suggests it's at least as important to do so by interacting with other people. If we're all spiritually connected anyway, then why not explore that through direct interaction?

Quiet reflection and meditation can be powerful spiritual practices to help you connect within, but it's best if they're combined with abundant social interaction. Allow yourself to gain spiritual lessons both from your inner world and your outer world. Sometimes your answers will come from stillness; other times they'll come from direct communication. Listen to both channels.

Personal relationships can be a tremendous source of spiritual growth. While it's possible for us to fall out of touch with reality if we spend too much time alone, such problems are less likely with abundant interaction. If we become too impractical in our thinking, the people around us will tell us we've gone off the deep end. The pursuit of spirituality is really the pursuit of accuracy, where our goal is to develop the most accurate model of reality we can. If we fail to include other human beings in this model, we toss away too much potentially valid information, and our model is doomed to inaccuracy.

Spiritual development requires the freedom to connect with different parts of reality in order to understand them more fully. The more you're able to explore, the more connections you can form, and the greater your spiritual growth will be. When you feel a strong desire to connect with something in your reality, listen to your intuitive guidance, and make the connection.

For example, I'm really not sure why I felt a strong affinity for the city of Las Vegas during my 20s. I made the 300-mile drive from Los Angeles to Las Vegas dozens of times, sometimes with friends, sometimes with Erin, and sometimes just by myself. Despite the city's reputation as a one-stop shop for every human vice, I felt a deep connection to this oasis in the desert. In January 2004, my family and I relocated from Los Angeles to Las Vegas; and in retrospect, it turned out to be one of our best decisions ever. Mentally, I had doubts about the move, but I could feel in my heart that it was meant to be. Now that I've been living here for several years, I love it even more. I feel much more centered and at home here than anywhere else, and I'm especially grateful for all the wonderful friends I've made here. I even wrote an article about what it's like to live in Las Vegas and why I love this city so much (**www.StevePavlina.com/vegas**).

As it turned out, moving to Las Vegas massively enhanced my spiritual development. Certainly, the people I met here helped facilitate some important new experiences. Another factor was that by living in a city filled with free alcohol, ubiquitous gambling, strip clubs, and gluttony-inducing buffets, I became better at tuning out distractions from my spiritual path. By following my heart, I was led to the growth experiences I needed to have.

At various times in my past, I chose to connect with shoplifting, drinking, gambling, and many other vices. Although those activities are socially condemned, I must admit that all of them contributed greatly to my spiritual growth. They all offered me valuable new insights. Sometimes we're drawn to paths that seem to lead us away from truth, love, and power, but which actually increase our principle-centered nature in the long run. If I'd never explored these vices, a very valuable part of my life would have been lost. A major reason I'm able to share myself honestly today is that I know what it's like to be dishonest. I'm also able to embrace conscious living because I know what it's like to live unconsciously.

Am I suggesting that you should deliberately go out and explore various vices? I can't tell you what to do here because it would violate the principle of authority. That's a decision you'll have to make for yourself. But I will say that regardless of what you decide, I'm in no position to judge you for it. The best advice I can give here is to follow your heart and see where it leads.

Spirituality and Power

One of the most empowering choices you can make is to decouple your spiritual beliefs from your identity. Despite how firmly held your beliefs may be, they can never define you. If you change your faith, you're still you. A fixed belief system can only limit your ability to grow; it's like permanently closing one eye and denying yourself access to your natural stereo vision.

Personal attachment to beliefs, especially cultural and spiritual beliefs, is unfortunately very common. While experiencing a belief system from the inside is generally a wise choice, equating your identity with any fixed notion is a disempowering mistake. As the principle of truth reveals, beliefs are lenses through which you can view reality. Every lens reveals some aspects of reality while hiding others. The more lenses you experience, the more complete your understanding of the whole. Even if you become incredibly attached to one particular lens, it remains simply a lens and cannot define you. Attachment to one specific view of reality limits your power and curtails your ability to connect with people who hold different lenses.

This is a difficult concept for many people to accept because we grow accustomed to identifying with our beliefs. It can be disconcerting to stop identifying with any fixed ideology and to realize that all beliefs are lenses and cannot define us. Social conditioning tells us we must turn one particular set of ideas into our personal identity.

Are you a capitalist? A Christian? A skeptic? The way these questions are asked assumes you must respond with a yes or no. But this is like asking if you're an eye, an ear, or a nose. It would be more sensible to ask questions such as "Do you understand the viewpoint of Christianity?" instead of trying to equate it with your identity. When you start linking specific beliefs to who you are, you artificially restrict your sense of self. This practice violates the principle of power.

Belief identification is a source of social conflict as well. Disagreements, arguments, and even wars are caused by an inflexible attachment to a fixed perspective. It's far more productive for us to learn to see reality through multiple lenses and seek higher truths together instead of fighting over who holds the most popular lens. Spiritual lenses are inherently value based, so they don't represent truth by themselves, although they can reveal different aspects of truth.

When people ask me what religion I am, I tell them the question doesn't make any sense. I'm a conscious being, not a religion. While I understand the perspectives of many popular belief systems, having experienced several of them firsthand, I don't identify myself with any of them. I see my beliefs as a toolbox of lenses to choose from; they're an extension of my senses. When working on my computer, I'll pay attention to what my eyes are seeing. When talking on the phone, I'll shift my attention to listening with my ears. When I'm doing my taxes, I might adopt a very earthy, atheistic perspective. When I'm discussing the life of Jesus with someone, I'll consider reality through a Christian lens. When I meditate, I might adopt a Buddhist or New Age philosophy. I select each lens based on how empowering it is for me in the moment.

When you first attempt to perceive reality through multiple lenses, especially those that seem to inherently contradict each other, it will feel as though you're trying to do the impossible. You'll be like a newborn baby trying to make sense of garbled blobs of light, noise, and pressure. You may feel overwhelmed and frustrated, as if you're flooding your mind with utterly useless information.

Be patient with yourself. With sufficient practice, you'll gradually learn to combine data from multiple viewpoints into a single coherent picture. At first, it will take considerable conscious effort as you mentally switch between different perspectives, asking questions such as: "How would a Buddhist view this situation?" or "How would a Christian solve this problem?"

Eventually, your subconscious will learn to do it for you, and you'll begin to sense the big picture that emerges from multiple viewpoints. As this begins to happen, you'll unlock a new level of clarity, like an infant realizing for the first time that the floating blob is its own hand. It won't be a perfect clarity, but you'll likely find that some problems that previously plagued you become much easier to solve.

In order to align yourself with the principle of power, you must shed limiting viewpoints that disempower you. Imagine trying to understand the intricate connections between your financial situation, your religious or spiritual beliefs, and your emotional states. Common cultural belief systems only offer a very dysfunctional understanding of these links, which helps explain why so many people struggle both financially and emotionally, despite investing a great deal of effort in their spiritual practice. But when you examine the connection from multiple points of view, it's easier to see the big picture. This panoramic view can enable you to find a practical solution that allows you to enjoy positive emotional stability, financial abundance, and deep spiritual development without so much struggle and conflict. By examining your problems from different philosophical viewpoints, you empower yourself. Holistic solutions finally start to emerge. You gain the ability to solve problems you were previously unable to solve.

For example, one way to balance yourself financially, emotionally, and spiritually is to center your life around service to others. If you focus your efforts on genuine value creation and contribution, you'll eventually be able to manifest happiness, wealth, and a sense of meaning. If you look at this solution financially, it makes sense. If you look at it emotionally, it also works. And if you look at it spiritually, it works there as well. When considered from multiple vantage points, the effectiveness of this solution is readily apparent. Yet most of us are socially conditioned to overlook the simplicity of across-the-board, high-level solutions because we cling to fixed belief systems that prevent us from seeing the big picture. We live in a manner that actually prevents us from solving our most challenging problems.

A sound spiritual practice should be flexible enough to help you handle the mundane parts of your life without having to compartmentalize them. Your spiritual beliefs should empower you to be able to pay your bills, resolve relationship problems, and feel good emotionally. A fragmented approach can't achieve such results. A multi-perspective approach works best because it brings you into alignment with truth, love, and power. Ultimately, the general solution to all your problems is to find the place of alignment with these principles, and a multi-perspective approach helps you achieve greater alignment than a fixed perspective.

Equating your identity with one spiritual viewpoint (such as "I am a Christian") is like blindfolding yourself and plugging your ears. It's a very disempowering approach to spiritual growth. Let go of such limits, and free yourself from a fixed perspective. Be open to using all of your spiritual senses, especially if you start picking up information that disagrees with what you've been taught to believe.

How can you effectively train your spiritual depth perception? Find others with different belief systems that seem to empower them in some specific way, and learn from them. Study people from other cultures. Find out why a Buddhist monk seems so calm, why an athlete can maintain such a high fitness level, or why a billionaire is able to enjoy so much financial abundance. Read books written by such individuals, meet them in person if you can, and find out what makes them tick.

Through such studies, you'll learn that certain perspectives are more likely than others to yield positive results. For example, if you can't get yourself to meditate regularly, then obviously you perceive reality differently from someone who meditates every day. But if you could learn how such people see the world, you could model their beliefs to improve your results. How do those individuals view things, and how can you use their perspective to improve your own meditation practice? What are they seeing that you're overlooking? What senses are they using that you're ignoring?

A multispectral philosophy of life—that is, one that combines input from multiple perspectives—aligns closely with what's considered common sense. When you find your beliefs incongruent with what your common sense is telling you, perhaps you just need to view the situation from another angle. This is more effective than clinging to limiting ideas that get in your way. Your common sense is probably right.

We all have a tendency to fear and resist the unknown, so the notion of giving your beliefs so much flexibility may give you pause. Will you lose your sense of self? Will you become totally amoral and ungrounded? In my experience, these worries are unfounded. Allowing yourself a greater richness of perceptual channels will only increase your power to make decisions that align with your most sacred values and morals.

The point of spiritual exploration is to help you make conscious, empowering choices. Cloudy or incomplete perceptions reduce your ability to do so. The richer your field of input, the better your decisions will be, and that in turn benefits all the lives you touch. In order to bring more power to your spiritual path, you must remain open and receptive to all points of view. Whenever you close your mind to new ideas, you fall out of alignment with power, and your spiritual practice will suffer as a result.

Spirituality and Oneness

Since we're all inherently connected, we constantly influence each other by the spiritual choices we make. Consequently, our spiritual practice isn't merely an individual issue. Our personal spirituality has a collective impact.

When I was about 12 years old, I met another boy who was an atheist. I assumed that meant he must be misguided or evil in some way, since that's how I was taught to view non-Catholics. He didn't believe in God, so I concluded there must be something terribly wrong with him. Why else would he be doomed to spend eternity in hell? However, as I got to know him, I discovered to my surprise that he was actually a very nice person, and he and I remained friends for years. As hard as I tried, I could find no evidence that he was evil. This was confusing to me because it conflicted with what I'd been taught all my life. My beliefs encouraged me to disconnect from this boy, but I chose to align with love and connect with him anyway, thereby experiencing an important step on my path of spiritual growth.

Many serious conflicts in the world result from the decision to pass on beliefs that label other human beings as unworthy, damaged, or evil. If we are to live consciously, such beliefs must eventually be abandoned because they're out of alignment with truth, love, and power. The health of the body cannot be maintained when the cells choose to fight amongst themselves.

Your individual spiritual duty is to ensure that you harbor beliefs that are aligned with the principle of oneness. To the extent that you neglect this duty, you cause harm to others by teaching separateness instead of unity. Only when we all learn to align ourselves with truth, love, and power at the individual level will we be able to achieve peace at the global level.

Spirituality and Authority

The principle of authority makes it clear that yielding control of your spiritual life to someone else is a mistake. You must be the ultimate authority in your life—not God; and not some guru, master, or teacher. Your spiritual practice is yours to direct. Feel free to consult with whomever you wish, but don't forget that you're in command. You can't delegate your spiritual authority to anyone else. Ultimately this is a quest you must pursue for yourself.

In order for your beliefs to be aligned with authority, they must be effective. This means that they must ultimately satisfy the following eight criteria:

1. **Accurate.** Effective beliefs must be consistent with your observations of reality. Your beliefs can't contradict any facts you know to be true.

2. **All-inclusive.** For your beliefs to be effective, they must collectively address your entire field of experience. If you experience things that lie outside your beliefs about reality, then your belief system is incomplete, and an incomplete belief system can never be fully trusted.

3. **Flexible.** Effective beliefs adapt well to new circumstances. They offer appropriate guidance regardless of your career, income level, relationship situation, lifestyle, and so on.

4. **Ethical.** It's never effective to adopt beliefs that lead you to harm yourself or others. Such ideas are rooted in fear and ignorance. Effective beliefs don't encourage violence or dishonesty.

5. **Congruent.** Either your beliefs must be internally consistent with each other, or you must have a clear method of resolving incongruencies.

6. **Consciously chosen.** You inherit your initial set of beliefs from your upbringing and social conditioning. But as a fully conscious adult, those beliefs should be identified,

examined, and then deliberately altered or reintegrated. This is an ongoing process that can take years, if not your entire lifetime.

7. **Pleasure-increasing and/or pain-reducing.** Effective beliefs make you feel good, either by elevating your emotional state or as a side effect of generating the results you desire. Effective beliefs also reduce fear by bringing truth to the unknown.

8. **Empowering.** Your beliefs should allow you to experience whatever is technically possible; they should never mislabel the possible as impossible. Subject, of course, to ethical and moral considerations, your beliefs shouldn't unduly limit your abilities. If you think something is impossible for you, then it must truly be impossible, regardless of your thinking. If a mental shift would alter your abilities via the placebo effect, then your belief is both disempowering and inaccurate.

Take a moment to write down some of your current beliefs about reality. What do you believe to be true about your health, career, relationships, finances, spirituality, and so on? Then go over the eight criteria above to see how your beliefs measure up. If you don't like what you see, craft more effective tenets to replace the old ones. Remember that your beliefs are not merely observations of reality; they also shape and define your experience of reality. Many of the thoughts you hold most sacred may reveal hidden falsehoods once you take the opportunity to consider the alternatives.

Spirituality and Courage

In today's world, it takes courage to think for yourself instead of blindly swallowing what others want you to believe. It's up to you to hold yourself to the path with a heart and to follow it wherever it may lead, regardless of how others judge you for it. In the end, your spiritual practice must be immensely personal and consciously chosen.

As you progress along your unique spiritual path, you may experience periods of prolonged confusion lasting several weeks or longer. During such times, you may feel distant and disconnected. Reality suddenly makes very little sense to you, and you become uncertain of everything.

This *dark night of the soul* is a time of massive cognitive restructuring. Your mind is reconsidering its previous model of reality in order to complete the jump to a new level of understanding. Unfortunately, there are times when your old patterns are scrambled beyond repair, but new ones haven't yet taken shape. When this happens, it can feel extremely unsettling. There isn't much you can do except ride it out. Fortunately, once you complete one of these leaps, you enter a period of incredible clarity. It's like your whole mind has been retuned to a new level of truth.

I recall going through one of these periods a few years ago. I was trying to reconcile my high-level personal spiritual path with the practical realities of running my business. On the one hand, I was very dedicated to helping people grow. On the other hand, I was a successful entrepreneur running a business. However, I lacked an overall spiritual philosophy that brought these two parts of my life together in a way that felt good to me. I was experiencing a conflict between running a business to generate income and wanting to help people as selflessly as possible. For many weeks, I lingered in this place of inner darkness and uncertainty. Eventually, my mind was able to perceive a new underlying order that made perfect sense to me. I realized that we are all cells in the same body, and that the health of the body depends on the health of the cells. This made it clear that if I wanted to effectively serve others, I had to make sure I was also meeting my needs, or my work wouldn't be sustainable.

Spirituality and Intelligence

In order for your spiritual practice to be truly authentic, you can't compartmentalize it. You can't be a spiritual person for an hour each weekend and then put that part of yourself on hold when you go to work on Monday morning. An intelligent spiritual practice is a holistic one. It integrates with all parts of your life, including your career, your finances, your health, and your relationships.

According to the principles of truth, love, and power, the highest level of spiritual attainment would be perfect alignment with those principles, which implies perfect intelligence. The ultimate ideal of any sound spiritual path is to be infinitely truthful, infinitely loving, and infinitely powerful. By extension, this also requires infinite oneness, infinite authority, and infinite courage. The ultimate spiritual pursuit is to strive to live congruently with all of these.

Since the principles of truth, love, and power are universal, a proper spiritual practice must be universal as well. This means that even when you're doing your taxes, your spiritual beliefs must be applicable to the task at hand. If you face any situation in life where your views can't be applied, then they aren't universal, which means they can't be aligned with truth, love, and power. Even if you think about something as mundane as mowing your lawn, you can use the values of truth, love, and power to help guide you. Any other universal spiritual principles must satisfy the same criteria.

✦ ✦

As you use the power of conscious choice to bring your life into greater alignment with truth, love, and power, the long-term result is spiritual wisdom and peace. Your life reaches a new level of clarity where all the parts begin working harmoniously together.

Our collective spiritual development is rooted in our common interest in truth, love, and power. These are our guides through all the challenges of human life. If it were somehow possible for everyone on earth to come together and agree on a single spiritual philosophy, it would be one that incorporates the universal principles of truth, love, and power. These are the ideals that guide us not only as human beings, but also as spiritual beings.

✦ ✦ ✦ ✦

Afterword

•————————————▶

Personal development for smart people is the approach that shifts you into greater alignment with the core principles of truth, love, and power (and by extension, the secondary principles as well). When your thoughts and actions are truthful, loving, and strong, you're living consciously and intelligently. This is the very best you can possibly do as a human being.

Despite being very motivated and driven to share the ideas in this book with you, this is also the book I most needed to read. When I follow the seven principles from Part I, my life just works. I stay focused on creative self-expression, I serve others willingly and effectively, I resonate with abundance, and I'm very happy and fulfilled. Whenever I stray from this path and begin to violate these principles, life becomes a struggle. I make poor decisions, I get overwhelmed by problems and obstacles, I drop into survival mode, and I feel disconnected and stressed.

If I could summarize the core message of this book, it is simply this:

Seek truth with open eyes. Courageously accept your discoveries and their consequences. Rid your life of falsehood, denial, and fear of what is. Make truth your ally, not your enemy. This isn't easy, but it is correct.

Share your love openly. Connect with yourself and others by tuning in to the connection that already exists. The risk of rejection is overshadowed by the rewards of loving connections. Whenever you feel disconnected, reach out and connect with another human being. Remember that you're always loved.

Fully develop your human abilities, and use your power in honorable service for the highest good of all. False power corrupts, but true power elevates. The more you resonate with truth and love, the greater your ability to wield power wisely. No one is served by your refusal to shine.

Embrace your unique path of growth. Use your intellect and emotions to guide you in the conscious pursuit of truth, love, and power. Invest in creative self-expression, service, and contribution, and you will suffer no scarcity. Your greatest gift to the world is to share who you really are.

Enjoy your incredible human journey. Accept the highs and the lows as equally valuable. Recognize that your deepest sorrows reveal your greatest joys. Share your stories with others, and know that you're not alone. Be grateful for your time on earth.

Live consciously.

✦ ✦ ✦ ✦

Resources

Here are some additional free resources to further assist you in your pursuit of conscious growth:

Personal Development for Smart People Support Page - www.StevePavlina.com/smart
Take advantage of free resources to support you in applying the seven principles to your life.

Steve's Blog – www.StevePavlina.com/blog
Enjoy deep and insightful personal development articles with frequent new content.

Steve's Audio Programs – www.StevePavlina.com/audio
Listen to free audio programs (i.e. podcasts) on a variety of personal growth topics.

Discussion Forums – www.StevePavlina.com/forums
Meet growth-oriented people from around the world, and get help from a highly conscious and supportive community.

Contact Steve – www.StevePavlina.com/contact
Send Steve a personal message, including your feedback about this book.

Erin Pavlina's Website – www.ErinPavlina.com
Visit the Website of Steve's wife, Erin, to explore spiritual wisdom for conscious people.

✦ ✦ ✦ ✦

About the Author

Steve Pavlina runs one of the most popular personal development Websites on the Internet, creatively named StevePavlina.com. He has written more than 700 free articles and recorded 20 free audio programs on topics such as productivity, relationships, and spirituality. Steve's Website is enjoyed by more than two million monthly visitors in 150 countries, and he continues to post new material every week.

Prior to launching StevePavlina.com, Steve founded and ran Dexterity Software, an award-winning computer-game development and publishing company, for more than a decade. He also served as president of the nonprofit Association of Shareware Professionals and was later inducted into their Hall of Fame. He willingly retired from game development in 2004 to begin a new career in the field of personal development, a decision he has found immensely rewarding. Steve lives with his wife, two children, and the Area 51 aliens in Las Vegas, Nevada.

Steve's purpose in life is:

To live consciously and courageously;
To enjoy, increase, and share peace, energy, passion,
and abundance;
To resonate with love and compassion;
To awaken the great spirits within others;
And to fully embrace this present moment.

✦ ✦ ✦ ✦

Notes

Notes

Notes

Notes

Notes

Notes

Notes

Notes

We hope you enjoyed this Hay House book. If you'd like to receive a free catalog featuring additional Hay House books and products, or if you'd like information about the Hay Foundation, please contact:

Hay House, Inc.
P.O. Box 5100
Carlsbad, CA 92018-5100

(760) 431-7695 or (800) 654-5126
(760) 431-6948 (fax) or (800) 650-5115 (fax)
www.hayhouse.com® • www.hayfoundation.org

Published and distributed in Australia by: Hay House Australia Pty. Ltd., 18/36 Ralph St., Alexandria NSW 2015 • *Phone:* 612-9669-4299 *Fax:* 612-9669-4144 • www.hayhouse.com.au

Published and distributed in the United Kingdom by: Hay House UK, Ltd., 292B Kensal Rd., London W10 5BE • *Phone:* 44-20-8962-1230 *Fax:* 44-20-8962-1239 • www.hayhouse.co.uk

Published and distributed in the Republic of South Africa by: Hay House SA (Pty), Ltd., P.O. Box 990, Witkoppen 2068 • *Phone/Fax:* 27-11-467-8904 orders@psdprom.co.za • www.hayhouse.co.za

Published in India by: Hay House Publishers India, Muskaan Complex, Plot No. 3, B-2, Vasant Kunj, New Delhi 110 070 • *Phone:* 91-11-4176-1620 *Fax:* 91-11-4176-1630 • www.hayhouse.co.in

Distributed in Canada by: Raincoast, 9050 Shaughnessy St., Vancouver, B.C. V6P 6E5 • *Phone:* (604) 323-7100 • *Fax:* (604) 323-2600 • www.raincoast.com

Tune in to **HayHouseRadio.com®** for the best in inspirational talk radio featuring top Hay House authors! And, sign up via the Hay House USA Website to receive the Hay House online newsletter and stay informed about what's going on with your favorite authors. You'll receive bimonthly announcements about Discounts and Offers, Special Events, Product Highlights, Free Excerpts, Giveaways, and more!
www.hayhouse.com®